W9-BVX-054

HF5500
H28

Managers' Performance and Personality

by

THOMAS W. HARRELL
Professor of Applied Psychology
Stanford University, Stanford, California

118669

NOV 15 1967

SOUTH-WESTERN PUBLISHING CO.
Cincinnati 27 Chicago 5 New Rochelle, N. Y. Dallas 2
Burlingame, Calif.

Copyright ©, 1961
by
South-Western Publishing Company
Cincinnati 27, Ohio

All Rights Reserved

The text of this publication, or any part thereof, may not be reproduced in any manner whatsoever without the permission in writing from the publisher.

Library of Congress Catalog Card Number 60-53299

K161
Printed in the United States of America

PREFACE

•

This book is written to managers, prospective managers, and students of personnel research. Many line managers are interested in the problems discussed here although they may wish to skip the numerous coefficients of correlation and other statistical data. It is hoped that the material presented will lead to research on the selection of business students and business managers.

Acknowledgments are due to several persons. Lewis R. McClellan has assisted in several important ways for twelve months. He has found many articles and books from the Stanford libraries. He has assisted in the preparation of the bibliography and has done considerable abstracting. The following men have read critically all or part of the manuscript and contributed useful suggestions for change: William Dill, Fred Fiedler, Ed Ghiselli, Ernest R. Hilgard, E. K. Strong, Jr., Lewis Ward, and Gerald Wentworth. To a considerable extent, this report is the result of home industry. My daughter, Susan, has typed the manuscript. My son, Tom, has drawn two figures. My wife, Margaret, has edited the manuscript. She has made many useful suggestions for changes and her questions have provided the impetus to improve the manuscript in numerous instances. She has been an intellectual companion with whom to discuss the important issues in the study throughout its prosecution. Grateful acknowledgment is made for the preparation of the manuscript to Mrs. Linda N. Miller and Mrs. Margaret E. Gragg, and of the index to Mrs. Marianne Gowen.

TWH

February 1, 1961

EDITOR'S SERIES

We are proud to present this book as the first in a special series — the Editor's Series.

Books in this series will be selected and published because of their scholarly nature, their contribution to advanced thinking and research, and their general professional contribution to the improvement of business and economic education. Appropriate manuscripts will be considered on their merit.

Books of the Editor's Series are those that every professionally minded person will want to possess. They should be in every library. Most of them will be useful as supplementary readings for students.

CONTENTS

CHAPTER		PAGE
1	Introduction	1
2	The Criterion Problem	18
3	Managers' Performance Related to Productivity	35
4	Recruitment from College	53
5	Who Gets Promoted?	67
6	General Managers	75
7	Sales Managers	100
8	Production Managers	109
9	Office Managers	127
10	Research and Engineering Managers	137
11	Personality Theory and Measurement	142
12	Summary and Conclusions	164
13	Future Research	175
	Bibliography	182
	Index of References	198
	Index of Topics	201

Chapter 1

INTRODUCTION[1]

Why the Problem is of Interest

The dominance by business in the American culture makes the question of managers' performance and personality a broad social one in terms of the actual and ideal goals of management. Whyte's castigation of the Organization Man, Huxley's accusation of over-organization and Mills' charges against the Power Elite are spectacular but not isolated instances of criticisms of the philosophy of business management.

Why there should be such interest in the qualifications of managers may be asked. It has been reported that only slightly more than 25 per cent of the men who become managers, officials, or proprietors hold these jobs throughout their life (Jaffe and Carleton, 1954).[2] While some of those who leave management go into the professions, the bulk of them drop into manual work; others into clerical and sales work. This would indicate that the job of management is hard to keep and deserves study.

Not only is the selection of managers not scientific as a rule but there is also little reason to expect that it will become so in the foreseeable future. The personal qualifications of a prospective manager comprise only one of several variables that are responsible for his becoming a top manager. Personal qualifications include relations with executives who count. Additionally, there are luck and timing.

An example of good timing is being in the right place at the right time for a good job or a promotion. An executive of a sizable company was able within a few years to make officers of several

---

[1]The study resulting in this publication was made under a grant by the Ford Foundation. However, the conclusions, opinions, and other statements in this publication are those of the author and not necessarily those of the Ford Foundation.

[2]The complete reference for each reference that is given briefly in the textbook may be found in the bibliography beginning on page 183.

of his classmates from a graduate school of business. Had he not known them in school, it is doubtful that at their age they would have become officers of that or of any other company.

Personal relations with executives who count are almost always necessary for high management position, but rarely are they sufficient. One vice-president of a nationally known company stated that, if his company had a different president, he did not believe that he nor any of the present vice-presidents would have been appointed to their positions. Further, he thought that, if another person had his position as vice-president, there might well be another slate of people who reported to the vice-president. This seems to be typical, or almost typical, although there are no systematic data available.

Perhaps there can be few generalizations about good managers because there are so many causes for differences among successful managers. Managers probably vary depending upon the functional field of sales, production, etc., and they probably vary with level of responsibility. There may be differences between industries, as between public utilities and the oil industry. There may be differences correlated with the growth pattern. Perhaps there are different personality requirements for a dynamic California electronics company and for a stable southeastern textile company. A growth company may promote aggressive men; stable companies, more easygoing people. There may be differences because of company policy or tradition not associated with the other variables mentioned. There are said to be big differences due to time. Gordon (1959) has written that the personality of the heads of corporations today is vastly different from that of fifty or seventy-five years ago. It has also been asserted that a manager can be a success on the job but use a different pattern of performance from another who is equally successful. These then are some of the variables that make it difficult to generalize about successful business managers. They point to the necessity of looking at the situation as well as the personality and performance of managers.

In looking for predictors of management success, the search is difficult because of the scarcity of complete information. Margaret Jones has pointed out that of the hundreds of reports of selection studies only a handful had complete information (Jones, 1950).

She specified the desirability of (1) a complete job description; (2) a complete description of the sample; (3) exact test titles; (4) a detailed description of the criterion; and (5) adequate statistical treatment. Her criteria for a satisfactory report have not been met by a single study of managers. The main need is to know the averages and dispersions of the criteria and predictors as well as the relationships between predictors and criteria. For example, if one study found that intelligence was an important predictor of management success while another study found that intelligence was not at all related to success, the apparent disagreement might be understood in terms of differences in the two populations, provided that the reports contained the essential information. Population A might have had a wide range of IQ from 70 to 130 with an accompanying high standard deviation. All the IQs in Population B might have been above 95.

The form of the relationship between predictor and criterion may be important. Almost all studies of management success have used linear or straight line relationships, although the University of Southern California series was an outstanding exception. There have been frequent suggestions that curvilinear relationships would be expected rather than straight line relationships. For example, it might be hypothesized that the best manager in a given situation would have a moderate amount of dominance, but that either a small amount or a large amount of dominance would be a negative factor for his success. Or it is thought that the true relationship in some instances is discontinuous rather than a straight line. An example would be a situation where a minimum amount of intelligence is desirable but where, above a certain level, there is no increase in the chances of success. Above a certain level, the correlation between intelligence and the criterion of success might be zero; below a certain level, the correlation could be +.30.

Purpose

The purpose of this study is to find out what is known about the qualifications and performance of successful business managers and to define the main issues as to what is not known and what needs to be known so that a research program can be built around these key issues. There is no scarcity of ignorance so there is an abundance of unsolved problems, but it is difficult to decide about the salience of these problems and the likelihood of research success with respect to them.

While the main purpose is to determine the qualifications of general managers, related purposes are to determine the qualifications of the main functional fields of management: (1) sales; (2) manufacturing and production; (3) accounting and finance; and (4) research and engineering.

Greatest interest is in the top and middle levels of management, but by far the greatest amount of material is available for first-line supervisors. Data from all available levels are included.

Although the qualifications of successful business managers constitute the central purpose, there have developed important ancillary purposes which seemed inescapable to a comprehensive look. One is the criterion problem—who is a successful manager and how does one decide? This in turn raises the problem of what is management and what are its important dimensions.

The definition of management and leadership has emphasized performance as well as personality. Consequently, the purpose was broadened to look at some of the newer studies on performance in relation to productivity and morale.

In trying to determine the qualifications of successful management, it has also been found necessary to look at personality theory for that theory which best fits the evidence and provides the greatest hope for fruitful research. Finally, there is the purpose of outlining research that will yield more insight as to the qualifications of successful general managers.

Scope

An attempt has been made to consider business management in broad terms. While the main goal is to seek ways of choosing students who will be successful managers and to seek research avenues that will lead closer to the goal, this does not mean that it is expected to find a simple answer. It is not expected to find any single unitary factor of management aptitude, or even any combination of personality factors that will provide a clear answer to the best qualifications of successful managers.

The scope of the present study is primarily business managers in the United States. There are some exceptions in the literature that will be cited. Some military and foreign studies will be cited because of their unusual interest. In addition to the dozens or probably hundreds of leadership studies that have been published from the armed forces, it is worth noting that some of the most interesting civilian studies have been paid for out of military research budgets. This was true of several of the Big Ten University studies at Ohio State, University of Michigan, and University of Illinois which have been outstanding in studying leadership performance. The military service has made a greater contribution to personnel research than has business. Military studies have added much to the understanding of managers as well as to other areas of personnel research. Rating of managers is an important example. The first systematic use of rating scales was that of the United States Army in World War I. Several of the most useful methods for appraising performance came from World War II—peer ratings or buddy ratings; forced choice; and critical incident. Still, the focus will be on business managers, their performance and personality, although there will be brief excursions to the military because of methodological developments.

Leadership Theory

Current definitions of leadership include the situation as well as the leader and his interaction with subordinates. The rejection of leadership traits, it seems to the author, has gone too far, admitting that there are no universal traits of leadership. Where Shartle has defined leadership completely in terms of performance, it seems to the author that this is less accurate than including personality as well as performance (Shartle, 1956). How a person performs will depend upon his personality. There is evidence that the personal characteristics of leaders have varied from one group of successful leaders to another and that the practices of leaders may be effective in one situation and not in another.

Personality has been defined either as the effect a person has on other people, or as the total of his habits (Gibb, 1958). By either of these two common definitions, personality seems to be inescapably an important part of leadership performance.

Stogdill's thorough and scholarly review of the literature published in 1948 has been a major influence on changing the research emphasis from traits to the situation. His review included all publications giving data about leaders — not just those in business. He concluded that:

> A person does not become a leader by virtue of the possession of some combination of traits but the pattern of personal characteristics of the leader must bear some relevant relationship to the characteristics, activities and goals of the followers. Thus, leadership must be conceived in terms of the interaction of variables which are in constant flux and change.[3]

An interesting proof for the effectiveness of leadership in relation to the characteristics of followers has been made with respect to the nearest rival for leadership as well as to the characteristics of the whole group (Ghiselli and Lodahl, 1958). Supervisors who did not suffer from the competition of a threatening rival were rated as more effective in a work situation. Supervisors who had a group which was less capable of making decisions without a leader were also rated as more effective.

Although many authors have followed Stogdill's lead of diminishing the importance of trait differences, some have gone beyond his conclusions. Actually his summary shows interesting and perhaps important generalizations about the characteristics of leaders:

> 1. The following conclusions are supported by uniformly positive evidence from 15 or more of the studies surveyed:
>   a. The average person who occupies a position of leadership exceeds the average member of his group in the following respects: (1) intelligence, (2) scholarship, (3) dependability in exercising responsibilities, (4) activity and social participation, and (5) socio-economic status.
> 2. The following conclusions are supported by uniformly positive evidence from 10 or more of the studies surveyed:
>   a. The average person who occupies a position of leadership exceeds the average member of his group to some degree in the following respects: (1) sociability, (2) initiative, (3) persistence, (4) knowing how to get things done, (5) self-

[3]Ralph M. Stogdill, "Personal Factors Associated with Leadership: A Survey of the Literature," *Journal of Psychology* (1948). Reprinted by permission of The Journal Press.

confidence, (6) alertness to and insight into situations, (7) cooperativeness, (8) popularity, (9) adaptability, and (10) verbal facility.

3. In addition to the above, a number of factors have been found which are specific to well defined groups . . . Intellectual fortitude and integrity are traits found to be associated with eminent leadership in maturity.

4. The items with highest over-all correlation with leadership are originality, popularity, sociability, judgment, aggressiveness, desire to excel, humor, cooperativeness, liveliness, and athletic ability, in approximate order of average correlation coefficient.

5. In spite of considerable negative evidence, the general trend of results suggests a low positive correlation between leadership and such variables as chronological age, height, weight, physique, energy, appearance, dominance, and mood control. The evidence is about evenly divided concerning the relation to leadership of such traits as introversion-extroversion, self-sufficiency, and emotional control.[4]

Stogdill's findings apparently were that while there are some generalizations as to the personality characteristics of leaders, these depend upon the situation which includes the competition for the leadership position. This would suggest that the student who aspires to leadership should, among other things, consider carefully his qualifications in relation to the competition.

The deemphasis of traits as the explanation of leadership and the increased emphasis on the performance of leaders has led many writers to express great hope for the training of leaders on the theory that the evidence tended toward showing that leaders are not so much born as made. While it is not within the scope of this book to look in detail at the evidence from the training literature, it is not much of an effort to consider the quantitative results. The almost complete lack of evidence for the effect of training on managers naturally leads one back to an examination of personality appropriate for the situation as a basis for improving the performance of managers.

In addition to the need for considering the situation to find any generalizations for traits, Stryker has written in *Fortune* that there is so little agreement by managers on the meaning of various "executive qualities" that they are not useful in communication

[4] *Ibid.*

(Stryker, 1958). His evidence is convincing and the writer has had some supporting experience. One implication is that if traits or qualities are to be used, they must be defined rather than the assumption being made that they will have an agreed definition.

One definition of leadership that has implications for management and that has been carefully explained is:

> interpersonal influence, exercised in situation and directed, through the communication process, toward the attainment of a specified goal or goals. Leadership always involves attempts on the part of a leader (influencer) to affect (influence) the behavior of a follower (influencee) or followers in situation.[5]

This definition differs from Shartle's in that it does not limit leadership to effective acts. The analysis of leadership in terms of communication broadly considered is an emphasis that is implicit in much of the stress on communication for management which *Fortune* a few years ago declared was management's number one problem. Later this was dethroned by the declaration that management development, including selection, was management's number one problem.

The analysis of leadership by considering the aspects of the leader's personality as well as the fundamental steps in the communication process between leaders and their subordinates has implications for the manager's performance as well as for his personality. The outline of the analysis made by Tannenbaum and Massarik was:

A. Leader Personality: Needs, Perceptual Capacities, Action Capacities.
B. Perceptual Flexibility.
C. Relevance Judged by Leader and "Actual" Relevance.
D. Social (and Nonsocial) Sensitivity.
E. The Psychological Map.
F. Action Flexibility.
G. Selection of Communication Behaviors Judged Appropriate by Leader and "Actual" Appropriateness.[6]

---

[5]R. Tannenbaum and F. Massarik, "Leadership: A Frame of Reference," *Management Science*, (1957). Reprinted by permission of the Institute of Management Sciences.

[6]*Ibid.*

This rather technical analysis suggests that the most effective leaders may not know what they are doing by these names. Still, the analysis has some suggestive value as a basis of theory and research planning.

Consistent with the conceptions of Tannenbaum is a typology of leadership that was developed from a study of MBA's who had been graduated for only a few years (Ward *et al.*, 1954). The classification emphasized personality development with the assumption supplemented by some evidence from observation that personality was changing on the job. In no instances were the changes attributed to formal training either on the job or at the university. The classification was based on attitudes toward management that emphasized the communication process and that related to people.

The emphasis on communication by Tannenbaum and Massarik and also by Ward is supported by some evidence in two companies. Both at Sears and at Lockheed managers who were higher in sales or persuasive interest kept their jobs (Pederson, 1953; Bentz).

The five types that Ward, *et al.*, have presented are interesting in that they suggest leads for selection of students and for research on selection and training. They are not necessarily tight types, *i.e.*, the assumption that they merge into one another runs through the classification. The first group of men had grown the most and were able to adjust better to stress effectively. They enjoyed the challenge and accomplishment of succeeding in business problems. They had good insights into their abilities, were optimistic, and welcomed new responsibilities.

A second group had apparently grown as much as the first but it differed from the first in important ways. The motivation of the second group was primarily competitive—to outdo someone—which apparently was developed from earlier trauma. They were more interested in material success than in successful human relations. They had been hurt once and apparently were trying to avoid being hurt again. Their too great sensitivity seemed responsible for their changing jobs more often than most workers because of real or fancied unfair dealings.

The third group had not advanced as far as the first but did have the capacity to adjust. They were somewhat anxious, which kept them from being quite as effective as the first group. As they found that their anxiety was not necessary, they could move into the first group.

Members of the fourth group had frequently developed defense reactions to shield them from anxieties. If these reactions broke down they would become more anxious, or if they found the defenses no longer necessary, they could adjust effectively. Initially the fourth group seemed more mature than the third group; but, if their defenses were crumbled, these men seemed more anxious than those in the third group. When their defenses were down they often showed hostility and prejudice. Where they could change their attitudes, they were judged capable of growing into the third group and from there possibly into the first.

Members of the fifth group could not relate satisfactorily to people and they had not developed defenses to cover up this lack. They lacked confidence in themselves. Their deficiency was not in intelligence but in emotional control, in personality. Their attitudes toward people had failed to develop beyond hostility and suspicion, but they had not learned any defense reactions to protect themselves.

The distinction between the first and second groups puts in question some of the interpretations of W. E. Henry, Gardner, and Warner and Abegglen reviewed in Chapter 6. This Chicago group places great stress on the competitiveness with one's father as does Spencer, also located in Chicago, in the results of the Young President's Organization surveys. There seems to be disagreement between the Harvard and the Chicago group in that the latter puts competitive value highest, while Ward, *et al.* are saying that such managers are effective, but less effective than those who get pleasure out of managing for the accomplishment itself.

Ward, *et al.* analyzed capacity for communication into perception as did Tannenbaum and Massarik, but used different words thereafter in their analysis although there may be no essential disagreement. In other words, being able to communicate depends to a great extent on how the communicator sees the situation. They suggested a clinical approach of examining a man's background to discover his reactions to home and school, and thus to determine whether he had developed the capacities to become effective in communicating through these essential processes. It is not clear how one could make such determinations, which presumably are intended to be done in an interview, but it might be worthwhile to attempt to develop such methods. The importance of feelings and objectivity rather than intelligence as measured by a test is stressed.

The combination of the attitudes for relating with people plus communication skills is an interesting one which gives a practical meaning to a human relations approach for management. It seems perfectly plausible to agree that management consists of communicating with or influencing people. It also seems plausible to stress that communication can be effective only under certain relations between the manager and his associates. Relating was defined as the ability to motivate another.

One assumption about the conditions of effective communication will be supported by evidence shown in Chapter 3, Managers' Performance Related to Productivity.

> The most effective communication seems to result from information transmitted when the communicants are in a state of relative contentment and happiness so that their attention is not disturbed by feelings of anxiety or anger and where their mood is such as to promote a continuing relationship.[7]

The Michigan writers have shown that, in general, work units in some situations are more productive where employees feel less pressure.

The stress by Ward, *et al.* on confidence in the communicator may be related to the generally high socio-economic status of

---

[7]L. B. Ward, *et al.*, "Status Report of the Selection Study." Unpublished. Harvard Business School, September 23, 1954.

successful managers. It was pointed out that the effective communicator needs to have confidence in his ability to motivate the person with whom he is communicating. The tremendous advantage of socio-economic status for highest management, which is reviewed in Chapter 6, suggests the self-confidence factor as an important one of the in-group, although there are, no doubt, other factors. Perhaps personality inventories that attempt to measure self-confidence have not done so validly.

Ward, *et al.'s* ideas on the importance of energy that can be mobilized for effective communication brings to mind that Procter and Gamble has emphasized energy as one requirement it seeks in prospective managers from college (J. H. Taylor, 1957). Although Taylor was specifying physical energy and Ward, *et al.* were emphasizing mental energy, there may be some common ground here.

It has been pointed out that even if characteristics are found that relate to the success of management at certain levels and certain functions after possibly being qualified further as to the situation, the question will remain as to whether these were required for success or whether they were a result of adjusting to the job (Krauss and Porter). One of the authors, Porter, was a coauthor in a study which does raise this question pertinently. It was shown that top executives showed a personality different from middle managers in being more self-confident and daring (Porter & Ghiselli, 1957). The question is whether or not the top executive was more self-confident and daring before he became president.

The same study, showing the difference between middle and top managers, might also be suggestive of a second question that was raised by Krauss and Porter. Does being good at one job qualify one for the next above? McMurry has vigorously written that coming up through the ranks of middle management in the large corporation guarantees that the man will not have the aggressive personality desirable in a president. Newcomer presents some evidence that companies have grown more with outside presidents (Newcomer, 1955).

Krauss and Porter point out an important difference between selection for schools and for a particular job in business. They bring out that, since business schools are preparing for a variety of business occupations, there is a much wider spectrum of traits appropriate than for a single occupation. This is a useful distinction; but, if graduate schools of business really want more alumni to be general managers, they still may be able to concentrate on a pattern of success for these jobs, even though the pattern may be broad and inexact.

Another literature survey which was published in 1951 has conclusions that for the most part seem to have relevance today.

> It is concluded from this study of leadership research that the following represent the qualities which make for successful leadership in working organizations:
>
> 1. The leader is somewhat more intelligent than the average of his followers. However, he is not so superior that he cannot be readily understood by those who work with him.
> 2. The leader is a well-rounded individual from the standpoint of interests and aptitudes. He tends toward interests, aptitudes and knowledge with respect to a wide variety of fields.
> 3. The leader has an unusual facility with language. He speaks and writes simply, persuasively and understandably.
> 4. The leader is mentally and emotionally mature. He has come of age mentally and emotionally as well as physically.
> 5. The leader has a powerful inner drive or motivation which impels him to strive for accomplishment.
> 6. The leader is fully aware of the importance of cooperative effort in getting things done, and therefore understands and practices very effectively the so-called social skills.
> 7. The leader relies on his administrative skills to a much greater extent than he does on any of the technical skills which may be associated directly with his work.[8]

What is Business Management?

The definitions of leadership given above apply to business management, but it may be desirable to look at several specific

---

[8]C. E. Goode, "Significant Research on Leadership," *Personnel* (1951). Reprinted by permission of American Management Association, Inc.

definitions of business management. While the broad outlines of business management are clear, the exact boundaries are not.

Management seems to imply two different definitions of management depending upon the purpose or context in which the term is used. When speaking of selecting managers, the definition is relatively narrow. Management then applies to someone relatively high in the organizational structure who is the superior of a supervisor or of a foreman. On the other hand, when management is talking about training managers, it adopts a different definition. Here manager is broadly defined to include everyone not classified under the standards of the National Labor Relations Act. This latter broad definition is even more clearly adopted when management is drawing the line for a labor dispute with a union.

A new and interesting definition was made as part of a Ford Foundation study by Whisler (1958). Whisler's definition would seem to say that managers are those whom executives treat as managers by relying on them for inferences and not just for information.

The General Electric Company has developed quite a long definition that is somewhat more conventional and that probably would be acceptable by business management generally, even though the definition is unusually long (Smiddy, 1955). It includes the steps of planning, organizing, integrating, and measuring.

While the definitions given may be useful in other situations, the definition of a manager preferred for the purposes of the current study is the broadest, namely, the incumbent of any job that any responsible company wishes to call a management job. While supervisors and foremen are sometimes distinguished from managers, they will be included for the purposes of this study. It is admitted that the performance and personality of supervisors and foremen may be distinct in part at least from that of higher managers. It is even harder perhaps to define staff managers than line managers, but again the broadest definition of staff managers is preferred. Except salesmen or others who are clearly not legitimately called managers, anyone who is seriously called a manager in any company would be acceptable for the purposes of this study.

Summary: What Do Managers Do?

Managers do so many different things depending upon so many variations in the situation that it is difficult to generalize on just what they do. Additional information on their duties is given in Chapters 6, 7, 8, 9, and 10. What managers do depends upon the level of the position, i.e., the first-line supervisor's duties are different from those of his boss, and so on up the line to the president. The manager's job differs with his function and to some extent with the industry. The metal production president does more inspecting than the banker. The job depends upon what has to be done, which at times depends upon the season of the year. Many managers are puppets who are pulled by the strings of their colleagues rather than deciding their actions on reflection. The job depends upon the company to some extent. But more important than the company is the job itself. There are consistencies in the positions of two sales managers in two separate companies, for example. The manager's job varies with the individual although this is probably most significant at the highest levels. Shartle points out that differences between the styles of one manager and another may be a cause of upset to an organization when there is a change in management (Shartle, 1956).

According to some writers, the heart of management is decision making and seeing that decisions are carried out (Carlson, 1951). In order to arrive at decisions managers spend the majority of their time in communicating. They are talking to people, attending meetings, telephoning, reading reports, or writing almost all of their working time.

Whatever executives do, they work hard. It has been difficult to find a case of employee fatigue in recent years, but there is no lack of material on the fatigue of executives. One of the *Fortune* editors has documented the long hours of executives (Whyte, 1954b). His survey shows that managers normally work 57 to 60 hours per week but that in a crisis the hours are even longer. Several other surveys show slightly different amounts, but almost all agree that it is an unusual group of managers who average as little as forty hours per week.

Changes in Management

There is agreement that the job of manager has changed through the years and some writers think that there is the prospect of greater changes in the years shortly ahead. One change that has occurred and that some predict will accelerate is the need for relatively fewer managers proportionate to the work force. In 1950, there were only 16 per cent of the working force who were proprietors, managers, and officials (Roe, 1956, p. 138). There had been a steady decline from 23 per cent in 1910. One prediction is that, by 1980, there will be many fewer middle managers due to the use of data-processing machines and that those middle management positions will be less important (Leavitt and Whisler, 1958).

The same prophets who forecast fewer middle managers also predict a lesser emphasis in human relations, although another prophet has forecast the reverse, *i.e.*, increasing emphasis on human relations (Mee, 1955). There has been in recent decades an increasing emphasis on human relations or getting work done cooperatively through people. This has been accepted more for the lower levels of management than for the higher levels (Bendix, 1956). The reason is probably that militant labor unions have forced the issue upon first-line supervision, while vice-presidents are still unorganized—even though they are Organization Men.

Organization of the Study

The difficult criterion problem of how to determine management success will be discussed in Chapter 2. Next, in Chapter 3, will be a presentation of the manager's performance related to productivity. Recruitment of managers from college and from graduate schools of business will be presented in Chapter 4. The paths to promotion in management are presented in Chapter 5, which describes some of the things that are done, some that are said to be done, and some that it is said should be done.

The selection of business managers requires five chapters. The main interest here is in general management. There is a good deal known about the educational and family background of general management; but because of the relatively small population of general managers, plus perhaps their inaccessibility, there is less known of their abilities than is known for some of the functional fields. Four functional fields of management are dealt with in separate chapters. These are (1) Sales; (2) Production; (3) Office: and (4) Research and Engineering.

Selection studies are of two general kinds as reflected in the information sections of the journal, *Personnel Psychology*. There are validity studies which compare the success of managers with varying amounts of some variable, *e.g.*, intelligence test scores. There are also studies presenting normative data, or just what are the qualifications for persons holding management positions. Each of these groups, general managers, sales managers, production and manufacturing managers, finance and accounting managers, and research and engineering managers, are discussed separately and respectively in the five chapters, 6–10.

Personality theory and measurement are considered in Chapter 11 as they apply to business management. An attempt will be made to develop an eclectic theory of personality that will best explain what is known about business managers and that appears most fruitful for future research.

A summary of what is known, a list of controversial issues, and conclusions are presented in Chapter 12. A program of future research on business managers' performance and personality is outlined in the final chapter, 13.

Chapter 2

THE CRITERION PROBLEM

Research workers have agreed for some time that the criterion problem is the most difficult hurdle in the process of determining the qualifications for success on a job. This is particularly true of management positions—even more so than for many rank and file jobs. Who is a successful manager? When the problem is seriously considered, businessmen as well as research workers see that it is extremely tough.

How Can Success as a Business Manager Be Defined?

Values. Success as a business manager depends upon the values held by the person defining success. There is some but not complete agreement about all of the values or goals that management should have and these goals have changed and are changing. While everyone is agreed on the necessity of profits for the survival of a business, some writers say that profit is the only legitimate goal of business, while others say that the over-all goal of business is to provide a service. The question of social responsibility is the most controversial value. While there is increasing stress by some writers on business' social responsibility, there are other students who do not accept this as a goal of business. Still, it is inconceivable that any business leader today would dare publicly restate the famous Vanderbilt remark, "The public be damned!" (Holbrook, 1953, p. 95).

Several goals for business have been stated clearly in the General Electric definition of the manager's job (Smiddy, 1955) wherein it was stated that there are obligations to customers, suppliers, employees, and stockholders. Just how one can balance these obligations, or how one should weight them is not clear and perhaps can not be mathematically given. That a conflict can occur was spectacularly shown in a Ford Motor Company lawsuit. The conflict concerned the importance of income to stockholders versus growth. Stockholders sued and got more dividends.

> The original Henry Ford "told the court that the profits of the Ford Motor Company were neither his nor the stockholders. After they (the employees) have had their wages, and a share of the profits, it is my duty to take what remains and put it back into the industry to create more work for more men at higher wages."[1]

The job of the manager is obviously to move his organization toward its goal, but what its goal is may not always be clear or simple. The goal may be variously defined by the person who is asked, and the goal may vary with time. One of the company goals that is often considered important but that is sometimes overlooked is the maintenance of the organization.

The most convenient method of defining the success of a manager is his remuneration, although no one is satisfied that this is completely accurate. Some of the problems in using remuneration as a criterion will be discussed in a later section. At an earlier period in history a businessman was not considered successful however high his salary because he could not be a real success unless he owned his own business (Wyllie, 1954). Opportunities for owning one's own business have become fewer, and now the position of corporation executive is more the success goal (Bendix, 1956).

Definitions by Managers. The meaning of success varies with the level of management defining success and with time. Some of the evidence as to managers' views on success fits a theory of motivation and personality which states that goals change depending on whether the person thinks that he can reach them. Managers defined success differently than lower level supervisors in one study (Pellegrin & Coates, 1957). The study included executives and supervisors who were from business, industry, and other organizations—all in a single town.

---

[1] Stewart H. Holbrook, *The Age of the Moguls* (Garden City, N. Y.: Doubleday & Company, Inc., 1953), p. 207. Reprinted by permission of Doubleday & Company, Inc.

Initially the goals of the executives and supervisors were similar and consisted of money, prestige, and high status. Over the years the goals changed somewhat for both the executives and the lower level supervisors. Higher level executives stated that their goals changed from money to the less materialistic ones of challenge and of recognition. Some of their comments were:

> I get the biggest kick out of being respected for my ability as a problem solver of both technical and human problems. . . .
>
> Success refers to the satisfaction of job accomplishment, to believing you are doing your job better than it has ever been done before.
>
> Money isn't everything. Success is the inner satisfaction of accomplishment—having the courage of your convictions, feeling good about what you have achieved, and realizing that people appreciate you and have confidence in you. . . .
>
> Success means recognition by your contemporaries, financial security, and being asked by big companies to accept new challenges.[2]

Lower level supervisors apparently adjusted to their goals by wanting to keep what they had, rather than expecting any greater challenge. Their goals became lower than those of the executives. Here are definitions of success by two of the supervisors:

> Success means happiness, peace of mind, security, family respect, and providing good starts for one's children.
>
> Success is the satisfaction of knowing you are accomplishing something, being personally happy, providing well for your family, and being recognized as a respectable citizen. Whatever money you make is only a means to these ends. . . .[3]

The difference in the definition of success by the two groups fits Maslow's motivation theory in that motives changed with varying degrees of success—level of aspiration varied. Executives did not define success in terms of giving their children an education because they did not doubt that they would be able to do so—at least at the time when their children approached college age.

---

[2]Ronald J. Pellegrin and Charles H. Coates, "Executives and Supervisors: Contrasting Definitions of Career Success," *Administrative Science Quarterly* (1957). Reprinted by permission of *Administrative Science Quarterly*.

[3]*Ibid.*

Attempts to Measure Management Success

The lack of a satisfactory measure of management success is commonly regarded by research workers as the primary retarding influence on the measurement of management potential. Until there is a measure of management success that is acceptable, *i.e.*, a yardstick not made of rubber, it will be impossible to have satisfactory predictors of the yardstick.

While everyone agrees that profit is necessary for the success of a business manager, there are many instances where it is difficult or impossible to measure the specific contribution to profit of a single manager. How long does a profit have to be made for the manager to be called a success?

Some of the questions dealing with measuring management success will be dealt with in this chapter, others in later chapters. Business success is less predictable than success in other occupations. Two explanations are available. Perhaps the low predictability is due to the fact that success in business is due more to luck and therefore is more unreliable. While this explanation appears to the writer to be the better or at least the main explanation, a second explanation is that management success is largely determined by intangible personality factors that as yet cannot be satisfactorily measured.

Emphasis on the performance rather than the personality of managers is given in Chapter 3 where studies which relate supervisory practices to productivity will be reviewed. Promotion to higher status management jobs has been considered as a criterion of management success in Chapter 6. While this criterion undoubtedly has some reliability and possibly some validity, there are some objections to it on the basis of nepotism or personal factors rather than performance.

Earnings are the criterion of success presented in Chapter 4. Earnings make the most convenient single criterion and have to be considered, although they are far from perfect. A businessman has said that he knows a manager earning $100,000 per year who is not nearly so good a manager as one in another company who is earning only $20,000 per year. Objective measures especially for factory supervisors will be considered in Chapter 8.

A look at some of the attempts to measure management success will be taken in this chapter. The Darwinian criterion of survival or merely holding the job will be examined. Job evaluation which puts a value on the job will be considered. The fairness of executive salaries will be explored. Objective measures will be considered briefly although these are treated at greater length in Chapter 8. Judgment is probably the most widely used administrative measure of management success. Examples of judgment that have been expressed in ratings will be discussed in this chapter.

Criterion Issues. Bellows (1941) presented three potential sources of error in the use of criteria which have some pertinence for management success. One source of error is "contamination by illicit use of predictor information." This danger is present wherever a person with authority for promotion has knowledge of a predictor, e.g., a test score or school grade. When a boss knows what grades a man has made in college, he may be influenced in his rating or in his decision to promote the man. In the typical management consultant appraisal of managers there is always the danger of contamination since the appraisal is often reported to the manager who makes a rating judgment on the man who was tested.

A second danger Bellows presented is "contamination by artificial limitation of production." This could happen with a manager who was successful because he had inherited a good crew or who was unsuccessful because he had inherited a bad crew. While this danger can be reduced or eliminated by rotating managers to a variety of situations, this is not always practical.

A third possible source of error with criteria is "contamination by differential influence of experience." This occurs where experience makes a difference to job performance.

Ghiselli (1956b) has pointed out two additional problems that have application to attempts to measure the success of managers and that are of fundamental importance in considering the criterion. One is the dimensions of the criterion. If the criterion consists of two or more factors, how should they be combined? For example, where a manager's job required productivity and morale, how should these two factors be combined? Will high productivity offset low morale, or will it be necessary to have a certain minimum score in each?

Ghiselli's second point is closely related to the first in that it pertains to the dimensions of the individual performance rather than to the job requirements. One manager's job performance is high in productivity but low in morale. Manager B, on the other hand, is low in productivity but high in morale. How can the two be compared?

Holding the Job. Holding the job is a frequently used measure of success. For research purposes, however, it may be desirable to have some standard as to a minimum length of time on the job. The criterion might be more reliable if some such interval as three years were adopted.

Job Evaluation. Job evaluation provides a possible method for deciding upon a criterion of success in the management job. For a given sample of management jobs in which they were all evaluated under the same system, the jobs could be ranked in order of their importance. For any study of the qualifications of the managers, it would then also be necessary to have appraisals of the job performance of the incumbents.

Dimensions of the Manager's Job. The preceding definitions of the job of manager gave some statements of the dimensions of the jobs of managers. There have been more attempts in the armchair than by empirical methods to spell out in detail the essential dimensions of the management job.

One effort that is of particular interest was part of the Executive Study made by the Educational Testing Service (Hemphill, 1958). The study was limited to executives who supervised one or more supervisors. Consequently, first-line supervisors were not included in the study. An "Executive Position Description," a questionnaire consisting of 575 questions about job elements, was developed. Ninety-three executives in five companies filled out the questionnaire. After a factor analysis the questionnaire was reduced to 191 questions which could be answered in an hour. A factor analysis of the results found that ten factors or job dimensions accounted for 99 per cent of the similarities among the positions.

These ten factors show the amazing diversity of business. The complexity of duties reflected in the descriptions of these factors show that the positions analyzed were from big business, as undoubtedly they were.

Three of the factors taken together relate to Whyte's concept of the Organization Man. These three—G., Exercise of Broad Power and Authority, with its stress on unusual freedom of personal action, implying that freedom of personal action is unusual; H., Business Reputation; and I., Personal Demands—point to the importance of personality and personal life in the business life of the executive. They show the necessity for conforming to the stereotype that is expected for the position. They suggest that stability is necessary and that nonconformity and creativity will be, or are believed to be, fatal in many executive positions. On the other hand, there are informed opinions which state that creativity and innovation are the heart of business success in the highest executive positions.

There was a fairly high degree of similarity between jobs of the same title from one company to another, but there was also a company pattern in job composition that showed itself to a lesser extent. This is a demonstration of the hypothesis of a company standard. There are other differences in the composition of jobs that are unique to the position. Table 2-1 shows the average factor loadings for the positions of Vice-President (Manufacturing), Division Manager, Plant Manager, Production Manager; General Sales Manager, District Sales Manager; and Section Superintendent (Research).

There is a hierarchy of the dimensions of the positions. Vice-President, the highest position represented, did not have a significant factor loading on the dimension of Business Control, which was a significant part of the lower Division Manager and Plant Manager positions. On the other hand, there were three factors prominently present in Vice-President's position which were not important in the positions of either Division Manager or Plant Manager. These were Business Reputation, Personal Demands, and Preservation of Assets.

Looking at the manufacturing and production positions in Table 2-1, the highest position, Vice-President, contains only

Table 2-1
AVERAGE FACTOR LOADINGS OF SEVEN EXECUTIVE POSITIONS ON EIGHT DIMENSIONS

Position Title	Staff Service	Supervision of Work	Business Control	Technical Products and Markets	Planning	Business Reputation	Personal Demands	Preservation of Assets
Vice President, Manufacturing (N = 3)						.40	.42	.30
Division Manager (N = 5)			.41					
Plant Manager (N = 3)			.38					
Production Manager (N = 2)			.37		.22			
General Sales Manager (N = 2)			.40	.30				
District Sales Manager (N = 2)	.35			.34				
Section Superintendent, Research (N = 2)	.31	.41	.22	.28	.36			

NOTE: Values are shown only where all positions with same job title had significant factor loadings, *i.e.*, .20 or higher, for a given factor.

Source: Adapted from J. K. Hemphill, *Basic Dimensions of Executive Positions*. Research Memorandum 58-2, Educational Testing Service, Princeton, March, 1958.

the three dimensions of Business Reputation, Personal Demands, and Preservation of Assets. The first two of these are personal or personality factors rather than technical factors. The only dimension that is required by the position of Plant Manager is Business Control. The position of Production Manager required Business Control but also included Planning.

Both levels of Sales Managers contained the Technical-Products and Markets factor. General Sales Manager also contained Business Control, and the District Sales Manager included Staff Service.

The position of Section Superintendent in Research had the greatest variety of duties of any of the positions, having significant weights in five factors. In order of their size, the factors were Supervision of Work, Planning, Staff Service, Technical-Products and Markets, and Business Control.

Hemphill's analysis is unique for executive positions although there are some similar studies for first-line positions in manufacturing. It would be interesting to have the Hemphill analysis include more positions and more companies. This will undoubtedly occur in time as his method of describing positions is being used in at least one or two additional samples of considerable size and may be used fairly extensively in research. This dimensional analysis is interesting and may be useful although it has been pointed out that there is no articulation on dimensions that can be used between such job analysis and man analysis (Tagiuri, 1958).

Remuneration. Remuneration as a criterion of a manager's success raises the question of whether it constitutes a fair value for the comparison of managers from one company to another. Within a company there is considerably less question about the fairness of earnings as a yardstick of success, although in any large company there are instances of managers who are thought by themselves and by others to be more valuable than their top management thinks. Comparisons from one company to another involve the question of whether the typically higher salaries in electronics, oil, and chemicals are comparable to the typically lower earnings in railroads and utilities. Attention has been called to the earnings of Bethlehem Steel Company officers who during several years have had more than one among the top five in the country. Is there reason for thinking that the value of these positions in one company is that high relatively?

It has been shown that the value of the president's salary has little if any relationship to the success of the company as measured by profits (Roberts, 1959). In good times and poor, a president may continue to draw his $100,000 per year. Patton (1958) found that while salaries were larger for larger companies they were not proportionately larger.

Several variables have been found which did correlate significantly with executive salaries although there was some unexplained chance variance (Howe, 1956). There was probably a significant correlation between a subordinate executive's salary and that of his chief (Patton, 1958). In divisions of companies with under $15 million in annual sales, the salaries of the division heads varied materially with the importance of the division (Howe, 1956). In larger divisions, however, there was a more definite hierarchy of salaries with functional fields as follows:

1. Sales
2. Manufacturing
3. Product engineering
4. Control
5. Personnel
6. Industrial engineering
7. Purchasing[4]

Other correlations with executives' salaries were sales volume and, especially, profits (Howe, 1956; Patton, 1958). The evidence then was varied with respect to profits. For presidents there was no correlation, but for executives other than presidents there was a correlation between profits and salary. In the latter instance, size of company, which was probably the only significant variable, has not been controlled.

Management opinion toward bonuses implies that salaries alone are not a fair measure of a manager's worth. A large number of companies pay bonuses, but the number has been somewhat less than half the total of companies (Stryker, 1956). Those that pay bonuses would justify them in part on the basis of salaries being an inadequate measure of the executive's worth. This suggests that in a study of remuneration as a criterion of management success, it would be desirable to deal only with executives in companies where bonuses were paid. On the other hand, every company paying bonuses appears to have its unique system although many of them taken alone sound convincing for their fairness and discrimination.

---

[4]Robert J. Howe, "Price Tags for Executives," *Harvard Business Review* (May–June, 1956). Reprinted by permission of *Harvard Business Review*.

An index of salary increase has been a useful measure in studies of Carnegie Tech alumni (Dill, 1960). This would seem to deserve more study.

Objective Methods. Company growth and other objective measures have been used in setting bonuses for high executives. One measure of the success of the top executive has been company growth (Newcomer, 1955, pp. 138–139). Fast-growing companies hired their executives from the outside in 17.1 per cent of the cases in contrast to only 8.9 per cent of the cases for slower-growing companies. It is not known whether the outside executives were more effective in causing growth, whether growth led to the recruitment from without, or both.

McMurry has supported the proposition that the most effective top executives are recruited from the outside, even though this is done in only about 15 per cent of the cases (McMurry, 1959). His argument is that the process of working one's way up through an organization prescribes a personality that is not sufficiently aggressive to lead to maximum company growth. While company growth and the other measures mentioned above in setting bonuses are about the only objective measures used for top executives, there are several instances of attempts to use or develop objective measures with lower managers, especially first-line production managers.

Criteria in a General Motors study (O'Neill & Kubany, 1959) included four objective measures. The objective criteria with their reliabilities in the two plants were "Scrap (.75, .92), Expense Material-Tools (.90, .93), Expense Material-Processing Supplied (.93, .82), and Efficiency (.46, .97)."

Related to the criteria that were used by the Ohio State people in the International Harvester Company is a very impressive criterion developed by the General Electric Company with the aid of the consulting firm, Richardson, Bellows & Henry (Merrihue & Katzell, 1955). A yardstick called the "Employee Relations Index" was developed to determine the extent to which employees had accepted the policies of management and were performing in accordance with them. Based on a set of guiding principles for the selection of variables which would statistically make up a general factor, eight personnel statistics were chosen out of thirty-three that were considered. Production data could not be included since it was not sufficiently comparable from one group to another. The eight components of ERI were:

1. Periods of absence
2. Separations (all types)
3. Initial visits to the dispensary for occupational reasons
4. Suggestions submitted through the suggestions system
5. Actions incurring disciplinary suspension
6. Grievances submitted through the foreman grievance procedure
7. Work stoppages
8. Participation in the insurance plan[5]

While these data seem to make a valid and reliable index in this company, the authors point out that perhaps other measures would be more appropriate for another company.

There are convincing validating data. ERI was found to correlate with several characteristics of a plant or of work groups. ERI was higher in smaller work groups, in plants that were not expanding rapidly, in plants where rank and file employees were predominantly of the same sex. It was higher in plants where "a large percentage of hourly employees work in teams in which the members must coordinate their work movements." It was higher in work groups where there were "older employees . . . and employees whose average length of service is greater (this last holds true even when the effects of age differences are discounted)."

ERI shows the possibility of an objective criterion. It could be used as a validity criterion for management selection although it has not been so reported. It suggests the expense of criteria research and how such a criterion can be established in a very large company, and it shows that each criterion needs to be tailor-made.

Ratings by Superiors. Although rating scales have not had an entirely happy and successful life as criteria for selection studies, they have been the most widely used criterion of management success for middle and lower managers. In spite of their wide usage, ratings of managers have not been shown to correlate with

[5]Willard V. Merrihue and Raymond A. Katzell, "ERI — Yardstick of Employee Relations," *Harvard Business Review* (November–December, 1955). Reprinted by permission of *Harvard Business Review.*

demonstrably valid criteria of performance. Cleven and Fiedler (1956), in their study of open hearth shops, found zero correlations between shop superintendents' ratings and productivity of open hearth foremen. This occurred despite the fact that superintendents had access to productivity records and expressed belief in the validity of the records. Ratings are often influenced by factors not relevant to productivity, such as compatible social and personality characteristics.

One study (File, 1945) did report such a lack of reliable ratings across company lines that the rating method was abandoned as a criterion. E. R. Henry (1959) has, however, described a Performance Description which he states has been successfully used in comparing managers in different companies of the Standard Oil (New Jersey) system. Since this was established for administrative purposes, one could expect the rating method to work even better for research purposes. Consequently, this method might be tried in research across other company lines.

The performance description consisted of two sets of 15 items each. Each item was made up of four positive statements. Each of the 120 statements was answered in terms of the extent to which it fitted the man whose performance was being described, using a scale from 0, "fits poorly," to 9, "fits well." Within a block of four items, the rater was instructed that there could not be a tie. If statement "A" was marked "4," then statements "B," "C," and "D" had to be marked other than "4." Statements were constructed and organized in such a way as to yield six area scores in addition to a total score. Area scores were more useful than the total score in the Standard Oil Company of New Jersey. It would presumably be necessary for one to develop local norms for the area scores. The six area scores were classified as follows:

I — Initiative; responsibility; leadership
K — Specific job-knowledge and skill
D — Dependability; thoroughness; follow-through
C — Ability to get along with others; cooperativeness
S — Stability under pressure; self-control
A — Effectiveness of appearance; manner; work habits[6]

[6]Edwin R. Henry, Unpublished paper presented at Harvard Graduate School of Business Administration Symposium, March, 1959. Printed by permission of Edwin R. Henry.

There have been many demonstrations of the reliability of rating scales for research purposes, although their success or failure in administrative use is another story. One short forced-choice scale was shown to have a satisfactory validity in the B. F. Goodrich Company (Taylor, Schneider, and Clay, 1954). Ten item scales correlated up to .62 with an objective criterion for store managers. Examples of the uses of rating scales in research with managers are given in Chapters 7, 8, 9, and 10.

What is rated on administrative rating scales as determined by three surveys is shown in Table 2-2 (Mahoney, Dohman, & Jerdee, 1957; Benjamin, 1952; Spicer, 1951). The results for 1957 were for managers; those for 1952 were for administrative, professional, and supervisory personnel; and those for 1951 pertained to salaried employees. The differences in the results of the three surveys suggest that the authors did not agree on how characteristics were to be classified. It seems unlikely that "Co-operation" which was listed 31 times in the 1952 survey and 18 times in the 1951 survey would have been completely absent in 1957 unless there had been a difference in classification. In 1957, it was reported that four companies thought that performance should be emphasized more and traits less. Both performance and personality were included in the questionnaries at each of the survey periods.

Ratings by Peers. While there have been several references to peer ratings in the military service and in school situations, only three were found that have been used in business management (Randle, 1956; Springer, 1953; Weitz, 1958).

Springer found much higher agreement among the ratings given by supervisors than for those given by peers who were lead men, but the relatively large numbers of peers and their opportunity to observe unguarded situations leads to the expectation that peer ratings may be more reliable and more valid than supervisory ratings. Peer ratings by life insurance agents were shown to be significantly correlated with superiors' judgments after 100 of the agents had been promoted to assistant managers (Weitz, 1958).

Table 2-2
WHAT IS RATED ON RATING SCALES

	1957	1952	1951	Total
Personal Characteristics				
Personality				
Social acceptance	9			9
Motivation	5			5
General personality	4		10	14
Responsibility	3			3
Character	2	27	19	48
Dependability	2			2
Self-control	2			2
Confidence	1			1
Cooperation		31	18	49
Attitude			14	14
Appearance			11	11
Mental				
Ability to learn, or intelligence	8		12	20
Initiative	7	22	26	55
Judgment	4	23	18	45
Analytical ability	2			2
Leadership	3	19	13	35
Skills				
Job knowledge	8	34	26	68
Verbal facility	2			2
Physical condition, health	3	6		9
Performance Measures				
General performance				
Quality of output	8	23	22	53
Over-all performance	5			5
Quantity of output	5	19	23	47
Attendance	4		19	23
Cost control	1			1
Safety	1			1
Working relations			12	12
Supervision				
General supervision	5			5
Training	5			5
Motivating	3			3
Directing	1			1
Organizing and planning	8	14		22
Coordination	6			6

Source: Adapted from American Management Association, *Personnel:* T. A. Mahoney, W. Dohman, and T. Jerdee. "Applying Yardsticks to Management," 33(1957), 556–562; R. Benjamin, Jr. "A Survey of 130 Merit-Rating Plans," 29(1952), 289–294; and L. G. Spicer. "A Survey of Merit Rating in Industry," 27(1951), 515–518.

Ratings by Subordinates. Employee opinion polls generally include a rating of the supervisor by subordinates, but the results are customarily not stated in such terms as to be useful for shedding much light on the performance or personality of supervisors. Subordinates usually find, however, that supervisors' performance has substantial room for improvement to meet their standards. This review does not include employee opinion polls generally. The studies of supervisory practice frequently include ratings by subordinates. These are reviewed in Chapter 3. Rupe (1951) focused on subordinates' ratings of superiors. From a factor analysis of the Purdue Rating Scale for Administrators and Executives, he found two factors, "(1) social responsibility to subordinates and society and (2) executive achievement." The use of subordinates has the advantage of providing a group of raters large enough to get more reliable results than are usually obtained from ratings by superiors. No doubt subordinates emphasize different factors in their ratings than do superiors.

Summary

The criterion of success as business managers depends ultimately on the values or what is wanted. The first thing that occurs to people when the question is raised is profits, but the use of profits as a criterion has not been of particular value. This is primarily due to the complexity of the situation where it has usually developed that profits are not acceptable as a valid measure of the competence of a manager.

Definitions of success by managers varied with the level of management and with experience. Initially both of the levels compared presumably had the same definition—primarily in terms of money and power. With age and experience the higher managers changed their definition to that of challenge and recognition; lower managers, to security for their families.

In looking closely at the study of criterion, a number of issues arise. Three difficulties are the contamination through illicit use of predictor information, the artificial limits put on production through the different opportunities inherent in the job, and the influence of experience. Where there is more than one factor involved in job performance, as there always is in the job of a manager, there is a question as to the best way of combining the factors of the job. Similarly, the same question occurs as to the best way of combining the factors of job performance of the incumbent managers.

The most commonly used measure of success in the research encountered are holding the job, for top managers, and ratings, for lower ones. A number of objective measures have been developed but even when they have been reliable, they have usually been abandoned for ratings, possibly because the objective methods have not had wide applicability. A forced-choice rating scale reported by E. R. Henry is said to have been useful even in cutting across company lines in the affiliates of the Jersey Standard Oil Company. This may be worth trying in future research.

Rating scales include an appraisal of personality or performance, usually both. There is a trend to emphasize performance as being more pertinent and to eliminate personality as being less pertinent and more difficult to judge.

Hemphill has shown that a variety of management jobs can be reduced to ten factors. There were similarities in the factorial composition of the same job in two or more companies, although there were also company differences as well as some uniqueness of individuals.

Remuneration has been useful as a measure in comparing various groups. It also seems to be the best measure of success for alumni surveys as reported in Chapter 4, but otherwise it has not been reported as a criterion of success. It has serious difficulties of fairness in evaluating an individual.

The Employee Relations Index that has been used within the General Electric Company seems to be a valid and objective criterion. It could be used by other manufacturing companies, but would have to be standardized separately within each company.

Chapter 3

MANAGERS' PERFORMANCE RELATED TO PRODUCTIVITY

While the focus in this study is mainly managers' personalities, it has seemed worth while to take a closer look at their performance. There have been increasing numbers of studies relating the performance of managers to productivity or morale or both. Most of the studies have dealt with first-line supervisors. Interest in performance is secondary to personality, but since there is an interaction between performance and personality it seems desirable to look at performance in some detail.

Current theory on management is that while there are some fundamentals of performance that apply generally, the effectiveness of much performance depends on the situation (Likert, 1958b). It is salient to know the expectations and perceptions of the manager's superior, subordinates, and peers before being able to make a good guess as to the effectiveness of the manager's performance.

This situational theory of management by Likert (1958a and b) is based on a motivational theory in which ego recognition of the individual employee is the key (Likert, 1952). The motivation of the worker will depend on what he wants and how he sees the situation. Since this will vary for work groups and for individuals within the work group, what is effective within one group may not be so in another.

Productivity was found to vary in small work groups to the extent that the immediate supervisor was employee-centered and production-centered (Foundation for Research on Human Behavior, 1958, p. 13). Within certain limits, productivity was higher when the supervisor was employee-centered. This meant that the supervisor was interested in his subordinates and showed them that he was. Productivity was also higher within certain limits where the supervisor was production-centered. For highest productivity, then, the supervisor needed to be interested in people and in productivity.

The highly specific nature of the situation was supported by analyses of questionnaire results in two government organizations (Comrey, Pfiffner, & High, 1954). There was little similarity among the relationships with criteria that were highly significant. The same authors found only one relationship between a criterion of group effectiveness and the questionnaire answers of 29 Lockheed foremen that was significant at the 1% level. This relationship was between favorable "Attitude towards paper work" and Production Rate where there was an *eta* of .55.

Two studies have found that ratings of leadership depended significantly on subordinates' behavior that was relatively independent of the manager himself. Ghiselli and Lodahl (1958) found that ratings of foremen were influenced significantly by two characteristics of the group they supervised. Where a foreman had in his group a subordinate who was rated higher on a supervisory scale than he was, his ratings by a superior were lower as compared to other foremen. The r was $-.50$, significant at the 5% level. Also, where the group contained more people who thought that they were capable of making decisions, the foreman was less highly regarded by his superior. Here the r was $-.57$ for 18 foremen and work groups studied, significant at the 1% level.

Scott (1956) made the other study which showed that ratings of leadership among Navy personnel depended significantly on subordinates' behavior relatively independent of the manager. Officers with strong petty officers received higher ratings from their superiors but lower leadership nominations from enlisted men. The enlisted men's leadership nominations went instead to the petty officer where he was effective. One could interpret the findings of Ghiselli and Lodahl and Scott to mean that a manager's performance is naturally graded in terms of his subordinates and, consequently, it is up to the manager to obtain effective subordinates. While this is true to some extent, these studies suggest that it is often practically impossible to have exactly the men a manager may want as subordinates. The point is that the qualifications of one's subordinates are an important part of the situation on which a manager's performance is rated.

An illustration of Likert's situational theory of management is shown in a study of the relations between productivity and group cohesiveness (Society for the Advancement of Management and Foundation for Research on Human Behavior, 1956). Some work groups with high group loyalty had high productivity; other groups with equally high group loyalty had low productivity. The explanation seemed to be in how the men saw the company. Those who saw the company as supportive or as being interested in the employees had higher productivity with high group cohesiveness. See Figure 3-1. Those who saw the company as threatening had lower productivity with their higher group cohesiveness.

Figure 3-1

INFLUENCE OF HOW MEN SEE THE COMPANY AND OF COHESIVENESS ON PRODUCTIVITY

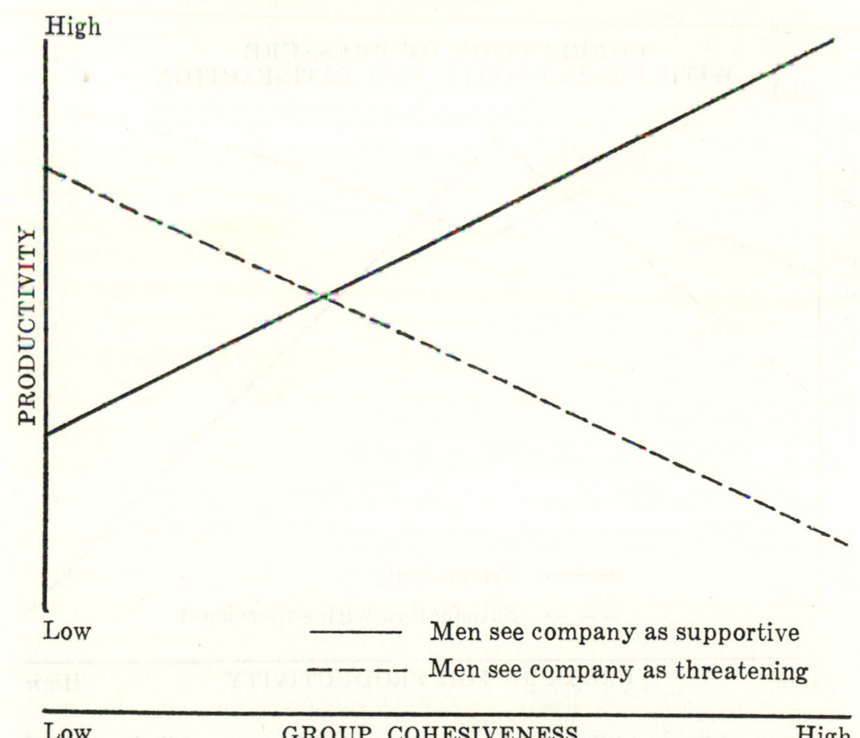

Source: S. Seashore. *Group Cohesiveness in the Industrial Work Group.* Ann Arbor: Institute for Social Research, 1954, p. 120.

Again the situational theory was supported in some results that showed how reaction to pressure depended upon the situation (Society for the Advancement of Management and Foundation for Research on Human Behavior, 1956). As shown in Figure 3-2, productivity generally increased with pressure, although the acceleration in productivity was greater when pressure was relatively low. Satisfaction with supervision, however, increased with pressure at low levels, but decreased sharply when pressure became moderate and continued to decrease with increases in pressure for productivity. When dissatisfaction with supervision became great due to increasing pressure for productivity, one might wonder whether this would not result in turnover which, in turn, would lower productivity.

Figure 3-2

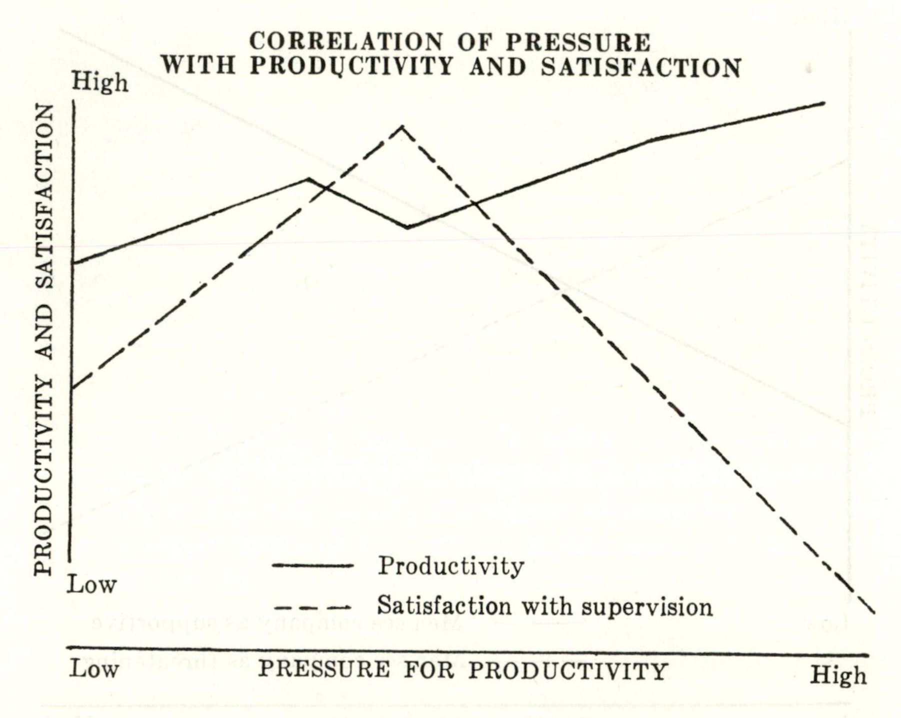

Source: R. Likert. "Developing Patterns of Management," in *General Management Series No. 178.* New York: American Management Association, 1955, p. 11.

Pelz (1952) showed that the effectiveness of supervisory practices in their response from subordinates depended upon the degree of influence which the supervisor had with his superior. Not just the supervisor's behavior, but the situation again had to be considered.

General Managers

Spencer (1957) has reported differences in the president's performance between high- and low-profit companies headed by members of the Young Presidents Organization. The high-profit companies increased profits more than 200 per cent from 1953 through 1957; the low-profit companies, about 20 per cent for that five-year period. A middle group, approximately equal in number to the high-profit group and to the low-profit group, was omitted from comparison. Since more manufacturing companies were in the high-profit group, only manufacturing companies were included. There were also product differences in profitability, so "high- and low-profit products were equally represented in both high- and low-profit groups. . . ."

Plans that had definite objectives were present somewhat more frequently in the high-profit group than in the low, 54 per cent and 47 per cent respectively. The presence of written plans was more frequent in the low-profit group, but apparently these were of a general nature. The fact that the plans were written did not necessarily mean that they would be ineffective, for of the companies with written plans, the high-profit companies had had written plans for about five years as contrasted to about three years for the low-profit companies.

The method of decision making differed between the high- and low-profit companies. Committee planning and decision making was used more frequently by the high-profit companies, especially in the areas of finance, profits, and personnel. Operational matters of production, physical facilities, and cost control were more frequently decided either by a committee or by the relevant staff member alone in the high-profit companies. In all of these areas the presidents of low-profit companies reported that they alone made the decisions.

Godfrey, Fiedler, and Hall (1958) found a different pattern for the optimal performance of the board chairman and the general manager in marketing cooperatives. The most successful companies financially had as chairman of the board of directors a man who was very permissive—who would listen to anyone no matter how silly his ideas. Under him, however, in the most successful cooperatives was a general manager who was task-oriented. In Fiedler's words, "he would fire his grandmother if she couldn't sell fertilizer, and she probably couldn't."

There is something new suggested for business in this finding of Godfrey, Fiedler, and Hall although it has also been suggested in some military research. There may be an optimal pattern for a pair of managers that is more meaningful than one optimal performance for every manager. This may be true in many situations. As one military research has suggested, every organization may need a stern father and a permissive mother.

Sales Managers

Likert (1952) found a number of differences in the performance of more successful life insurance management. Ten of the most successful agencies in the United States were compared with ten of the least successful. Questions about the local manager were answered by the agents in each agency. Seven of the actions showing the greatest differences between the superior agencies versus the mediocre agencies are shown in Table 3-1.

Manufacturing and Production Managers

"Position performance," which is defined as "how well the executive carries out the duties of his present job," was a discriminating characteristic between manufacturing executives who were promotable and those who were rated as inadequate (Randle, 1956). Forty-eight per cent of the promotable executives were rated as outstanding in position performance and only three per cent of the inadequate executives were rated as outstanding in position performance. Other performance characteristics that discriminated between the two groups were administration and

Table 3-1

FAVORABLE COMMENTS ON MANAGERS' PERFORMANCE IN "SUPERIOR" AND "MEDIOCRE" LIFE INSURANCE AGENCIES

Comments	Favorable Comments as Per Cent of Total Comments		
	"Superior" Agencies	"Mediocre" Agencies	Difference
Unselfish in dealings with agents	100	26	74
Cooperative with agents	92	35	57
Sympathetic toward agents	88	32	56
Interested in agents' success	100	54	46
Democratic toward agents	81	36	45
Sincere in dealings with agents	91	55	36
Capable planner and organizer	35	5	30

Source: R. Likert. "Motivational Dimensions of Administration," *America's Manpower Crises, Institute on Manpower Utilization and Government Personnel, Stanford University, 1951*. Chicago: Public Administration Service, 1952, pp. 89–117.

planning. Forty-nine per cent of the promotable manufacturing executives were rated outstanding in administration versus only three per cent of the inadequate executives. Forty-five per cent of the promotable executives were rated as outstanding in planning versus only seven per cent of the inadequate executives. The outstanding characteristics approach zero for the inadequate executives, but they do not approach 100 per cent for the promotable executives. Promotable executives can be promotable through a variety of patterns, not just one.

Kay (1959) found sixteen critical requirements for production foremen which were said to be highly similar to those independently found in another company. The sixteen requirements which were determined by the critical incident technique were:

Competence in administrative matters
1. Planning operations
2. Following instructions
3. Attention to details
4. Adherence to company policy
5. Selection of work for active supervision
6. Willingness to assume responsibility
7. Tact and discretion

Competence in supervising subordinates
8. Development of subordinates
9. Correction of undesirable behavior
10. Giving credit where due
11. Equality of treatment
12. Concern for employee's welfare
13. Keeping subordinates informed

Relations with equals and superiors
14. Adherence to chain of authority
15. Acceptance of criticism and suggestions
16. Communication with equals and superiors[1]

The General Electric Company (General Electric, 1957a) found differences between good and poor foremen through an observation study, but no significant differences were found by observation in two General Motors plants (O'Neill & Kubany, 1959). The differences between the good and poor foremen in the General Electric Company were that the good foremen were not as busy as the poor foremen because they did not try to do so many things during the day as the poor foremen. The good foremen spent more of their time in planning, for example, in the personnel, equipment, and methods areas. They spent more time in talking with their subordinates, in giving information, or in two-way discussions. There was no difference in the total time spent with employees; the poor foremen had more contacts with their employees but spent more time in trying to get information from them. The good foremen supervised more generally; the poor foremen spent more time with immediate problems.

---

[1] B. R. Kay, "Key Factors in Effective Foreman Behavior," *Personnel* (1959). Reprinted by permission of American Management Association.

It is not clear whether the positive results in the General Electric study and the lack of positive results in the General Motors study were due to the differences in research methods or to differences in the situations in the two companies. The GE study used 12 foremen who were rated as good both by their superior managers and by their subordinates and 12 who were rated "poor" by their superior managers and by their subordinates. Other foremen who were rated poor by either the superior or the subordinates and good by the other were not included in the study.

The University of Illinois (Fiedler, 1958), as well as the University of Michigan, has been studying the performance of supervisors in relation to productivity for a number of years. The design of the series at Illinois has been similar to that at the University of Michigan. There has been an objective measure of production with every group studied in the Illinois series. Only one industrial group, open-hearth furnacemen, has been included, along with several other groups from the military service and schools. Tank crews from the Army, bomber crews from the Air Force, survey gangs from college, and high school basketball teams have been studied. Only first-line supervisors, not higher management, have been studied. The attitudes of the leader have been measured and compared with the productivity of his group.

Fiedler has concluded that the leaders with the highest productivity maintained some "psychological distance" between themselves and some members of their work group. He found that groups could be highly productive when the leader was on close terms with his first lieutenant so to speak, or the group could be highly productive when the leader was buddy-buddy with the rank and file but not with the first lieutenant. Where, however, the leader was on intimate terms with everyone in his work group — his lieutenant and rank and file — productivity was not high. Fiedler's interpretation was not in support of the cliché, "familiarity breeds contempt," but rather that where there was no psychological distance between the leader and members of his work group, he became too involved with them personally. He could not be sufficiently detached to make decisions, which might be unpleasant, about members of the group. This interpretation would qualify the Michigan finding that supervisors who were employee-centered had higher production. Perhaps it means that supervisors can be too interested in their people, although optimum results can be obtained where there is more interest than normally occurs in industry today.

There was a thorough study of production and nonproduction supervisors in an International Harvester plant by Ohio State University (Seashore, 1957). The supervisors' behavior was similar to that of his superior. Supervisory behavior was measured in terms of two scales, "consideration" and "initiating structure" (Fleishman, Harris, & Burtt, 1955). The scale for Consideration measured the extent to which the foreman was friendly and did things for his subordinates. Initiating Structure measured the extent to which the foreman was bossy and organized things for the subordinates so that they did not have to think for themselves. The higher up in management men were the lower were their scores on the Consideration scale and the higher on the Initiating Structure scale (Fleishman, 1953). Foremen's attitudes on Consideration were between those of their employees and superiors but were closer to those of their superiors. This is another documentation for Likert's situational theory, showing evidence that managers adjust to the views of their superiors and subordinates. Subordinates whose foremen were high in Consideration and low in Initiating Structure had higher morale. Superiors in production departments rated foremen higher when they were high in Initiating Structure.

An attempt was made to develop objective criteria of the success of each work group. Production criteria were not retained for study because there was contamination with them or they were not independent. Four objective criteria were retained in addition to the criterion of employee morale and superiors' ratings. The four objective criteria were (1) turnover; (2) accidents; (3) absenteeism; and (4) grievances. These were essentially independent; the highest correlation between any pair was .37. They had respectable reliabilities running from .85 to .59.

As the results show in Table 3-2, there is a difference between the production and nonproduction or service departments. Presumably the explanation is primarily in the time pressures that are present in the production departments. Proficiency as judged

Table 3-2

RELATION BETWEEN FOREMEN'S CONSIDERATION OR INITIATING STRUCTURE ON WORK BEHAVIOR IN PRODUCTION AND NON-PRODUCTION DEPARTMENTS

	Proficiency	Absenteeism	Accidents	Grievances	Turnover
Consideration					
Production	−.31*	−.49*	−.06	−.07	.13
Non-production	.28	−.38	−.42†	.15	.04
Initiating Structure					
Production	.47*	.27†	.15	.45*	.06
Non-production	−.19	.06	.18	.23	.51+

*Significant at or beyond the 1-per cent level of confidence.

†Significant at or beyond the 5-per cent level of confidence.

Source: E. A. Fleishman, E. F. Harris, and H. E. Burtt. *Leadership and Supervision in Industry*, Bureau of Educational Research, Monograph 33. Columbus: The Ohio State University, 1955, p. 85.

by superiors' ratings in the production departments was positively correlated with Initiating Structure, but negatively correlated with Consideration. Even in the production departments Consideration did show a pay-off in being associated significantly with freedom from absences. In the nonproduction departments the only significant correlation with Consideration was freedom from accidents.

While Initiating Structure accompanied higher proficiency ratings by superiors, it also accompanied more grievances and, still significantly but to a lesser extent, absenteeism. Initiating Structure among foremen accompanied turnover in the nonproduction departments.

In another company Consideration as measured by the supervisors' attitudes correlated .29 with ratings of effectiveness in supervision by higher management (Bass, 1956). This was significant only at the 5% level. One production supervisor whose Consideration was low but whose Initiating Structure and financial results were very high was observed and reported in great detail (Argyris, 1954).

Production rate in the Lockheed Aircraft Corporation correlated significantly with Good Conference Practice of superiors as reported by supervisors (Comrey, High, & Wilson, 1955 a & b). Ratings correlated at the 1% level of confidence with Pride in Work Group, Pressure for Production, and Adequate Authority. The last three variables were obtained from scores on a questionnaire filled out by supervisors. The relationship was measured by *eta* which does not assume linearity. Low Work-Rework Ratio, the index of the amount of work that had to be done over, correlated significantly with Sympathy.

Also at Lockheed, a similar questionnaire was given to rank and file employees with respect to their supervisors (Comrey, High & Wilson, 1955a). Low Work-Rework Ratio correlated with supervision as seen by workers for Job Helpfulness, Job Competence, Consistency, Planning, Good Judgment, and Pride in work group. Work Acceptance Rate correlated with Planning. Production Rate correlated with Communication-down and with Social Nearness. These results were significant at the 1% level of confidence.

The Lockheed studies were unusual in having several reliable objective criteria and also in reporting in full detail the results in the same groups for employees, supervisors, and foremen. This completeness of publication has not been done for the important Michigan series. The University of Southern California study at Lockheed measured and reported so many variables that it is somewhat difficult to follow. The analysis was unusual in using *eta* rather than r. While the results seemed to favor a human relations pattern of supervision, this is not entirely true, and the important aspects of performance varied from one criterion to another, so that the picture appears quite complex. The study is also unusual in having a large sample of supervisors as well as of rank and file employees.

Two of the series of studies made by the University of Michigan Institute of Social Research have concentrated on production foremen (Kahn, 1956). One of these studies took place at the Caterpillar tractor plant. As in the earlier studies of office supervisors and of supervisors of railroad right-of-way maintenance gangs, the investigators concluded that the supervisors of the groups which were above average in production were concerned about the needs of their employees and were skillful in meeting those needs. These supervisors were also interested in production, but did not give their employees the feeling of pressure for production as much as the supervisors of less productive groups. Employees in the highly productive groups thought that their supervisors put a high value on production but that it was not the most important thing.

The Michigan investigators changed their theory from hypothesizing that satisfaction would cause high productivity since they had found that the most productive workers were not the ones who were most satisfied. Their new theory was that people would try hard for what they wanted. Therefore it would be necessary to find out specifically what employees wanted and how they saw a possibility of getting what they wanted. The first opportunity to test this theory was in an appliance manufacturing company. The results were positive but still left a good deal to be explained. Of a group of employees who said that they wanted high wages and who saw an opportunity of getting them, 66 per cent were high producers as determined by time study men. Of those who either did not say that they especially wanted high wages or did not see that they could get them by harder work because of the limitations such as an assembly line, only 17 per cent were in the high producing group. One thing that explained high group productivity according to the foremen's reports was that men helped each other out more (Katz & Kahn, 1952).

While not exactly production, the maintenance work of right-of-way gangs on the railroad seems closer to production than to the other functional fields. The Michigan investigators (Katz, *et al.*, 1951) sought supervisory practices in the Chesapeake and Ohio Railroad that could be related to a rating criterion of production. As mentioned above, the foremen of the high production groups were interested in their employees' needs and were skillful in meeting them. Their men said that these foremen were interested in them, that they were more understanding and less punitive, and that they spent more time in training them. The foremen of the high production groups differentiated their roles to a greater extent than did the foremen of the low production groups. They seemed to see their supervisory responsibilities better and spent more time in supervision.

Office Managers

How autocratic leadership can be effective in an office over a year's time was shown in an experiment conducted by the University of Michigan at the Prudential Insurance Company (Morse & Reimer, 1956; Likert, 1958a). Four experimental groups which did not differ in competence or ability from the control group were chosen. Two groups were led autocratically, or were "hierarchically controlled," in that decisions formerly made by the supervisor were made by the supervisor's superior. Scientific management was used to show that the groups were overstaffed and the forces were reduced.

Two groups were more democratically led and were called the "participative" groups because rank and file employees were encouraged to participate in making decisions that formerly their supervisors had made. Both the hierarchically controlled groups and participative groups were more productive than a control group, but the hierarchically controlled groups were the highest in productivity. Their costs were 25 per cent lower than those in the

Table 3-3

DESCRIPTIONS OF SUPERVISORS BY HIGH AND LOW MORALE GROUPS OF EMPLOYEES

Supervisor's Behavior	High Morale %	Low Morale %
Enforces the rules	54	54
Arranges work, makes work assignments	67	69
Supplies men with materials and tools	36	41
Recommends promotions, transfers, pay increases	61	22
Informs men on what is happening in the company	47	11
Keeps men posted on how well they are doing	47	12
Hears complaints and grievances	65	32

Source: R. Likert. "Motivational Dimensions of Administration." *America's Manpower Crisis, Institute on Manpower Utilization and Government Personnel, Stanford University, 1951.* Chicago: Public Administration Service, 1952, p. 98.

control group, while the participative costs were reduced by only 20 per cent. Productivity as measured by cost reduction was best in the hierarchically controlled group. The participative group had the best morale. Morale was lowest in the hierarchically controlled groups. Attitudes deteriorated with respect to getting the work done; attitudes became less favorable toward the high producers in the work group, toward the managers and assistant managers, and toward the company. One might wonder how long productivity could stay high without being hurt by excessive turnover or a strike.

In the Detroit Edison Company a study was made to compare the ratings made of supervisors by their superiors with what the subordinates thought of the same supervisors (Mann & Dent, 1954). There was substantial agreement between employees and superiors about which supervisors were good and which were poor. Where superiors had called supervisors "Immediately Promotable," their employees said:

> He is good at handling people.
> He is a man with whom employees feel free to discuss important things about their jobs.
> He is also one with whom employees feel free to discuss personal problems.
> He goes to bat for them.
> He pulls for both the company and the men.
> He lets employees know where they stand.
> He lets his employees work pretty much on their own instead of supervising them closely.
> He holds group meetings where problems can be discussed.
> He is a "leader of men," "likable," "reasonable." He is not "bossy," "quick to criticize," a "driver," or "unnecessarily strict."
> He gives recognition for good work done.
> In particular, he gives employees recognition by training them for better jobs.[2]

The detailed descriptions of some supervisory performance in groups of high and low morale are shown in Table 3-3 (Likert 1952, p. 98). In clerical work groups the extent to which super-

[2]F. Mann and J. Dent, *Appraisals of Supervisors and Attitudes of Their Employees in an Electric Power Company* (Survey Research Center, 1954). Reprinted by permission of the Survey Research Center, University of Michigan.

vision was close or general followed the pattern of the supervisor's superior (Likert, 1952, p. 91).

Belongingness and the ego motives rather than the reward systems set up by management were believed effective in the office as well as in the factory by Katz and Kahn (1952). Girls more frequently helped each other out in high-producing work groups, whereas in the low-producing work groups, a girl would do only the work specifically assigned to her.

Kinds of group discussion varied in high- and low-production sections of an insurance company office (Likert & Katz, 1948). There was more problem-solving discussion in the high-producing groups, although the total number of discussions was essentially equal between low- and high-production groups. The discussions in the low-producing groups consisted of the supervisor giving instructions to employees rather than encouraging participation. In the high-production groups the supervisors more frequently began in such ways as "Here's a new situation. Now, what's the best way of going about it?" or, "I thought of thus and so. Does it make sense?"

Research and Engineering Managers

The Michigan Institute for Social Research has reported two studies which include the performance of research managers correlated with productivity. Performance seemed to be due in part to the contacts which the first-line manager had with his scientists (Pelz, 1957). For both scientists and scientific supervisors who saw their superiors frequently, productivity was correlated with their freedom to decide how to do their work. In a study of 20 medical laboratories with 310 research scientists, Baumgartel (1956) found that scientists' internal motivation was more important to their productivity than the effect of management upon them. Research men who had more contacts with other scientists whose backgrounds were different from theirs were more productive.

Summary and Conclusions

Kahn and Katz (1953) have reviewed the Michigan series of studies which have included the factory, office, and research organization, but not sales organizations, and have concluded that four supervisory practices were generally associated with higher than average productivity.

1. Differentiation of duties. This meant that the supervisor spent more of his time in activities which differed from those of his subordinates. He spent more time in planning, in personnel matters, and in doing specialized tasks which he could do better than his subordinates. He spent time in talking with subordinates, in training them, and in motivating them. Differentiation of duties — especially the planning and communicating with people — is supported by a number of other studies in addition to the Michigan series.

2. Lack of close supervision. Supervisors with higher than average productivity gave general rather than close supervision. All supervisors attempted to raise productivity and enforce the rules, but some breathed down the necks of their employees. That high productivity results from general supervision has support from some other studies, but there is a suggestion that at least some production jobs have high productivity with close supervision; and the Prudential experiment also showed this in the office, although morale was terrible, and perhaps continued high productivity was impossible.

3. Employee-centered. Supervisors with higher than average production were interested in their employees and their employees said that the supervisors were interested in them and that the supervisors did things for them. These supervisors were more understanding and less punitive when mistakes occurred. They more often sided with their subordinates when there was a conflict between employees and higher management. There is also some support for this from other studies, although Fiedler's interpretation would qualify this to say that the maximum amount of interest for all employees is inconsistent with the highest productivity. An alternative explanation for Fiedler's data is simply that supervisors of the most productive groups were highly aware of individual differences between the best and worst employee.

4. Group Relations. There were better group relations in the work groups with higher than average productivity. It was concluded that productivity was improved by group relations, and,

in turn, group relations were improved by the success experience of high productivity. Specifically, what seems to happen is that if people in a work group like each other, they will more willingly help each other out. This effect on productivity happens only, however, when the employees look on the company as supportive; otherwise productivity goes down with an increase in group cohesiveness.

Pfiffner (1955), summarizing the University of Southern California studies, concluded broadly that effective management included a human relations approach plus a concern for productivity. This seems to be true from all the evidence.

Supervisors in the factory and in the office were shown to follow their superiors' example. In the factory they also followed their employees' expectations, but the superior's example was stronger.

The situational theory of Likert seems to be essentially supported by all the data. While there are some fundamentals of good management, such as being responsible, planning, and motivating people, the effect of one practice or another often depends upon the situation. Some of the important elements of the situation are what one's superior, peers, and subordinates want and how they see the situation. This calls for flexibility and wisdom on the part of managers.

Chapter 4

RECRUITMENT FROM COLLEGE

This chapter deals with the recruitment of prospective managers from colleges and graduate schools of business. It deals with what business says it is looking for and what it gets. The chapter also reviews studies of management success with information that was present when these men were in college. Finally, it reviews studies on predicting grades in undergraduate and graduate schools of business.

What Business Wants

A survey (Gordon & Howell, 1959) among 84 companies found that the qualities that businessmen most frequently said that they wanted in college men were skill in human relations—given by 42 companies—and motivation or ambition—answered by 35. Stryker (1958) found that top executives listed integrity as the prime requirement for young managers. Integrity was defined broadly and did not mean just "not taking money out of the till. . . ."

A survey, which had 552 returns from 800 questionnaires sent to companies (Adams, *et al.*, 1959), found that the seven qualities businessmen said were wanted most in college graduates at the bachelor level were:

1. Integrity
2. Ability to think logically
3. Enthusiasm, initiative, drive
4. Dependability
5. Ability to communicate, orally and in writing
6. Emotional stability
7. Ability to get along with others[1]

[1]John Adams, *et al., What Industry and Business Looks For in the College Graduate* (*Bachelor Level*) (Western College Placement Association, 1959). Reprinted by permission of the Western College Placement Association.

Several people have observed that business managers look for young men who are like themselves (Hinchliffe, 1959; Dalton, 1959). Managers naturally look for prospective managers that they like, and people typically like people who are similar to them. Social stratification may occur through the interview and also through personality testing where the procedure is to get more managers like the present ones. While the process is perhaps less vicious where the purpose is to get more managers like the present good managers, it still may be a stifling of opportunity to some extent.

Young Presidents seemed to want MBA's who were similar to themselves (Spencer, May 1957). The Young Presidents thought that the most important characteristics for success were hard work and drive, while business students thought that getting along with people was most important. There is a contradiction between the answer that the Young Presidents gave for the key to success and their answer on another occasion to the factors that contributed to their success. In that instance they answered in terms of dealing with people. In other words, the Young Presidents gave the same answer then that the business students gave.

Recruiting Methods. Indiana University (Steele, 1949) concluded that the three tests most frequently used by employers using the University's placement service were (1) Wonderlic Personnel Test, (2) Kuder Preference Record, and (3) Bernreuter Personality Inventory. Consequently, in the school year 1949–50, all graduating seniors were given these tests so that the results would be available for prospective employers.

Procter and Gamble Company (Uhrbrock, 1949) constructed a test of ability and knowledge for recruiting college graduates. This correlated .48 with a rating by superiors in the manufacturing division. College grades correlated .24 with the same rating. A combination of the test and the grades gave a multiple R of .56.

At Stanford a study was made of 12 companies recruiting management trainees among prospective MBA's (McConnell &

O'Neill, 1958). The companies agreed fairly generally on what they said that they wanted, namely:

> experience, ability to get along with people, personal stability, leadership, attitude, interest, appearance, intelligence, participation in extra-curricular activities, poise, drive, initiative, ambition, loyalty.[2]

They agreed less well in their decisions to offer a job. Of twenty men who were interviewed by three or more companies there was no man who was offered a job by all companies who interviewed the candidate. There were four men who were not offered a job by any company. One man was offered a job by four companies. The twenty- to thirty-minute interview could hardly be expected to yield more reliable results with respect to such broad qualities.

Leaderless group discussions were compared with the interview in three companies recruiting for supervisory trainees at Ohio State University (Bass, 1951). Reliability was said to be the same for the leaderless discussion groups as for the individual interview.

Whom Business Gets from College

Ability. The ability of students who attend undergraduate business schools is slightly lower than the average of all college students but there is a great deal of overlap (Wolfle, 1954). Graduate students in business were slightly more able than undergraduates and slightly less able than graduate students generally. There are, of course, many college students who enter business who did not attend business schools.

Interests. Interests of graduate students of business are not as clear cut as are the interests of students of medicine, engineering, or law (Strong, 1943, p. 420). This is due in part to the fact that business is broad, that it includes people with quite diverse interests who, when averaged, reduce the peaks of interest. It is also due to the fact that many men go into business because they are not genuinely interested in any occupation. The average

[2]P. McConnell and P. O'Neill, "A Study of the Selection Interview." Unpublished paper. Stanford University, 1958.

graduate business student showed no clear primary interest pattern. Two secondary patterns that were frequently found were business detail and sales-contact. Also there were a number of B ratings for production manager and personnel manager. Another complicating fact is that scores on the business manager scales showed more increase over a period of years. In other words, the interest test was less valid for young business students when comparing their interests with mature men, than for other occupations of college men.

The Kuder Preference Record was given to a sample of alumni from the Indiana University Schools of Business and Law (Shaffer & Kuder, 1953). The interests of accountants differed from those of other business alumni, being higher in the Computational and Clerical scales, and lower in Social Service and Persuasive. Aside from the accountants, business alumni had higher Persuasive and Mechanical scores than the lawyers but were lower in the Literary and Scientific scales.

Attitudes. Business students at Mississippi State College had attitudes that differed from both business administrators and business employees (Anikeef, 1954, 1955). The attitudes of the students were closer to those of the employees than to those of the administrators. The main difference from employee attitudes was that students disapproved much more of equality in distributing profits. The main difference from business administrators' attitudes concerned government control which was favored more by students than by administrators. To generalize these two findings it would appear that these students were intermediate on a radicalism-conservative axis between administrators and employees, but were somewhat closer in attitudes to employees.

Predicting Success from College

There have been several studies which correlated success in business with information that was available at the time the man left college. Some interesting information is contained in the results of a survey that was made by *Time* and analyzed at Columbia University (Havemann & West, 1952, pp. 27–187). College graduates were much more likely to be managers than were men with less education. Of all men graduates 34 per cent were proprietors, managers, or executives, compared with only 13 per cent for all nongraduate United States men.

Men who worked their way through college did not do so well in business as those who were family-supported. Among businessmen 40 years of age and older, 41 per cent of the men who worked their way through college and 53 per cent of those who were family-supported were earning $7,500 and over.

While the bulk of college graduates had important jobs, there was a difference in the percentage of graduates who became managers depending on religious preference. Thirty-four per cent of Protestants, 33 per cent of Jews, and 26 per cent of Catholics became proprietors, managers, or executives.

Husband (1957) found several predictors in college to correlate with success thirty years after graduation of his Dartmouth class of 1926. He used earnings as a criterion for most of his comparisons but he also used a second criterion, ratings of how well a man had done with respect to the opportunities in his chosen occupation. Being outstanding in college in anything was associated with higher earnings, and being outstanding in more than one thing made financial success even more probable. College grades were generally associated with earnings. Men with the highest grades — over a B average, 3.30 and over — had the highest average earnings of $20,000 plus. Those with the lowest grades, 1.50–1.69, where D was 1.00, had the lowest median income, $10,625. There were a few inversions, but generally grade-point average was correlated with income. The median income for the class was $14,950.

A similar finding was reported in 1928 for the Bell Telephone System (Gifford, 1928). Five years after graduation men who had been in the highest third of their graduating class had 48 per cent of their number in the highest third of their salary group and 27 per cent in the middle third salary group. Of those in the lowest third of their graduating class, only 22 per cent were in the highest third of their salary group and 31 per cent were in the middle third of the salary group. By chance there would have been 33 per cent in each of the three salary groups. Bellows has pointed out that there could have been a contamination of criterion here since the promoting authorities had access to the college records. While this is possible, it is doubtful that the contamination was very important.

Husband (1957) found that although men with lowest intelligence scores had low earnings, so also did the men with the highest intelligence test scores. The latter he attributed to the fact that so many of those with the highest intelligence went into the teaching field.

Extracurricular activities also were associated with high earnings in the study of Dartmouth students although not quite as much as were grades. Men with no extracurricular activities had median earnings of $13,840 versus $20,000 and over for those with outstanding success in extracurricular activities. Those who had participated moderately in extracurricular activities had intermediate incomes.

Athletes who had won their letters had incomes higher than those who had not, although again the difference was not as great as for the extremes in grades. Those who had not been in athletics averaged $14,280 while the winner of a single letter averaged $18,575. Those who had won numerals but not letters were intermediate in income. Also below the winners of a single "D" were those who had won two letters, although there were only nine of these men. Husband reported contrary findings by Tunis who had reported that although good scholars had high earnings, athletes from Harvard had relatively low earnings.

Those who had been editors or held top staff jobs in literary or musical organizations in college had somewhat higher earnings than the average, namely, $16,250. Men who had participated but not held office in these organizations had earnings a few hundred dollars above the class median of $14,950.

Political activities as shown by being a member of leadership organizations which included most of the class offices also were correlated with earnings. Those with no activities averaged $14,250; those with two or more averaged $20,000 plus. Those in one activity had an intermediate income.

The rating criterion of success was also correlated with undergraduate records of grades, extracurricular activities, and social activities.

Table 4-1

CORRELATION OF TEST SCORES AND GRADES IN ADMINISTRATIVE PRACTICES WITH SALARIES FOR HARVARD MBA'S
(N = 150)

Tests	Salaries	
	1955*	Starting**
Personnel Problems (AMP Differential Key)......	.35	.24
Individual Background Survey (MBA Differential Key)..	.30	.24
Emotional Maturity Rating.....................	.27	.33
Administrative Practices Grade................	.26	.33
Caution Score on Business Problems Test......	−.21	.03
Objectivity Score on Guilford-Zimmerman.......	.20	.36
Productivity of Ideas on Imaginary Events Test..	−.18	−.22

*1955 salaries were normalized by standard scores for length of time out of school.

**Starting salaries were normalized by standard scores for each class sample separately.

Source: Adapted from L. B. Ward. "Tentative Summary." Unpublished. Harvard Graduate School of Business Administration, 1958.

Graduate School of Business Alumni Surveys

Ward (1958) has made a thorough study, including many important possible predictors in relation to salaries, of a sample of five classes of Harvard MBA's. The first class was that of 1948 and the other four were of succeeding years. Results in Table 4-1 show the predictors which correlated highest with salaries received after five years out of school and show the order of their correlation. There were many other variables which did not correlate significantly, but some of these did correlate significantly with starting salary. Human relations and personality variables are essentially the only significant ones, with the exception of the negative relationship with Productivity of Ideas which perhaps is a combination of the intellectual and nonintellectual components of personality. The AMP Differential Key for the Personnel Problems Test was based on answers by members of the Advanced Management Program, differentiating the most able from the least able students as judged by the faculty. The MBA Differential Key for the Individual Background Survey was based on answers of the MBA's correlated with 1955 salaries. It was cross-validated with half of the sample, after setting weights on the other half of the sample.

The Emotional Maturity Rating was made by the Research Staff on all information available at the time of graduation. What this information was is not known. Administrative Practices Grade is a grade in a human relations and organization course.

It is interesting that 1955 salaries were negatively correlated with the Caution Score and with Productivity of Ideas. If these results mean anything, they mean that business success is retarded by caution and creativity.

A study of Stanford MBA's showed four variables that correlated significantly with earnings (Williams, 1959). Results are shown in Table 4-2 for men who had been out of school for 15 years or more.

Table 4-2

CORRELATIONS OF PREDICTORS WITH EARNED INCOME FOR STANFORD MBA'S

(N = 196)

Variable	Income after 15 or more years
Number of offices as an undergraduate	.24
Grade point average in elective graduate courses	.22
Masculinity score on the Strong Vocational Interest Test	.19
Ratings by undergraduate professors	.18

Source: F. J. Williams. "Predicting Success in Business." Unpublished Ph.D. dissertation, Graduate School of Business, Stanford University, 1959.

Grades in required courses in graduate school and undergraduate grades had no correlation with earnings, nor did intelligence test scores. The average IQ of the students was between 125 and 130.

Predicting Grades for Graduate Business Students

Harvard. Ward (1958) obtained a multiple correlation of .60 with first-year grades from a combination of test scores and undergraduate grades. Undergraduate grades were adjusted for the scholastic standards of the schools. The tests that correlated higher than .30 with First-Year Grades were "Deductive Reasoning, Quantitative Relations, Business Analogies, Practical Judgment (AMP Key) and Individual Background Survey (MBA Compensation Key)." Since the reliability of the grades was only .65, Ward concluded that there was little expectation of raising the multiple correlation.

Vatter (1958a) found some interesting relations between Harvard Business School grades and fathers' occupations. Sons of laborers and farmers were underachievers in terms of predictions from scores on the Admission Test for Graduate Study in Business (ATGSB) and their undergraduate grade averages. Their underachievement was −.78 of a grade point with respect to the predicted graduate grades. The grades of sons of professional men and businessmen were more accurately predicted. Sons of professional men were very slight underachievers, −.07, and sons of businessmen, slight overachievers, +.06. One interpretation is that the study of business is culturally embedded. There is less learned about business in the homes of laborers and farmers than in the homes of businessmen and professionals. This information is of interest in terms of the occupational mobility studies reported in Chapter 6 which show that father's occupation as a businessman is a very positive factor in the son's becoming a business manager. While family influence, especially in getting a job and perhaps to a lesser extent in promotion, is a factor, the Harvard results suggest that possibly there is a factor of knowledge or problem-solving ability that is family-embedded and independent of general intelligence and scholarship. There is probably a personality factor, including such things as poise, self-confidence, assurance in communications, or "smell-of-the-hive," that helps.

Vatter (1958b) found that low scores on either the Verbal or Quantitative parts of the ATGSB were associated with low grades at Harvard Business School. The ATGSB total score consists of more than these two separate scores, which are the only separate scores reported. The Quantitative score correlated .32 with grades, the Verbal, .21. The Quantitative Score alone did not add to the prediction of first-year grades over the total score but it and the verbal scores predicted weaknesses in separate courses. The Multiple R was .47 between Verbal, Quantitative, and College Grades on the one hand and first-year grades on the other. Students who had Verbal scores of 22 or lower often had trouble in two courses, Administrative Practices and another course. Students who had Quantitative scores of 25 or less often had low grades in three courses, Control, Production, and Finance.

Stanford. Essentially the same, but slightly higher multiple R's were found by Pietrowski (1958) at Stanford. Results are shown in Table 4-3. There was a practice effect on the ATGSB

Table 4-3

CORRELATIONS OF TEST SCORES AND UNDERGRADUATE GRADES WITH STANFORD GRADUATE SCHOOL OF BUSINESS FIRST-YEAR GRADES

Grades or Test Score	Class of 1958 (N = 158)	Class of 1959 (N = 144)
Undergraduate grades	.39	.34
Verbal Score, ATGSB	.41	.38
Quantitative Score, ATGSB	.53	.64
Total Score, ATGSB	.59	.64
ATGSB combined with Undergraduate Grades	.63	.66

Source: R. F. Pietrowski. "Predicting Success in Graduate School of Business." Stanford: Mimeographed, 1958.

test. For 81 students who had previously taken the test, the initial score was 521; the score the second time was 552. This is a difference of 31 points due to practice. The standard deviation for applicants to all schools was 100 points.

Stanford second-year students scored 568, taking the test for the first time during their second year. First-year students scored 525. Perhaps not quite all this difference of 43 points can be attributed to the year's education inasmuch as some of the weaker first-year students might have dropped out of the second-year class.

Tables 4-4 and 4-5 on pages 64 and 65 show some of these same results in percentages. Table 4-4 shows that no one made below the passing grade of C or 2.0 who had scored as high as 475 on the Admission Test. Requiring a score of 475 would, however, bar too many students who do get passing scores. Of those who score between 450 and 474, 91 per cent had grades above C.

Table 4-5 shows a similar expectancy of first-year grades from undergraduate grades. The prediction is much less accurate than for the test score. All students with undergraduate grades of 3.25 (3.0 is B) had an average in the Graduate School of Business above the required C, in fact above 2.5 or C +.

Carnegie Tech. ATGSB correlated .49 with first-year grades at Carnegie Tech (Miller).

Minnesota. The Miller Analogies Test correlated .63 with grades of 40 students in a Master's program in Industrial Relations at the University of Minnesota (Yoder, 1959).

Clinical Versus Statistical Prediction. Stanford uses a clinical method of appraising applicants in that an attempt is made to make a judgment on the total record of the applicant rather than on specific required scores on ATGSB or on grade-point average. Harvard's admission procedure is similarly clinical. One study was reported in which a comparison was made between the clinical and statistical methods (Sarbin, 1942). The statistical prediction correlated slightly higher with grades, but not significantly so. A review of the literature has failed to find any convincing superiority for the clinical method; results have generally favored the statistical method (Meehl, 1954).

Table 4-4

EXPECTANCY TABLE OF FIRST-YEAR STANFORD G.S.B. GRADES FROM ATGSB SCORES (FIRST-YEAR STUDENTS)

Shows Per Cent at Each Interval

ATGSB Scores	First-Year Graduate Business G.P.A.										N
	1.5	1.75	2.0	2.25	2.5	2.75	3.0	3.25	3.5	3.75 4.0	
725–749								100			1
700–724						100					1
675–699								25	25	50	4
650–674						20	40	20	20		5
625–649			14		14	14	14	29	14		7
600–624					17	17	25		33	8	12
575–599				15	8	46	8	8	15		13
550–574			10	15	27	21	27				19
525–549			8	8	8	60	8		8		13
500–524			15	38	8	15	8	8	8		13
475–499			7	29	7	14	36	7			14
450–474	6	13	31	6	25	19					16
425–449	7	18	18	9	18	18	9				11
400–424			33	67							3
375–399		25		25	25		25				4
350–374		33	67								3
325–349		67		33							2
300–324	100										1
275–299		100									1
Totals	2	6	12	15	13	22	15	5	8	2	144

Source: R. F. Pietrowski. "Predicting Success in Graduate School of Business." Stanford: Mimeographed, 1958.

Table 4-5

EXPECTANCY TABLE OF FIRST-YEAR STANFORD G.S.B. GRADES FROM UNDERGRADUATE GRADES (FIRST- AND SECOND-YEAR STUDENTS)

Shows per cent at each undergraduate G.P.A. interval

Under-graduate G.P.A.*	First-Year Graduate Business G.P.A.										N
	1.5	1.75	2.0	2.25	2.5	2.75	3.0	3.25	3.5	3.75 4.0	
3.75–3.99						50				50	2
3.50–3.74							50		33	17	6
3.25–3.49					13	26	18	30	4	9	23
3.00–3.24	3	5	3	10	3	26	24	10	8	8	38
2.75–2.99	2		11	9	23	24	17	6	6	2	53
2.50–2.74		3	7	21	16	24	17	9	3		58
2.25–2.49	2	2	11	23	29	18	9	2	4		55
2.00–2.24	5	8	18	18	12	15	12	8	3		61
1.71–1.99		17		17		17	33		17		6
Totals	2	4	10	15	16	21	16	8	5	3	302

*Adjusted for Stanford norms.

Source: R. F. Pietrowski. "Predicting Success in Graduate School of Business." Stanford: Mimeographed, 1958.

Summary

Businessmen say that they want many characteristics in the college graduates they hire, but heading the list are integrity, skill in human relations, ability to think, and drive.

Good scholars in college make more money after college. This was shown in studies by Havemann and West, Gifford, and Husband. Husband's study found that several leadership characteristics were associated with higher earnings, but scholarship had the closest association.

On the other hand, earnings of MBA's are not associated with undergraduate grades or, for that matter, only to a slight extent with graduate grades. Perhaps the reason is that the MBA's had been sufficiently selected so that scholastic aptitude of the selected group was no longer an important factor. What correlated with MBA earnings were number of important undergraduate offices, grades in elective graduate courses, masculinity, and professors' ratings for a Stanford group. For a Harvard group, the things which correlated highest with earnings were scores on a Personnel Problems test, scores on an Individual Background Survey, an Emotional Maturity Rating, and grades from an Administrative Practices course, which is a course in human relations. The Harvard and Stanford results together indicate that personality, including leadership, maturity, and understanding of people, is the most important factor found.

Grades in graduate school are satisfactorily predicted by the Admission Test for Graduate Study in Business.

Chapter 5

WHO GETS PROMOTED?

The qualifications of people who are promoted are discussed in several other chapters, but in this chapter a detailed look will be taken at promotion policies and at some results of and ideas about the promotion process. Undoubtedly promotion often depends upon the answers to the questions raised in Chapter 2 about who is a successful manager and how is success determined. Promotion also is inferred in Chapter 6 in relation to the characteristics of men who somehow get promoted to top management, and also in Chapters 7, 8, 9, and 10 where studies of the qualifications of men in the four most prominent functional fields of management are reviewed.

That promotion is not an exact science is attested by all the informed opinion and results that have been assembled. McMurry (1952) has been one of the most articulate critics in pointing out that promotion occurs for reasons other than the pertinent ones of the qualifications of the new job. He listed eight extraneous reasons why people were promoted to high management jobs.

T. Brooks (1958) reported from a survey of leading New York companies that promotion policies, and procedures differed widely, sometimes because of the company situation but more often because of differences of opinion. In fact he concluded that every company was different in its promotion policies and procedures. While no doubt there were no companies that were completely identical in the working of their free answer responses, one would expect that some generalizations about similarities could have emerged. With all the differences it is clear that each company had made its policies with the belief that it would get its best men to do its particular management jobs. The tremendous diversity of policies is therefore a corollary to the fact brought out in Chapter 2 that a determination of who is a successful manager is such a difficult step that it is rarely achieved.

One of Brooks' responding companies mentioned a policy of promoting only college graduates. Several managers have recently mentioned this, with some misgivings, as an implicit, if not written, policy of their companies.

While it is difficult at best to formulate policies that could be expected to be sound, some of Brooks' respondents appeared pretty far off base:

> There are those who emphasize sustained hard work, or seemingly minor traits such as promptness, on the theory that these virtues keynote more subtle potentialities; there are even companies that deliberately seek out idiosyncrasies — such as the boss who picks out men with their ties habitually askew, theorizing that they are concerned with *work*, not appearance; or the boss who does *not* promote typical "organization men" because they have no faults to set them apart from, and above, their fellows.[1]

A very different emphasis in the interpretation of promotion policies was found in a report by the National Industrial

Table 5-1

DIFFERENT METHODS USED TO FILL EXECUTIVE VACANCIES, AS ESTIMATED BY SIXTY-TWO COMPANY PRESIDENTS

Method	Per Cent of Vacancies Filled By This Method	Number of Times Mentioned
Pirating (men are hired from other companies)	10	45
Automatic (able men naturally come to the top)	15	41
Consultants (candidates are studied, investigated and recommended by consultants)	10	35
Compromise (least unlikely candidate is appointed)	5	24
Merit (men are promoted from within the company on the basis of demonstrated ability and favorable work records)	55	50
Miscellaneous (nepotism, seniority, politics, etc.)	5	31
Total	100	

Source: From National Industrial Conference Board. "Selecting Company Executives," *Studies in Personnel Policy, No. 161*. New York: National Industrial Conference Board, 1957.

[1]T. Brooks, "Promotion Practices," *State of New York Industrial Bulletin* (1958). Reprinted by permission of the Office of Public Information, State of New York, Department of Labor.

Conference Board (N.I.C.B., 1957). Results of a survey of 62 company presidents showed that methods were classified to include all responses in only six ways. The modal response, "merit," which accounted for 55 per cent of the replies, could, however, no doubt have been broken into as many different classifications as there were respondents. In other words, there is no complete agreement about how merit should be judged in considering the promotion of a man to executive status.

How top executives have been promoted within the largest companies in the United States was outlined by Newcomer (1955). A summary of her results is given in Table 5-2. This shows that just about half of the top executives have worked their way up in the company rather than coming from the outside and that this percentage has been increasing over the years.

Table 5-2

PRINCIPAL FACTORS IN OBTAINING EXECUTIVE OFFICE

Principal Factor	Percentage of Executives		
	1900	1925	1950
Working up within company	18	37	51
Success in another company	14	12	18
Inheritance	5	14	14
Investment	19	15	7
Work in organizing company	30	16	6
Other	14	6	4

Source: Adapted from M. Newcomer. *The Big Business Executive: The Factors That Made Him, 1900–1950.* New York: Columbia University Press, 1955, Table 45, p. 102.

The entry occupations of 1950 business leaders are shown in Table 5-3, and the last functional field before going into general management for essentially the same population of top executives is shown in Table 5-4. These are the presidents and board chairmen of the largest industrial, railroad, and utility companies in the United States. Clerical work shows an advantage of more

Table 5-3

ENTRY OCCUPATIONS OF 1950 BUSINESS LEADERS

Entry Occupation	Per cent
Clerk (including minor administrator and retail salesman)	33
Laborer	14
Engineer	14
Salesman	10
Other professional	10
Manager (including foreman)	9
Lawyer	8
Owner	2
Total	100

Source: Adapted from L. W. Warner and J. Abegglen. *Big Business Leaders in America.* New York: Harper and Brothers, 1955, p. 116; and M. Newcomer. *The Big Business Executive: The Factors That Made Him, 1900–1950.* New York: Columbia University Press, 1955, 87.

than twice that of the next most frequent entry occupations, laborer and engineer. Presidents were recruited from operations or production almost half the time. Finance was a poor second with sales and advertising third.

Table 5-4

LAST FUNCTIONAL FIELD BEFORE GENERAL MANAGEMENT—1950 BUSINESS LEADERS

Functional Field	Rails and Utilities (N = 115) %	Industrials (N = 268) %	Total (N = 383) %
Operations and production	60.9	39.2	45.5
Finance	13.0	21.3	18.8
Sales and advertising	2.6	20.5	15.1
Legal	13.9	11.9	12.8
General and others*	6.1	6.0	6.0
Receivers	3.5	0.7	1.5
Personnel	—	0.4	0.3
Total	100.0	100.0	100.0

*Assistant to the President and others not attached to special divisions.

Source: M. Newcomer. *The Big Business Executive: The Factors That Made Him, 1900–1950.* New York: Columbia University Press, 1955, p. 107.

The type of experience which most often preceded promotion to general management was determined for alumni of the Stanford Graduate School of Business (Pederson, 1953). Sales was first, with the next four functions in order of their frequency being (2) industrial and production management; (3) purchasing; (4) controllership and office management; and (5) organization planning and control. Twenty-one other functions were mentioned.

Randle (1956) made a study of the characteristics of executives, which accompanied judgments as to whether or not they were promotable. He included four major functional fields and three levels of management. The most discriminating characteristics in order of their importance were: (1) position performance; (2) drive; (3) intellectual ability; (4) leadership; (5) administration; (6) initiative. Leadership was defined as "Receives loyalty and cooperation from others. Manages and motivates others to full effectiveness." These and other characteristics were rated by superiors and associates who were peers.

Benge (1956) found from a survey that American industry reported the following practices in promoting technical men:

a. Recommendation of the present superior
b. An interview by the proposed superior
c. The candidate's personnel file
d. Merit rating[2]

While management believes that it is promoting on the basis of merit, there are several studies which show that rank and file employees do not see it quite the same way. Again the fact that there is no clear criterion of management success is no doubt responsible. Eighty per cent of the supervisors in an insurance company office thought that promotion was dependent on merit, but only a little over half of rank and file employees believed this. Almost none of the supervisors thought that promotion depended upon whom you know or luck, but approximately 25 per cent of the rank and file employees thought that these factors were controlling.

---

[2]E. J. Benge, "Promotional Practices for Technical Men," *Advanced Management* (1956). Reprinted by permission of the Society for Advancement of Management, Inc.

Dalton (1959, pp. 159–187) reported on a manufacturing company where he studied factors associated with promotion. He failed to find any generalization about age at the time of appointment to the management position; in other words, persons could be appointed to management positions at any adult age. A study of experience likewise led to the conclusion that it did not appear to be an important consideration in appointment to management. Education was of some importance. Average education was highest for the staff managers and next highest for superintendents, the highest level of line managers studied. General foremen had a slightly higher average educational level than first-line foremen. There was a range of education of at least nine years in each management level. There was little agreement between job placement and educational specialty for the college graduates.

Dalton made the unique interpretation that the advantage of a college education in getting men into management was the social skill that it reflected. Specifically he thought that college had taught men to compromise effectively. He did not question that ability was present as a criterion for promotion, but his view was that no formal efforts were made to assess ability and that ability alone was not judged to be sufficient.

Dalton presented data to indicate that there were unofficial requirements to promotion to management and also to higher levels within management. In the one company he studied, he concluded that these unofficial requirements were Masonic membership, ancestry or ethnic composition favoring English and German, membership in a yacht club, and affiliation with the Republican party. There were exceptions, but there were correlations with each of these four variables. There was no relation to father's occupation such as other studies of higher management have shown. Previous top management within the company had been Catholic and was reported as then favoring Catholics for management. Dalton's interpretation was that the in-group of management, not completely consciously, but out of a desire to have people who would be loyal and congenial, favored people like themselves.

One implication is that men who act like their bosses will be promoted. Aping the boss for promotion or preferment has, of course, been known for centuries as a way to get ahead. This and other studies suggest that variables should be subtle rather than crude to be effective.

A second study by sociologists (Coates & Pellegrin, 1957), which emphasized informal factors not usually found in management books, included respondents from more than one company and managers from organizations other than business in a single southern city. Opinions were obtained on informal factors in promotion from 50 top executives and from 50 first-line supervisors. The factors that were called most important numbered nine, although no data were given to document them. They were:

> (1) Family social standing and connections . . . very important in securing initial occupational contacts and opportunities. Their influence in subsequent career progress was said to decline, however, unless at least satisfactory ability was demonstrated . . .
>
> (2) Memberships in social and civic organizations . . .
>
> (3) Memberships in professional organizations . . .
>
> (4) Recreational activities and hobbies . . .
>
> (5) Judicious consumption . . . If you live too high on the hog, you'll be suspected of being a crook or running a wheel.
>
> (6) Influence of wives . . .
>
> (7) The acquisition of the attitudes, values, and behavior patterns of successful superiors. After ruling out the "copycat" and "yes-man" types, the majority of executives considered this factor very important in the learning process, and therefore a very important factor in career progress . . .
>
> After referring scornfully and sometimes profanely to "bootlickers," "apple polishers," and so on, the majority of the supervisors tended to agree that this factor was a very important informal influence in promotion . .
>
> (8) The establishment of higher-level friendships. After excluding the "pusher" type, the majority of executives and supervisors conceded that this process favorably affects career progress, provided it is exercised judiciously and unobtrusively... A favorable reputation in high-level circles inside and outside the organization reflects credit on the company and therefore puts the individual in a favorable light.
>
> (9) Retaining lower-level friendships . . .[3]

---

[3]Charles H. Coates and Ronald J. Pellegrin, "Executives and Supervisors: Informal Factors in Differential Bureaucratic Promotion," *Administrative Science Quarterly* (1957). Reprinted by permission of *Administrative Science Quarterly*.

The operation of these informal factors can explain some of the data shown in Chapter 6 on the advantage of being the sons of businessmen and of having the high status Protestant religions — Unitarian, Episcopalian, Congregational, and Presbyterian.

In England as well as in the United States there were different perceptions of why people were promoted (The Acton Society Trust, 1956). Promotions to the higher levels of manufacturing management were said to meet with more suspicion than promotions to the first level of management. A detailed study was made of the most advantageous and disadvantageous items in promotion to high management. The most advantageous item was having been a graduate of Oxford or Cambridge. The most disadvantageous item was having been a foreman. Graduates of Oxford or Cambridge apparently did not begin as foremen.

Discussion

It is probable that especially at the level of company president the way in which a man is promoted to that position is by the recommendation of the incumbent. True, the present president must have the concurrence of the board of directors and cannot go counter to their views. He often nominates a single candidate. This was documented in *Time* when only one man was said to have been nominated for the presidency of General Electric. At lower levels of management more higher levels consider a promotion and probably more choices are typically considered although the nomination of the incumbent is no doubt still very important.

Summary

The basis for the promotion of managers is far from a scientific procedure. There are many different criteria applied which often merely represent differences in management opinion. While most managers believe that they are promoting on the basis of merit, their definition of merit frequently differs. One fundamental which is implicit to almost all promotions is the personal acceptability of the prospect to the appointing manager.

Heads of the largest companies have worked their way up in the company rather than being brought in from elsewhere. They have generally begun as clerks and were generally in the operations or production field before getting into general management.

Chapter 6

GENERAL MANAGERS

"General manager" means here a breadth of management and, in large companies, the general manager is a man who heads several functional fields. In a smaller number of studies a general manager is one who does everything about managing a store, *e.g.*, a bake shop.

The characteristics of general managers, as well as those given for the functional managers in the following four chapters, are presented in two ways in the literature, as *Personnel Psychology* has pointed out, and will be organized separately here. One method is the presentation of normative data or the description of people who are now in general management. More crucial studies present validity information which specify the characteristics of successful managers versus those of men who have been less successful.

Qualities of General Managers

A look will be taken first at the qualities of general managers as determined by the armchair method; later in the chapter the published evidence will be introduced. There are numerous books and articles on executive qualities, mainly containing little or no data that would stand careful scrutiny. This account is not by any means intended as encyclopedic. As Calkins pointed out in 1946 when he was Dean of the Business School at Columbia University:

> What qualifications make for competence in the careers for which we train? Frankly, I do not know, and I can think of no one who does. But it is high time we found out.[1]

[1]R. A. Gordon and J. Howell, *Higher Education for Business* (Columbia University Press, 1959). Reprinted by permission of Columbia University Press.

Gordon and Howell declared that "The situation is not a great deal better today," but that "With few exceptions, the business schools have paid too little attention to such evidence as is available."

Stryker, after writing a series of articles reviewing the literature and his experience, decided that innovation was the heart of the highest business leadership. This may be true at the highest management levels, but there is some negative evidence that Ward presented to the effect that imagination of Harvard MBA's was negatively correlated with earnings received after five years out of school.

Greenewalt (1958), the president of the DuPont Company, emphasized the coordination function of the top manager who must bring about successful teamwork. Perhaps this should be in the performance section rather than listed as a quality.

Several writers have noted the conflict between the quality of aggressiveness needed by executives and the quality of getting cooperation (Learned, Ulrich, & Booz, 1951). This seems particularly pointed with the Young Presidents Organization in those instances where there is the problem of building an executive team.

Bavelas (1959) has suggested that the following characteristics are essential for successful managers: good judgment under stress; above average available energy; wanting to go up in management; not being afraid to use authority (this does not necessarily mean being authoritarian); communications skills; not being the brightest in the group; and a compulsion to clean up disorderliness.

Change in Thinking. In the history of American business there have been important changes in the qualities judged to be desirable for successful managers. These changes have been traced with much insight by Bendix (1956, p. 300–304). There has been a shift from the qualities of the individual to a stressing of the need for a manager to win cooperation:

> In the 1840's the "habits of business" were said to include "industry, arrangement, calculation, prudence, punctual-

ity, and perseverance." In 1918, intelligence, ability, enthusiasm, honesty, and fairness were the qualities listed.[2]

Later on there was more orientation toward employees. The manager was supposed to be interested in helping the employees develop and even in learning from them. The concept of the ideal manager had turned from one who worked hard and saved his money to one who put at least some emphasis on considering the needs of his employees.

Studies of management have generally been at the first-line supervisor level. There have been surveys but no experiments at higher levels, although, of course, opinions have been expressed about the optimum behavior for top managers. Although there is much lip-service to a human relations approach of getting co-operation — especially for first-line foremen who deal with members of militant labor unions — there is practically no information as to the extent to which a considerate approach is used by top management. Bendix (1956, p. 333) has opined that top management is less human-relations-minded than lower management.

Characteristics of Young Presidents. The most detailed information about presidents has been about young presidents who are members of the Young Presidents Organization. Spencer has reported annually on various characteristics and problems of this group since 1953. Information from several of these reports will be given later as it fits into the outline of this presentation. The qualities of these young presidents have been contrasted with those of the organization man (Klaw, 1956). Even though there are relatively fewer entrepreneurs today, it is extremely interesting to learn about the characteristics of these young presidents. The relative decline of the entrepreneur is shown by the fact that there was a decrease in self-employed businessmen and professionals from 9.4 per cent to 7.5 per cent of the working population between 1910 and 1940 (Bendix, 1956). During that same time the percentage of salaried employees rose from 16.1 per cent to 24.7 per cent.

[2]R. Bendix, *Work and Authority in Industry: Ideologies of Management in the Course of Industrialization* (John Wiley & Sons, 1956). Reprinted by permission of R. Bendix.

The Young Presidents Organization has a high concentration of owner-managers although the presidents are not all owners by any means (Klaw, 1956). They have been described as "aggressive egoists" and appear to be much more independent than are organization men.

Performance

Four functions of the members of the Young Presidents Organization were stated by Spencer (1955b) as being most important; although, later in another approach, definite planning appeared to be the key to high profits. The four essential functions of a president were said to be (1) picking key men; (2) setting the objectives of the business, reviewing them from time to time, and possibly making changes; (3) acting as chief financial officer even where there was a competent staff man as financial vice-president; and (4) representing the company in negotiations in times of emergency. The biggest difficulty in performance, the presidents said, was that there was not time to do all that one wanted to do and therefore it was a problem to choose just what one should do. Most mistakes were made in procrastinating, especially in unpleasant jobs such as getting rid of a key man who was not satisfactory.

Spencer (1954) found that the Young Presidents spent almost all of their working day in communicating. More than 80 per

Table 6-1

TOPICS DISCUSSED DURING WORK DAY, AS REPORTED BY YOUNG PRESIDENTS

Topic	Percent
Production	27%
Sales	25%
Community and Public Relations	10%
General Executive Administration	10%
Finance	10%
Personnel	10%
Other	8%

Source: L. M. Spencer. "What YPO Presidents Think About: Preliminary Findings of the 1954 Survey." New York: Young Presidents' Organization, Inc.

cent of their time was spent in talking with people; this did not include telephone conversations or time spent in dictating correspondence. What they talked about is shown in Table 6-1. Production and sales accounted for over half the discussions.

The big corporation executive has reported a slightly longer working week, with a median of 56 hours, than that of the Young Presidents, 53 hours, although the difference may not be significant (Klaw, 1956).

Table 6-2

DISTRIBUTION OF MANAGERS' TIME BY TYPE OF ACTIVITY

Activity	Per cent
Supervising	25%
Planning	20%
Coordinating	15%
Evaluating	12%
Investigating	11%
Negotiating	10%
Staffing	5%
Representing	2%

NOTE: Based on 250 jobs.

Source: D. Yoder. *Industrial Relations Center, University of Minnesota Chart Book*, 1958.

The distribution of managers' time as found by the University of Minnesota (Yoder, 1958) is shown in Table 6-2. These classifications are different from those used by Spencer for the Young Presidents and consequently there is almost no basis for comparison. The only classification that seems comparable is time spent by managers in Staffing of 5 per cent versus 10 per cent for the Personnel activities of the Young Presidents.

Carlson (1951) studied what nine managing directors of Swedish companies did for four weeks. Eight of the directors were studied for four weeks, the ninth for a lesser time. The term "director" meant that they were among top management but not necessarily on the board of directors. Nine different companies in a variety of industries were represented. The method used was a diary by the director, his secretary, and the telephone operator plus a study of correspondence and reports. A convenient form was developed for the director to report those with whom he had had a contact, what sort of problem was discussed, and what action was decided upon. The bulk of time, between 65 and 90 per cent, was spent in contact with other people. The median day at the office was 9¾ hours. Additionally, the average time spent per day in working at home was an hour and one half. There were memory errors concerning inspection tours. Directors frequently stated that they had made visits more recently than the diaries showed that they had.

Brooks (1955) reported on a study of executives within the Moore Business Forms Company. From 96 executives, 12 who were rated excellent and 10 who were rated below average were chosen by their superiors. Between these two groups of excellent and below average executives, the superiors rated four acts as being present 90 per cent of the time among the excellent ones and only 10 per cent of the time among the below average ones. These were:

> He has the members share in decision-making.
> He sees that the work of members is coordinated.
> He makes full use of the skills and abilities of members.
> He evidences improvement in his leadership ability.[3]

In the same company Brooks had subordinates rate the executives with the result that 41 were rated excellent and 18 were rated "average" or "below average." The executive acts, as reported by subordinates, which discriminated most between the groups in favor of the excellent group were:

> He does things which make it pleasant to be a member of the group.
> He keeps well informed about the accomplishments of the group.
> He lets members know what is expected of them.
> He helps members improve their job performance.
> He facilitates exchange of information within the group.[4]

---

[3] E. Brooks, "What Successful Executives Do," *Personnel* (1955). Reprinted by permission of American Management Association, Inc.

[4] *Ibid.*

Brooks' study is interesting despite its limitation of reporting on only one company and on only a small number of cases at the extremes. Further, it is not clear to what extent the reported behavior was in fact behavior, or whether there was some halo represented in the reports. There is, in spite of these limitations, some support from the related work reviewed in Chapter 3 of the Big Ten universities of Michigan, Ohio State, and Illinois. There is support for Likert's situational theory of management in showing the importance of the expectations of both subordinates and superiors. The results agree generally with those at Michigan in showing that the effective executive, as seen by both his superior and subordinate, is people-oriented. Further agreement is shown with the Michigan people in the emphasis on group problem-solving or participation. While the people Brooks studied were called executives, it is not known just what their level was; and, judging by their relatively large numbers, it is quite possible that they included some first-line supervisors.

There is agreement with the Ohio State results in that the subordinates were more interested in consideration and the superiors were more interested in results. There is one point of agreement with the Illinois results in that the most effective executives did not attend subordinates' parties; or in the Illinois terminology, "maintained psychological distance."

Normative Data

Ability. General managers are high in ability but are not usually the most able in their group; the most able are customarily staff people, usually accountants, lawyers, or engineers. One group of 250 executives in more than 12 companies and including various functional fields was found to have an average mental ability of the 96th percentile of the general population (Huttner, Levy, Rosen, & Stopol, 1959). Their highest scores were in numerical ability, their next highest in word fluency. Lowest scores were in spatial relations and in abstract reasoning. Even in spatial relations and in abstract reasoning, executives were still considerably above the average of the general population. These results are typical of those found in smaller samples.

Wald and Doty (1954) obtained the identical percentile for a group of 33 executives which measured at the 96th percentile for a general population of business and industrial workers. All except two of the 33 were above the 86th percentile.

Bingham and Davis (1924) found that 69 executives scored higher than 11 sales managers on the Army Alpha, but there was no information as to the significance of the difference.

Terman and Oden (1959) included 79 general managers in business in their thirty-five year followup of gifted children. This number did not include managers and executives in specific functional fields. The total group numbered 757, of whom the largest per cent, 46, were in professions not including business management. In the total group there were 18 MBA's whose median income was reported for 1954 as $11,430. This income was a little more than half that of the M.D.'s whose median was $22,000; it was also below that of the LL.B's whose median income was $15,250. The MBA income was higher than that of the Ph.D's and other occupational groups. Among the gifted executives in major businesses or industries, a 1954 income of $17,680 was reported, which was second among the occupational groups to practicing physicians who reported $23,500.

The vocational satisfaction of executives in higher business or industry was just below the average for that of Terman's entire group of superior children. Of ten occupations, executives were in 6th place. Forty-seven per cent of the executives reported a deep satisfaction and interest in their vocation and 43 per cent of them said that they were fairly content. The most satisfied group by far was physicians where 84 per cent stated that they had deep satisfaction and interest in their vocation.

Thorndike and Hagen (1959) followed up on the occupations for Air Force air crew men who had taken a thorough series of aptitude tests during World War II. Three occupations of the group seemed to belong in general management — president, vice-president, and secretary of a company. The test scores of those in general management gave a profile of Perceptual Speed, B; Reading Comprehension, B; Arithmetic Reasoning, B; Math Knowledge, B+; Numerical Operations, B –; Psychomotor Coordination, B –. The letter grades were based on standards for the population studied where B was high average.

Speer (1957) found that executives scored higher on an Arithmetic Reasoning test than a group of males employed in a variety of occupations. The difference was significant at the 1% level of confidence.

Personality. Based on his annual surveys of the Young Presidents Organization, Spencer (1954; 1956) has made some observations about the personality of the Young Presidents in which he emphasized the drive and independence of these men. For some of them he attributes their motivation to a need to compete with successful fathers. When the Young Presidents themselves gave the personality bases for their success, Table 6-3, their most frequent answers had to do much more with getting work done through people than with a personal drive to accomplish through one's own efforts. If Spencer is more nearly correct, is this lack of insight on the part of these Presidents an important part of their personality?

Table 6-3

CHARACTERISTICS THAT YOUNG PRESIDENTS' ORGANIZATION THINK HAVE BEEN MOST IMPORTANT

Getting along with people	28%
Talent for analyzing, organizing and delegating work	20%
Enthusiasm, honesty, sincerity	17%
Influencing people	16%

Source: L. M. Spencer. "What YPO Presidents Think About: Preliminary Findings of the 1954 Survey." New York: Young Presidents' Organization, Inc.

Personal Data. The education of general managers is much higher than that of the average for the population. With varying amounts of education one's relative chances of becoming head of a large company are shown in Table 6-4 on page 84. Being a

Table 6-4

CHANCES OF AN INDIVIDUAL'S BECOMING A COMPANY PRESIDENT OR BOARD CHAIRMAN[a]

	Percentage
Education	
College graduate	78.1
Attended college (not graduated)	15.0
Attended high school	6.3
Attended grammar school	0.6
	100.0
Father's Occupation	
Business	54.5
Professional	36.1
Farmer	4.6
Other	3.3
Worker (including white collar)	1.5
	100.0
Religion	
Unitarian[b]	30.5
Episcopalian	27.0
Presbyterian	16.5
Congregational	13.4
Methodist	2.4
Jewish	2.3
Lutheran	1.0
All other	1.0
Baptist	0.7
Roman Catholic	0.7
No preference given	4.5
	100.0
BIRTHPLACE (foreign-born excluded) (data based on white population only)	
East	34.2
West	29.2
Middle West	24.4
South	12.2
	100.0
Urban	72.7
Rural	27.3
	100.0

[a]Chances in 100 of attaining a given position as a business leader — based on backgrounds of business leaders of 1950. Assumes number of each group desiring to become business leaders is proportional to number of that group in the population.

[b]The sample included only 8 Unitarians. Total sample numbered 882.

Source: Adapted from S. Keller. "The Social Origins and Career Lines of Three Generations of American Business Leaders." Unpublished Ph. D. dissertation, Columbia University, 1953; M. Newcomer. *The Big Business Executive: The Factors That Made Him, 1900–1950.* New York: Columbia University Press, 1955; and *U. S. Statistical Abstract, 1950.*

college graduate meant that the odds were 78 out of 100 that one could get to the top, whereas they were only 6 out of 100 for men who had gone only as far as high school.

Presidents of smaller companies also have had higher than average education although the data here are not directly comparable with those for the largest companies, in Table 6-4, because they have not been adjusted for total population figures. Spencer (1954) found that 59 per cent of members of the Young Presidents Organization were college graduates and nine out of 10 of them had attended college.

That science and engineering have produced the modal number of heads of American corporations is shown in Table 6-5. In smaller companies, however, Spencer (1954) found that business administration had been the most frequent major of the Young Presidents, with engineering second, and social sciences third.

Table 6-5

COLLEGE MAJOR FOR EXECUTIVES[a]

Major	Number	Per cent	% of Those Under 50
The arts	46	8.9	12
Law	77	14.8	17
Business economics	160	30.8	39
Science and engineering	238	45.5	29

[a]Sample drawn from executives of 1950.

Source: "The Nine Hundred," *Fortune*, 46(5), 1952, p. 135.

The colleges that have produced the heads of American corporations are shown in Table 6-6. In 1950, one out of four of the presidents and board chairmen of the largest railroads, public utilities, and industrials had attended Harvard, Yale, or Princeton. This is the same population on which education data were given in Table 6-4.

Table 6-6

COLLEGE OR UNIVERSITY ATTENDED BY TOP MANAGERS
(Based on 657 Executives of 1950)

College or University	Per cent Attending
Harvard*	11
Yale	9
Princeton	5
Cornell	5
Michigan	5
Columbia	4
M.I.T.	4
Wisconsin	3
Pennsylvania	2
California	2
Other (160 institutions)	50
	100

*13 of 74 executives attending Harvard attended the Harvard School of Business Administration.

Source: Adapted from M. Newcomer. *The Big Business Executive: The Factors That Made Him, 1900-1950.* New York: Columbia University Press, 1955, Tables 27 and 28, pp. 73–74.

Next to education, the variable which is most discriminating for top executives has been father's occupation. The chances of becoming president or board chairman of the country's largest railroads, public utilities, or industrials are shown in Table 6-4. Being the son of a businessman gave one the best chance, although this by no means was due solely to nepotism. Nepotism is present much more in smaller companies than in these giants. Almost half of the Young Presidents became president through family influence (Spencer, 1958a).

Religion is different for the presidents of large companies as compared to the presidents of small companies, and the religion of all presidents is a different mix from that of the population in general. Religions to which the presidents of large companies most frequently professed, shown in Table 6-4, were Unitarian, Episcopalian, Presbyterian, and Congregational. Since there were only eight Unitarians in the sample, this result is likely to be unstable in additional populations. The modal religion for the Young Presidents, however, was Jewish, with approximately 28 per cent being of that faith (Klaw, 1956). These small enterprises are also likely to be relatively new ones which thus require more aggressiveness.

Birthplace is another variable that determined differences in the chances for becoming president. Again these data in Table 6-4 have been adjusted for differences in size of population in the various regions. A man in the East had almost three times the chance of becoming president as one born in the South. No doubt this as well as the results on colleges was due in large part to the fact that the largest company headquarters were located in the East.

The hobbies of Young Presidents as reported (Klaw, 1956) were masculine ones, "deep-sea fishing, shooting, sailing." This ties in with Williams' finding of a correlation between masculinity scores and earnings. Klaw's interpretation was that these outdoor hobbies were part of a pattern of having a lot of energy. More than average energy has been found among other management groups.

Gowin (1915) reported that executives were taller than other employees although there has been little or no publication on the physique of executives since this. Is the slightly greater height of presidents due to taller men having attracted favorable attention and hence being promoted higher? Or is it due to greater poise, to self-assurance, or to a slight correlation between height and intelligence?

Inventories. Huttner, Levy, Rosen, and Stopol (1959) gave the Minnesota Multiphasic Personality Inventory and the Bernreuter Personality Inventory to 250 executives from the major functional fields of sales, production, accounting, and research in more than a dozen companies. The results have not yet been published in detail but some information about the results has been presented. The highest score on the MMPI was defensiveness. This and two other scores on the MMPI

> indicate the executive's relative lack of insight into himself and his motivation. Coupled with the very high self-confidence scores in the Bernreuter, these findings bear out the picture of the typical executive as a man with a strong and effective superego.[5]

Perhaps Klaw (1956) was right that the Young Presidents have a big ego and an aggressive one.

The highest score for the 250 executives on the Bernreuter was extroversion and there were also high extroversion scores from the MMPI. This interest in people was coupled with a "strong need to belong (social dependence score is high on both the Bernreuter and the MMPI)."

The scores on both dominance and social dependence were one standard deviation above the average for the general population on Bernreuter. There is then a strange combination of independence and dependence:

> Independence is evidenced by his strong strivings for status, position, and authority, his competitiveness, and his belief in being a leader. Dependence is shown by his need to achieve popularity and his generally positive attitudes towards others.[6]

The authors concluded that the average executive is better adjusted and mentally healthier than the average person.

Wald and Doty (1954) published data on 33 top executives which Wald has stated have been confirmed on a larger sample. These data, based on the Adams-Lepley Personal Audit (Form SS), are in essential agreement with the above the average for general population norms in every instance. Listing them from high to low they were Firmness, 93%; Frankness, 82%; Seriousness, 70%; Tranquility, 70%; Tolerance, 60%; and Stability, 56%.

Richardson and Hanawalt (1944) also found with the Bernreuter Personality Inventory that supervisors were better adjusted and mentally healthier than the general population. Adjustment

---

[5] L. Huttner, S. Levy, E. Rosen, and M. Stopol, "Further Light on the Executive Personality," *Personnel* (1959). Reprinted by permission of American Management Association, Inc.

[6] *Ibid.*

and dominance were correlated with management status (Meyer & Pressel, 1954).

Thirteen traits were measured for 240 Managers and compared with Male College Student Norms (Yoder, 1958). Although in some instances they were almost the same, managers were higher than students on all traits except Flexibility where the managers' percentile was approximately 38. Managers were highest in Dominance, Confidence, and Poise. Data were given on a graph rather than in numbers so all results are approximate. The other percentiles for managers are shown in Table 6-7.

Table 6-7

COMPARISON OF MANAGERS WITH COLLEGE STUDENT NORMS ON PERSONALITY TRAITS
(N = 240 Managers)

Personality Trait	Average Percentile Score*
Dominance	76
Confidence	74
Poise	73
Leisureliness	73
Ambition	73
Responsibility	72
Tolerance	72
Sociability	72
Impulsiveness	71
Cooperation	71
Conservatism	70
Resourcefulness	70
Flexibility	38

*College students average 50.

Source: Adapted by permission from unpublished data of a research study conducted by the Management Development Laboratory, Industrial Relations Center, University of Minnesota.

Projective Tests. Warner and Abegglen (1955, pp. 77–83, 146–156) have reported results and interpretations from the Thematic Apperception Test for a number of top level executives. They found that personality differed for the mobile elite who had had to work their way up and the birth elite who already belonged to wealthy families. The results were given in a clinical and not a statistical form. They attributed the fundamental motivation of the mobile elite to their relations with their mothers. They were slightly negative toward their mothers, however, for the mothers' attempts to control the sons. They were not close to their fathers who seemed to have withheld psychological support. Part of the motivation of the mobile elite was interpreted as a demonstration on the part of the sons that they were worthy of the support of the fathers.

The lack of a close relationship with the father is similar to that found with many delinquents and criminals; so one might ask why these mobile elite stayed on the track of social conformity. Part of the answer was in their relations with their mother plus their relations during childhood with some other father substitute figure — usually a teacher.

After childhood these men were able to relate satisfactorily to men in authority, but did not get so close to them that they could not move away when there was an opportunity for a better job. Fiedler's interpretation of the importance of psychological distance comes to mind here.

Warner and Abegglen were impressed that the birth elite could focus their energies effectively on a single goal. Ward, *et al.* were also impressed with the capacity of the best adjusted MBA's to focus their energies. The mobile elite were said to depart completely from the stereotype that managers are ruthless and would hurt anyone to reach their goals. The mobile elite were essentially oblivious of the feelings of others in their path to the goal; they had no energy for personal duels.

A second popular conception is that the dynamic businessman is a gambler; this was not borne out by the mobile elite. Instead, they were highly realistic in setting their goals within attainable limits and then driving hard to reach them. Again this brings to mind the description by Ward, *et al.*, of the most effective young businessmen being those whose insights into their abilities are consonant with reality. Carnegie Tech graduates who got ahead faster also seemed to be active agents in their own progress. (Dill, 1960).

The personality of the birth elite was not described in nearly so great a length by Warner and Abegglen as that of the mobile elite. It appeared that there was not so clear a type for the personality for the birth elite. They were found to have a relatively free impulse life with respect to sex, although this did not imply unconventional behavior — just thinking. Independence was shown to have been able to function in important executive positions, but some dependence due to having played second fiddle to a father for a number of years was evident.

Interests. An occupational scale was developed for presidents of manufacturing companies. Strong (1943, pp. 142–320) has written, however, that it is one of the poorest scales of the Vocational Interest Blank because, for one thing, only 10 per cent of the sample contacted responded. Another deficiency in the scale is that the average education was 13 years for the group responding which is significantly lower than that for a representative group of manufacturing company presidents today. A factor analysis of the scores of a number of occupations showed that the scores for the manufacturing company presidents were low on a humanitarian factor.

It has been suggested that the interests of general managers are broad, but there has been no convincing publication of evidence. Barnabas (1958) found that executives had broader interests than another group of men as measured by scores on the group scales of the Vocational Interest Blank. Ninety-four per cent of a group of 52 executives had three or more scores above a T-score of 40 on the group scales whereas in a control group of men of equal age who were not executives, only 15 per cent had such scores.

Dooher and Marting (1957a, p. 269) placed a similar emphasis on the desirability of breadth of interest for general managers and went further in specifying the scales in which breadth is desirable and the scales in which it is undesirable. They have referred to an unpublished manuscript of Strong and to one of his publications (Strong, 1945). Dooher and Marting concluded that it is desirable for a manager to have only a moderately high interest test score in his entry occupation, *e.g.*, engineer, and that it is also desirable for him to have a breadth of interest that includes moderate interest in personnel management and production management.

The interests of 33 high-level executives in large companies as determined by the Kuder Preference Record were:

Mechanical, about 29%; Social Service, about 29%; Scientific, about 38%; Clerical, about 46%; Computational, about 53%; Musical, about 55%; Artistic, about 59%; Literary, about 79%; Persuasive, about 91% (Wald and Doty, 1954).

Validity Information

Ability. Ghiselli (1955a, p. 111) published a comprehensive literature review of the measurement of all occupational validity studies in which he included results on studies of managers, supervisors, and foremen. Correlations with several ability tests for general supervisors with a proficiency criterion are shown in Table 6-8.

Table 6-8

VALIDITY COEFFICIENTS FOR GENERAL SUPERVISORS

Type of Test	Proficiency
Intelligence	.36c
Cancellation	.32a
Arithmetic	.20a

a100 to 499 cases
c1,000 or more cases

Source: E. E. Ghiselli. "The Measurement of Occupational Aptitude." *University of California Publications in Psychology,* 8(2), 1955, p. 111.

Arithmetic as measured on the Wechsler Adult Intelligence Scale was the only part of the test, including the total score, which correlated significantly with a criterion for 39 top management personnel in one middle-sized company (Balinsky & Shaw, 1956). The coefficient of correlation was .42 between the Arithmetic part score and performance ratings.

A contrary result was found by Pederson (1946) with a different criterion in another company. Mental ability was lower for the managers and foremen who were retained in contrast to those who were demoted at the Lockheed Aircraft Corporation after World War II. The fact that men with lower intelligence were kept might have been due to the influence of seniority. The group included "foremen, assistant foremen, department managers, and assistant department managers" in "Manufacturing, Material, and Finance Branches."

Of a group of 33 bake shop managers the upper 16 scored significantly higher at the 5% confidence level than the lower 16, on the Wonderlic Personnel Test (Knauft, 1949). The criterion was a very thoroughly developed and considered one, consisting of three values — total controllable costs, raw material costs, and a superior's rating. The correlation between the scores for the 33 managers and the criterion was only .26, which was not significant.

Thorndike (1955) found that in a small number of owners or managers the high income men had higher Reading Comprehension scores. There were only nine in the low income group and the number in the high group was not given.

Another study (Huttner, Levy, Rosen, & Stopol, 1959) found that mental ability was higher for higher earning executives than for lower earning executives. Mental ability was measured by Thurstone's tests for Primary Mental Abilities. The number of cases was not given but was taken from 250 executives in larger companies.

Jones and Smith (1951) found that "problematic questions" were the most valid ones in predicting ratings by either superiors or subordinates in two groups of supervisors. Different items were valid for the two sets of ratings.

Table 6-9

RELATIVE IMPORTANCE OF THE REASONS FOR FAILURE AMONG EXECUTIVES
(N = 177)

Rank	Reason for Failure	Weight*
1	Lack of breadth of knowledge	197
2	Inability to delegate responsibility	186
3	Inability to analyze and evaluate	170
4	Lack of personnel and administration knowledge	168
5	Inability to judge people	146
6	Inability to cooperate with others	145
7	Decision inability	127
8	Lack of drive	126
9	Lack of responsibility	84
10	Lack of knowledge of technical processes	53
11	Lack of perseverance	51
12	Lack of knowledge of marketing and distribution	50
13	Lack of liability knowledge	44
14	Lack of corporate organization knowledge	40
15	Lack of accountancy knowledge	30
16	Lack of labor law and labor relations knowledge	19
17	Lack of finance knowledge	16
18	Lack of knowledge of materials	18

*A high number represents greatest importance.

Source: Adapted from F. J. Gaudet and A. R. Carli. "Why Executives Fail," *Personnel Psychology, 10* (1957), 7–21. Reprinted by permission of *Personnel Psychology.*

Personality. Personality factors were given more frequently as causes of executive failure than was lack of knowledge (Gaudet and Carli, 1957). In the survey by Gaudet and Carli no effort was made to compare the relative importance of behavior versus personality, and what was called personality was in effect a combination of behavior and personality. A questionnaire was sent to three hundred executives — chairmen, presidents, and vice-presidents — asking them to fill in the reasons for the failure of an executive they had known. There were 177 replies among which were a few that had been filled in by subordinates of the addressees. The level of the reported failures is indicated by the fact that the median number of men they had supervised was slightly under 200. Results are shown in Table 6-9 where the items reported are shown in rank order of their importance for failure.

Personal Data. Ghiselli (1955a) found that personal data had been studied for between 100 to 499 General Supervisors. Average correlation with a proficiency criterion was .36.

Personal history items were found by Jones and Smith (1951) to be valid for predicting ratings in two groups of supervisors. Results were not given separately for the personal data section of the "Supervisory Inventory."

Inventories. Personality inventory questions were also found by Jones and Smith (1951) to be valid for predicting ratings in two groups of supervisors. Ghiselli (1955a) in reviewing the literature reported that personality tests were reported as averaging a correlation of only .16 with training criteria for general supervisors. There were less than 100 cases where such studies had been reported. Personality tests averaged a correlation of only .20 with proficiency criteria for general supervisors. Here there were over 500 cases.

Forced Choice. Knauft (1949) found that Jurgensen's Classification Inventory correlated .39 with a criterion of success for 33 bake shop managers. By comparing the top 16 and bottom 16 on the criterion, the Jurgensen score difference was significant at the 5% level.

A forced-choice adjective check list developed by Ghiselli has shown differences between top managers and middle managers and between supervisors and rank and file employees. Porter and Ghiselli (1957) reported on interesting differences between top managers and middle managers, although it is not clear whether the differences were present before these men were in their positions or whether their positions in part brought about personality

Table 6-10

ITEMS DIFFERENTIATING TOP AND MIDDLE MANAGEMENT*

Top Management	Middle Management
See themselves as:	See themselves as:
capable	discreet
determined	courageous
industrious	practical
resourceful	planful
sharp-witted	deliberate
enterprising	intelligent
sincere	calm
sociable	steady
pleasant	modest
dignified	civilized
sympathetic	patient
Do not see themselves as:	Do not see themselves as:
unambitious	reckless
unfriendly	self-seeking
stingy	shallow
irritable	tense
apathetic	egotistical
rattle-brained	disorderly
pessimistic	opinionated
cynical	aggressive
dissatisfied	outspoken
sly	excitable

*Each of these pairs of adjectives were given in the list, where only one was to be chosen.

Source: From L. W. Porter and E. E. Ghiselli. "The Self Perceptions of Top and Middle Management Personnel," *Personnel Psychology*, 10 (1957), 397–406.

changes. The check list was given under operational rather than research conditions. There were 64 items or pairs of adjectives, of which 21 showed differences as high as the 5% level of significance. The differentiating items are shown in Table 6-10.

The interpretation by Porter and Ghiselli is that the top managers saw themselves as being daring to the extent of making decisions even in the absence of complete data. This relates to the observation of Spencer that the presidents of high-profit companies made intuitive decisions with their staffs but without the formality of outside research and advice on which low-profit presidents depended. On the other hand, the Porter and Ghiselli interpretation seems counter to the conclusion by Warner and Abegglen that the mobile elite were not gamblers but realists. Maybe the chances taken by Porter and Ghiselli's top managers were also realistic.

Porter and Ghiselli interpreted the middle managers as seeing themselves as more cautious, less daring, and less dynamic than the top managers. To repeat, the question arises as to whether these personality differences had existed prior to the business experience of these men. The differences are interesting. The device is simple.

This same forced-choice adjective check list was used to yield a measure of initiative in which managers scored high (Ghiselli, 1956a). Seventeen of the 64 items were used in the initiative scale.

> The scale was presumed to be valid because the scores it yields were related to other characteristics in certain ways that were postulated for initiative. Scale scores were found to (a) correlate positively with ratings of initiative, (b) correlate positively with ratings of proficiency of supervisors, (c) correlate positively with ratings of proficiency of management personnel and negatively with ratings of proficiency of line workers, and (d) differentiate among persons in different levels of office work.[7]

The one hundred and ten top managers had the highest score of any of six occupational groups, and 80 middle management personnel were second of the six groups. Fifty-four per cent of the top management personnel and 39 per cent of the middle

[7]E. E. Ghiselli, "Correlates of Initiative," *Personnel Psychology* 9(1956), 311–320. Reprinted by permission of *Personnel Psychology*.

management were in the upper 25 per cent of the general population on initiative.

Initiative scores for management personnel increased with age. This was presumably due to two reasons, although their relative importance is unknown. First, people without initiative had probably been eliminated from the management group. Second, being in a management position that permits the expression of initiative probably develops it.

Projective Tests. Gardner (1948), and W. E. Henry (1949) have concluded that there were clear differences between successful and unsuccessful executives on the TAT, although Ward (1958) did not find any significant correlation for six of the TAT cards and earnings five years after school for Harvard MBA's. The specific pictures used in the TAT referred to by Gardner and Henry were chosen by Henry and Moore. Gardner and Henry have presented a very plausible account of the personalities of successful and unsuccessful executives, but they have not presented any results. Henry has written that the two most significant questions are what the executive thought of his mother and father and what he thinks of at five o'clock. The crucial point about the latter question is whether he is interested in continuing work or whether he is ready to relax.

Henry has concluded that successful executives got their main drive from their mothers, but that they also have respect for their fathers. There seems to be a conflict between this interpretation and that of Warner and Abegglen who reported that mobile executives had been rejected by their fathers.

Situation Tests. One of the few validity studies of situation personality tests has been reported from South Africa (Arbous & Maree, 1951). Two hundred and nineteen applicants for positions as administrative trainees were given two situation personality tests. One was a leaderless group test. The other was a test of assigned leadership where, in groups of eight — the same number as were used in the leadership groups, each person was given a different task of leading a discussion. After a year on the job, criterion ratings were obtained, although the study is not clear as to the number of cases on whom criterion ratings were obtained. The three assessors had correlations of .48, .60, and

.60 between their final ratings and the criterion ratings. The assigned leadership appeared to contribute a little more than the leaderless group.

Interests. Ghiselli's (1955a) literature review found that interest tests had been reported as correlating .53 with a proficiency criterion for general supervisors. There had been less than 100 cases reported. Pederson (1946) found differences on the Kuder Preference Record between managers and foremen who were retained as contrasted with those who were demoted by Lockheed after World War II. Managers who were retained had higher scores on "administrative supervisory interests, sales interests, and human relations interests." Scales developed at the Lockheed Company were more discriminating than the Kuder scales. Interests from the Strong Vocational Interest Blank were not correlated with success for bakery shop managers (Knauft, 1951).

Summary

The man with the best chance of having been president of the largest industrial company, railroad, or public utility was a white Harvard graduate, whose father was a businessman, born in the East, and a high-status Protestant. The man with the best chance of having been president of a smaller company was similar except that the Jewish religion was the mode rather than high-status Protestantism.

There is just as much opportunity for a poor boy to become president of a company as there ever was. There never was a good chance, but there was and still is a mathematical possibility, especially if he gets a college education.

Top managers have much drive and dominance. There is some evidence that they get this in large part from their relations with their parents. Their ability is above the 90th percentile for the general population. A breadth of interests seems to be more desirable for general managers than great depth. General managers are better adjusted than the average person.

Chapter 7

SALES MANAGERS

The personality of sales managers has been studied at some length and their performance has been explored in one study. While there are major differences between sales managers as a group and other occupational groups, differences are not clearly generalizable between effective and ineffective sales managers.

Performance

Randle (1956) found that Position Performance and Administration were discriminating for sales executives who were promotable in contrast to those who were inadequate. Position Performance was defined as "How well the executive carries out the duties of his present job." Administration was defined as "Organizing own work and that of others; delegation, follow-up, control of position activities." Fifty per cent of the promotable executives were rated as being outstanding in Position Performance contrasted to only 18 per cent of the inadequate sales executives. Thirty-four per cent of the promotable sales executives were rated as being outstanding in Administration contrasted to only three per cent of those who were inadequate. It is likely that Randle's ratings were contaminated by the knowledge of who were good performers.

Davis (1957, pp. 346–354) has studied the performance and evaluation of field sales managers in 54 companies. His findings are illuminating with respect to questions about sales management. Performance of field sales managers was found to be concentrated in five areas: "development of salesmen (selection and training), the supervision of salesmen (control and motivation), personal selling, office administration, and providing local title and prestige." The biggest failing of field sales managers was to spend too much time in personal selling and not enough in management. This was also found by Spencer (1956) to be true for sales managers.

Davis found several false assumptions about the promotion of sales managers. These were that a man is qualified for a higher job because he is good on a lower one, that "Outstanding men naturally will want promotion," and that "Age and experience are essential for promotion."

Normative Data

Ability. On Army Alpha, Bingham and Davis (1924) found 11 sales managers to score slightly higher than salesmen and lower than executives. There was no indication of whether the difference was significant. Again without reporting the significance of the difference, Huttner, Levy, Rosen, and Stopol (1959) reported that sales executives scored higher on verbal tests than they did on nonverbal and that they made more errors on ability tests than executives in general. Ability was tested by Thurstone's tests for Primary Mental Abilities.

Personality. Huttner, Levy, Rosen, and Stopol (1959) also gave the Minnesota Multaphasic and Bernreuter Personality Inventories to a group of sales and other executives. They reported personality differences in the direction that popular stereotypes would expect, although they have not yet published the detailed results. Sales executives were:

> highly dominant, sociable, and extroverted, and tend to be more generally more people-oriented, more open and relatively more thick-skinned, more optimistic, and more self-assured, than other executive groups. Along with these traits there is some evidence on self-centeredness and selfishness.[1]

The authors warn that the traits of sales executives may cause trouble because of their dominance plus their higher propensity for errors. Once they make errors they may be capable of talking themselves out of their difficulties because of their verbal skills.

To generalize, one gains the impression that sales managers will dominate business management, but that they know less about what they are talking about than other major management groups. Further, it appears that with respect to the general

[1]L. Huttner, S. Levy, E. Rosen, and M. Stopol, "Further Light on the Executive Personality," *Personnel* (1959). Reprinted by permission of American Management Association.

population, sales managers are more different than any other group of managers, being the extreme, in optimism and dominance, to general managers who are intermediate between sales managers and the general population.

J. S. Guilford (1952) found that 208 executives in a grocery chain scored higher than 143 supervisors on a number of scales from three of Guilford's inventories. Eight differences were significant at or beyond the 1% level. In order of their magnitude these were (1) Social Introversion-Extroversion; (2) Ascendance or Social Boldness; (3) Cooperativeness; (4) Depression; (5) Inferiority Feelings; (6) General Activity; (7) Objectivity; (8) Nervousness. All differences were in the favorable direction for the executives over the supervisors who in turn had more favorable scores than those of the general population.

Interests. The interests of sales managers provided a scale showing that their interests were different from men in general and different from those of several dozen other occupational groups (Strong, 1943, pp. 319–320). The interests of sales managers were highly similar to those of successful real estate salesmen and life insurance salesmen. Their interests were more similar to those of salesmen than to the interests of other managers, *i.e.*, production managers and office managers. A factor analysis showed that the scale for sales managers had a negative loading in a factor which probably meant interest in creativity and lack of competitiveness; and a positive loading in a third factor that was not completely clear but which probably meant interest in being sociable.

Validity

Ability. Randle (1956) found that sales executives who were promotable had higher ratings in intellectual ability and creativeness than inadequate sales executives. Forty-four per cent of the promotable executives had ratings of outstanding intellectual ability contrasted to 23 per cent of the inadequate sales executives. Thirty-four per cent of the promotable executives had ratings of outstanding creativeness contrasted to only 18 per cent of the inadequate sales executives.

High intelligence was a disadvantage, or at least not an advantage, for section managers of the R. H. Macy Company.

The average IQ of section managers who were rated "Poor" was 116 compared to 112 for those who were rated "Good." This might not have been a significant difference. The reverse results were found with another criterion, stability. Those who had the longest length of service had higher than the average intelligence.

Dunnette and Kirchner (1958) found that high intelligence went with high ratings for sales managers in the Minnesota Mining and Manufacturing Company. Fifteen sales managers who had IQs of 125 or higher on the Wechsler Adult Intelligence Scale had significantly higher ratings than 11 sales managers whose scores were lower. The *t* test was 2.77, which was significant at the 1% level. The *r* between test scores and ratings was .47. No one of four ability tests correlated with ratings of 17 section sales managers of a tobacco manufacturing and distributing organization (Bruce, 1954).

Sears, Roebuck has been following up on the results of ability and other tests for managers with more continuity than any but a few companies (Worthy, 1951). The executive battery included the American Council of Education Psychological Examination (ACE), which has two part scores, Linguistic and Problem Solving, as well as a total score. Two groups, one a Parent Junior Reserve Group and the other a Released Failure Group, have been contrasted, as shown in Table 7-1 (Bentz). All of the members of both groups had been hired on the basis of test scores. Men in the failure group had been released from the company. The members of the Parent Junior Reserve Group were outstanding among those retained in that they were looked on as having unusual potential for higher management. The greatest difference was in the Problem-Solving score, although all three differences were significant beyond the 1% level of confidence.

Twenty of the men in the Released Group appeared to be separated specifically because of lack of ability:

> These reasons ranged from such phrases as "can't cut the mustard in this organization," or "can't cut the buck here," to "just doesn't have it," or "not sufficient ability to do the job."[2]

[2]J. C. Worthy, "Planned Executive Development: The Experience of Sears, Roebuck and Co.," *AMA Personnel Series No. 137* (1951). Reprinted by permission of American Management Association.

Table 7-1

A.C.E. MENTAL ABILITY SCORES FOR A PARENT JUNIOR RESERVE GROUP AND A RELEASE GROUP OF CHECK-LIST FAILURES

A.C.E. Test	Mean of Parent Junior Reserve Group (N = 102)	Mean of Released Failure Group (N = 68)	"t"*
Linguistic	81.90	71.45	3.89*
Problem Solving	48.90	41.00	5.09*
Total Score	129.80	112.45	4.42*

*All differences exceed the 1% level of confidence. A "t" as large as 3.291 is indicative that the difference between the means could not have occurred by chance alone in one in a thousand times.

Source: V. J. Bentz. "A Study of Psychological Components Related to Success and Failure of Sears Executives." Chicago: Sears, Roebuck Co., Mimeographed, undated.

A comparison of the scores for these twenty men with those of the Parent Junior Reserve Group showed an even greater difference than that in Table 7-1. Here the greatest difference was on the gross score, with Linguistic second in discrimination.

Sears has unusually able executives as measured by scholastic aptitude test scores. The Junior Reserve Group was above the average for all Sears executives, being at the 68th percentile but was at the 99th percentile for college freshmen. The Released Group was just about average for Sears' executives, being at the 48th percentile, but was at the 84th percentile for college freshmen. Mental ability was more important in differentiating the failure group from the Reserve than were measures of personality and interest.

The ability of 39 Sears' store managers was correlated with morale scores of their employees (Psychological Services, 1956). Correlations were computed between each of the Problem-Solving, Linguistic, and over-all ACE scores and each of fifteen parts of the Morale inventory plus an over-all morale score. Of these 48 coefficients of correlation only three were significant at the 1% level of confidence. Problem-Solving correlated .47 with Supervisory Employee Relations, and .47 with the Technical Competence of Supervisor as the employees rated it. The over-all ACE test score correlated .46 with scores on the morale inventory of Status and Recognition. With 48 coefficients some would be expected to appear significant on the basis of chance. Schultz (1936) found that intelligence scores above the 50th percentile went with high ratings for 31 assistant managers in the insurance industry.

Personality — *Personal Data.* Soar (1956) found that 14 personal data items held up under a cross validation procedure for predicting success in service station management. The criterion was ratings by superiors. The five most valid items were (1) over 5′ 6½″ in height; (2) no more than 200 lbs. in weight; (3) between 25 and 39 years of age; (4) held a blue-collar job while in high school; and (5) no more than one child. Kurtz (1948) found that an Experience Record Form correlated .48 with success of life insurance sales managers, using a cross-validating sample.

Inventories. Bentz found two differences between a group of managers who had been fired and a group of managers judged to have superior potential that were significant above the 1% level on the Guilford-Martin Personality Inventory. The superior managers showed less feelings of Inferiority and higher scores in Cooperativeness. The only score on the Allport-Vernon Scale of Values which differentiated the two groups beyond the 1% level of significance was the Political Values scale, where members of the Reserve group scored higher than those who were fired. The political values scale is an attempt to measure an individual's motivation for personal power.

Sears Roebuck has conducted two studies of managers in which personality as measured on inventories has been correlated

Table 7-2

SIGNIFICANT CORRELATIONS BETWEEN TEST RESULTS AND MANAGERS' RESPECTIVE DEPARTMENTS' MORALE*
(N = 42)

Tests	II Working Conditions	IV Employee Benefits	VI Supervisory Employee Relations	X Adequacy of Communication	XII Status and Recognition	XIII Identification with the Company	XV Reaction to Inventory
Guilford-Martin							
G — General Activity		42					
A — Social Leadership							42
M — Dominance						41	
O — Objectiveness						40	
Co — Tolerance			39			43	
Allport Political	40			52	44		

*All coefficients of correlation were significant at above the 1% level. Decimals omitted.

Source: From V. J. Bentz. "A Study of Psychological Components Related to Success and Failure of Sears Executives." Chicago: Sears, Roebuck Co., Mimeographed, undated.

with morale of subordinates. In one, men who were in staff positions in the home office, called Parent Supervisors, showed six results on personality inventories which correlated to the extent of at least the 1% level of confidence with some measure of subordinates' morale as determined from a subscore from the employee morale survey. Results are shown in Table 7-2. Seven measures of subordinates' morale were predicted by one of the personality scales. All of the results do not sound plausible and in spite of the criterion of significance applied, there may be some chance results that have spilled over in such a large number of correlations that were originally in the Sears study. The non-significant results are not reported except by inference. Some of the results in this study, when considered together as were some in the second Sears' study, do suggest a meaningful pattern.

The second study in which the personality of Sears managers was correlated with morale of subordinates included 39 store managers. Dominance scores from the Guilford-Martin Personality Inventory correlated .38 with subordinates' total score on a thorough morale inventory. Dominance scores also correlated significantly at the 1% level with two part scores on the morale inventory, .40 with Confidence in Management and .38 with Security of Job and Work Relations. This together with the general tenor of the results in Table 7-2 suggests positive evidence for the autocratic personality leading to good morale.

Projective Tests. Sinaiko (1949) found that two scores from the Rosenzweig Picture-Frustration test correlated with job ratings of 53 department store section managers. Ego-Defensiveness was negatively correlated to the extent of −.48. Need-persistence, measured by the frequency of reactions giving a solution to the problem pictured, correlated .38. Kurtz (1948) found no validity for the Rorschach in predicting success among life insurance sales managers.

Understanding Employees. There has been a growing interest in measuring the understanding of people by managers as one of their important qualifications. Marchetti (1954; Marchetti & Malone, 1956) has attempted to measure understanding and correlate it with several criteria in a grocery company. He has measured what he calls "detached understanding" by counting the manager's errors in predicting employees' responses to Kerr's *Tear Ballot for Industry.* He has measured what he calls "participant understanding" by counting the manager's errors in predicting employees' responses to a questionnaire which was a modification of Fleishman's *Supervisory Practices Questionnaire.* For 11 managers there was a correlation significant at the 5% level for participant understanding; this was a correlation of .56 with job satisfaction of the subordinates.

Interests. A group of Sears managers who were rated as being potentially valuable had higher Persuasive scores on the Kuder Preference Record than a group of managers who had been fired (Bentz). This seems to support Pederson's finding of higher Sales interests on the Kuder for Lockheed managers who were retained. This was a local Lockheed Scale.

Computational interests of Sears store managers on the Kuder Preference Record correlated .40 with a Supervisory Employee Relations score from a morale inventory by their respective employees. This was significant at the 1% level of confidence.

Summary

The main activities of sales managers have to do with personnel function of salesmen. The biggest deficiency of sales managers appears to be spending too much time in selling and not enough in managing.

Sales managers are highly verbal and aggressive. Their interests are more similar to those of salesmen than to those of managers in other functional fields.

Higher-rated sales managers had higher intelligence in four groups, but no higher in two additional groups.

Personal data has been found valid for sales managers but it must be standardized on each group of managers separately.

Similarly, personality inventories have shown valid results for several groups of sales managers, but the results have appeared to be specific for each group. At least there has not been cross-validation, therefore no generalizations can be drawn about the personalities of sales managers except that they are better adjusted, more optimistic, and more dominant than the average manager, who in turn is better adjusted, more optimistic, and more dominant than the average employee.

Chapter 8

PRODUCTION MANAGERS

Dalton (1951) has stated the goals of production managers very plausibly; these goals also have application to other kinds of managers:

> (a) To maintain a low operating cost record, a low accident record, a low grievance record (with no "wildcat strikes"), and a high production record; (b) to make "good contributions" (helpful ideas, suggestions, etc.) toward the solution of critical issues; (c) to achieve "good relations" in the department and between departments; and (d) to place organizational loyalty above personal aims.[1]

Spencer (1956) has emphasized the profit goal for the production manager in discussing their performance. Although production managers produce the goods, to succeed it is necessary to do so with profit to the company.

Performance

Creager and Harding (1958) found that the performance of 141 first-line production foremen in 23 companies could be analyzed into three factors. Information about their performance was obtained from ratings by immediate supervisors. The most important factor was Social Relations including Job Instruction. This accounted for 50 per cent of the nongeneral common variance. Second in prevalence was Technical Job Knowledge, 27 per cent of the variance. The third factor was called Administrative Skills, which included Planning and Control. This accounted for 19 per cent of the nongeneral common variance.

Wallace and Gallagher (1952) and the University of Minnesota Industrial Relations Center have also published accounts of the

[1]M. Dalton, "Informal Factors in Career Achievement," *American Journal of Sociology* (56, 1951), 407–415. Reprinted by permission of the University of Chicago Press.

performance of production foremen. These essentially agree with the results of Creager and Harding and with each other although the classifications differ in wording. The method used by Wallace and Gallagher and by the University of Minnesota was observation. The Minnesota results are given in Table 8-1 which shows that more than half the time of foremen was spent in communicating.

Table 8-1

HOW FIRST-LINE SUPERVISORS SPEND THEIR TIME
(Based on 931 work sample observations of 5 first-line supervisors in manufacturing over a three month period.)

	Time Spent
Communicating	58%
Observing Subordinates	12%
Traveling	12%
Personal	10%
Performing Operative Duties	8%

Source: Adapted by permission from unpublished data of a research study by the Personnel and Labor Relations Laboratory, Industrial Relations Center, University of Minnesota.

Wallace and Gallagher (1952) reported on a study in which two observers watched and recorded the activities of 171 production foremen in five plants. Their observation was continued until it appeared that additional information was not adding anything new. The observations were classified by action; with whom a contact was made; place; and topic. The emphasis on communication in the two studies reported above was supported. More than half the foremen's actions was talking, primarily with subordinates. The next most frequent action was looking at something, and close to that in frequency was doing manual work. The foremen's work was analyzed under 41 topics. The mode of topical classifications was the general one of "operation and maintenance of machines and equipment" and the provision of stock. One third of the foremen's performance had to do with this broad topic. Just under one-third of the foremen's actions had to do with implementing the production schedule. This included reassigning personnel and other specific acts.

> One-fourth of supervisory activities are directly or indirectly related to quality of production . . . One-tenth are administrative activities, centered upon such matters as meetings, safety, and housekeeping.[2]

Jasinski (1956) found that "the most effective foremen spend more time outside their work group than with their own employees."

Normative Data

Ability. Colby and Tiffin (1950) reported that the reading ability of supervisors in seven Indiana plants, as reported in 1950, was slightly above tenth-grade level.

Production managers among a group of Air Force enlisted men had a mean of 118 on the Army General Classification Test with a range from 82 to 153 (Harrell & Harrell, 1945). The mean for all enlisted men was approximately 100 with a standard deviation of 20.

File and Remmers (1946) reported that supervisors and persons selected as qualified to be supervisors had higher scores on the How Supervise? than those not judged to be qualified as supervisors. This is a test of supervisory judgment which correlates highly with intelligence tests.

Personality. The production manager is more likely to have come from the ranks than any other member of the first team of management (Spencer, 1956). This rising from the ranks was judged extremely important to the personality of foremen by More (1954) who had 60 men fill out a Sentence Completion Test. His description is interesting and, in spots, highly plausible,

---

[2]W. L. Wallace and J. V. Gallagher, *Activities and Behaviors of Production Supervisors, Technical Research Report 946* (30 April, 1952). Personnel Research Branch, Research and Development Division, The Adjutant General's Office, Department of the Army, Washington, D. C.

although the validity and reliability are unknown. He concluded that the production foreman was generally suspicious of his subordinates and was dominating toward them. The foreman could not defend himself against his boss because of his relatively low verbal skills, and so he had to take out his hostility on his subordinates. Much of his hostility had to be pent up, often leaving him in a tense state.

Rosen (1959) found among a group of over 200 executives that production managers were intermediate between sales managers and research managers who were least mentally healthy. Executives as a group were found to be more mentally healthy than people generally, supporting all other reports of this nature as given in Chapter 6. Production managers showed:

> marked defensiveness, strong control, relative lack of insight into themselves and their motivations, and a tendency to shy away from too much self-analysis. . . . The typical executive regards his father as helpful, wise, and strong — someone to imitate and to lean on in case of need, though not excessively. Actually, the executive has a certain ambivalence toward his father, admiring him yet wishing to surpass him. His attitudes toward his superiors seem to reflect the same ambivalence . . .
>
> The executive also has a marked preference for the practical as opposed to the theoretical approach . . . Perhaps connected with this trait is the apparent ability of many executives to tolerate frustrations but not ambiguity. . . .
>
> . . . The executive strives for success to assure himself and others that he is not a failure. . . .[3]

While people generally want to get their job done, the executive seems to be trying harder than most people.

Rosen's population of production managers was included in the group of executives reported by Huttner, Levy, Rosen, and Stopol. The description of their relations to their fathers agrees with the report of W. E. Henry rather than that of Warner and Abegglen. The neurotic basis for ambition disagrees with the more idealistic approach of Ward, *et al.*

Interests. There is a separate occupation scale for the production manager on the Strong Vocational Interest Blank which does not belong to any of the groups of occupations based on similar

[3]E. H. Rosen, "The Executive Personality," *Personnel* (1959). Reprinted by permission of American Management Association.

interests. This indicates that the pattern of interests for the production manager is not very similar to that of any other occupation for which a scale has been developed. Strong (1943, pp. 319-320) gave the results of a factor analysis in which the production manager was high in a factor which seemed to indicate masculinity, a dislike for competitiveness, and had a negative loading in a humanitarian factor.

Attitudes. Larke (1955) presented some results which indicated that the pro-management attitudes of foremen were due mainly to their being foremen. The attitudes of future foremen, before they became foremen, were not so pro-management as they became after being made foremen. When a group of foremen were demoted, their attitudes returned to being more critical of management, as they had been before their promotions. Results here were interpreted as favoring a role-theory of personality. Foremen took on the attitudes that they were expected to have.

Validity

Three companies, Procter and Gamble (Taylor, 1957), the Standard Oil Company (New Jersey) (Radom, 1950), and General Electric (Meyer, 1956) have reported over-all positive validity results on very careful and thorough approaches to selecting foremen. The Procter and Gamble Company was said to have had no failures among the men it had promoted to foremen in the more than 10 years in which it had been using very careful selection procedure. Some transfers which might be called failures were necessary. In the Standard Oil Company (New Jersey) a refinery was said to have had 33 successes out of 35 whereas before the scientific selection procedure was adopted the batting average had only been .500. The use of tests in selecting 101 General Electric supervisors resulted in only 13 per cent of the group being rated low in job performance, whereas 58 per cent of a group of 19 supervisors who had not been so carefully evaluated before hiring were rated low in job performance. The difference in performance between the evaluated and nonevaluated groups was significant at the 1% level.

Ability. — *Intelligence.* Ghiselli (1955a) found in the literature that the average correlation of intelligence tests with a proficiency criterion for foremen was .25 and the correlation of arithmetic tests with proficiency was .20. In each instance 1,000 or more cases had been reported.

Randle (1956) found that intellectual ability and creativeness were discriminating between manufacturing executives who were judged to be promotable versus those who were rated as inadequate. Forty-one per cent of the executives judged promotable rated outstanding in intellectual ability but only three per cent of those who were inadequate were rated outstanding. Thirty per cent of the promotable executives were rated outstanding in creativeness versus only three per cent of the inadequate ones.

Huttner and Stene (1958) found that Verbal, Reasoning, and Word Fluency scores from the Primary Mental Abilities Test correlated .48 with rankings of 87 Pillsbury Mills supervisors. The Wonderlic Personnel Test correlated .42 for the same population. Because of the convenience of administering the Wonderlic, it was given to another group of 59 supervisors, with a correlation of .32.

The aircraft industry in general, and the Lockheed Company in particular, has provided an unusually large group of production supervisors for study. In the case of Lockheed there have been reliable objective criteria as well as the more usual superior's ratings. Stockford (1957) reported that intelligence test scores predicted an objective criterion at Lockheed 17 per cent over chance. Parsons (1958) found that two ability tests correlated with ratings at the 1% level of significance. These were Visual Speed and Accuracy, .25, and Verbal Reasoning, .22. Thompson (1950) obtained a multiple correlation of .72 for the optimal weighting of five subtests from the California Test of Mental Maturity to predict a criterion of "over-all standing with the company." Using their best weights, four tests of the Guilford-Zimmerman Aptitude Survey correlated .57. In both the California Test and the Guilford the single best test was vocabulary. Stockford (1947) found that an IQ of 110 was a convenient cutting point for Lockheed supervisors. Of a sample of 478, "42% of the men in . . . Fair and Poor groups had IQ's under 110, whereas only 20% of the men in the Good and Superior groups had IQ's under this level." Shuman (1945) found that the Otis Quick Scoring Test of Mental Ability correlated .42 $\pm$ .04 with ratings of 297 supervisors in three aircraft companies.

The Otis Self-Administering Examination correlated .37 with ratings of 42 cotton textile supervisors (Harrell, 1940). If the minimum IQ had been set at 101, there would have been no cases rated unsatisfactory by superiors. Eight of the 27 supervisors with an IQ below 101 were rated as unsatisfactory. Fifteen supervisors with IQ of 101 or higher were rated by their superiors as being average or above in job performance.

The Adaptability Test has been reported as being valid in four studies. In the General Mills Company with 800 foremen "approximate validity coefficients" were published (Dooher & Marting, 1957b, p. 164). Scores from the Adaptability Test correlated .57 with rank order ratings. This result is somewhat higher than most, especially for such a large number of cases; therefore it would be interesting to know more details. Lawshe (1949) reported two studies on his Adaptability Test. In a rubber company, out of 70 men who were made supervisors, 17 had left the ranks of supervisors. All of the 13 men scoring 18 or higher on the test remained as supervisors. There was a consistent trend that, the lower the score on the test, the higher percentage to have left supervision. In Lawshe's second study, 44 plants designated their two best and their two poorest first-line supervisors. There was a consistent trend toward a higher percentage of "best" supervisors with higher Adaptability Test scores. At scores of 30 or higher, 100 per cent of the supervisors were in the "best" group, although there were only five in the group. The results for the 176 cases are conclusive in showing a steady improvement in test scores with increasing ratings. Poe and Berg (1952) also found the Adaptability Test as well as the California Short Form Test of Mental Maturity Total Score to differentiate between high- and low-rated steel supervisors.

The Wonderlic Personnel Test was found to be valid with a group of first-line supervisors by Owen (1951) and by Meyer (1956) who obtained a correlation of .27 with ratings of subsequent supervisory success for 142 supervisors.

Tests measuring separate factors of ability have proved to be valid, but not especially more valid for production supervisors than have general intelligence tests. As Ghiselli has pointed out, spatial relations has not been outstandingly valid for production jobs. He found that the average correlation for spatial relations was .21 with a proficiency criterion for 1,000 or more foremen. Of the parts in the Differential Aptitude Test, Language Usage — Sentences, correlated highest, .27, with ratings of 99 foremen in an aircraft manufacturing company (Grant, 1954, p. 301). Abstract Reasoning was the only one of the Differential Aptitude Tests to correlate significantly at the 1% level with ratings of supervisory potential in the Minnesota Mining and Manufacturing Company (Dunnette & Kirchner, 1958).

J. P. Guilford (1956) found that the Verbal Comprehension test of the Guilford-Zimmerman Aptitude Survey correlated .52 for 84 supervisors. General Reasoning was second at .29.

Mechanical Aptitude. Bennett's Mechanical Comprehension Test appears to be the most popular mechanical aptitude test for foremen. Ghiselli (1955a) found mechanical comprehension to average a correlation of .23 with proficiency criteria for 1,000 or more foremen in his study of the literature. Studies which have come to the attention of the author appear to show somewhat higher validity. One that was lower, however, was .13 with ratings of 99 foremen in an aircraft manufacturing company (Grant, 1954). This was Form BB which was also the form used by Meyer (1956) who computed a correlation of .29 for 68 supervisors with ratings of subsequent supervisory success. Mechanical Comprehension Test Scores also correlated significantly at the 1% level with success criteria for two groups of first-line production supervisors at two other General Electric plants (Cuomo & Meyer, 1955; Cuomo, 1955). In one instance the correlation was .46 with rankings for 45 men, in the other .38 with job-grade level achieved under a salary plan for 47 men. Carter found that the Bennett Mechanical Comprehension Test correlated .62 with ratings of 36 supervisors rated by fellow supervisors in metal fabrication plants. Form AA correlated .45 ± .04 with ratings for 297 supervisors in three aircraft companies (Shuman, 1945).

The Science Research Associates Mechanical Aptitude Test correlated at the 1% level of significance with ratings of 173 foremen at the Carrier Corporation (Hable, 1957). Scores on a test of Mechanical Ability correlated .27 with ratings of 107 foremen in a tobacco manufacturing company, and a Clerical aptitude test, the B-B-S Inventory, correlated .26 with the same criterion.

Judgment. There have been several efforts to measure supervisory judgment which have been reported for production foremen and managers. The How Supervise? test has been, however, by far the most popular test. This had slightly the highest correlation, .29, in comparison with several general and mechanical ability tests which were correlated with ratings for 99 first-line foremen in an aircraft manufacturing company (Grant, 1954, p. 301). How Supervise? had the amazingly high "approximate" validity coefficient of .64 in the General Mills Company with 800 foremen (Dooher and Marting, 1957b, p. 164). The term "approximate validity coefficient" is not explained. Carter (1952) reported a correlation of .63 between How Supervise? and ratings of 36 supervisors in metal fabrication plants. The ratings were made by fellow supervisors. "How Supervise?" asks about stereotypes of what a good supervisor should do. The correlation here may mean that the man who knows the right answers, as far as the test is concerned, also knows how to butter up his own supervisors.

A supervisory Judgment Test was valid in three refineries of the Standard Oil Company (New Jersey) (Employee Relations Depts., 1955, 1951). Meyer (1951) devised a test of Social Judgment of Human Relations which correlated .36 with ratings on human relations performance for 113 trades and operation supervisors in the Detroit Edison Company. His interpretation was that ". . . the good supervisor regards others as individuals with motives, feelings, and goals of their own, whereas the poor supervisor is more likely to perceive others in relation to his own motives or goals."

Meyer's interpretation that the more effective supervisor has clearer judgment about individual differences of motives might also apply to the results of Fiedler on his test of Assumed Similarity of Opposites, although Fiedler has a different interpretation in terms of the more effective supervisor maintaining a certain psychological distance. Cleven and Fiedler (1956) found that the

Assumed Similarity of Opposites correlated −.71 (Rho) with Tap-to-Tap Time in 16 work groups. Tap-to-Tap Time was an objective measure of productivity in terms of the time required to do a certain amount of work. This was significant at the 1% level. Assumed Similarity of Opposites is a measure of what one thinks about the responses for the man with whom "one can work best, versus the responses for the man with whom one can work least well." The negative result meant that production was highest for those supervisors who assumed less similarity of opposites.

Ratings of analysis and judgment were found by Randle (1956) to be discriminating between manufacturing executives who were judged to be promotable versus those who were inadequate, although such ratings were not discriminating for promotable sales executives, engineering and research executives, or finance and accounting executives.

Table 8-2

DISTINGUISHING PERSONALITY CHARACTERISTICS FOR MANUFACTURING EXECUTIVES

Characteristic	Percentage Present as an Outstanding Quality	
	Promotable Executives	Inadequate Executives
Drive	52	10
Leadership	47	4
Initiative	49	6
Acceptance	52	20
Motivation	31	1
Flexibility	37	7

Source: Adapted from C. W. Randle. "How to Identify Promotable Executives," *Harvard Business Review*, 34(3), 1956, 122–134.

Personality. — *Ratings.* Randle (1956) found that six characteristics of personality, Table 8-2, discriminated between promotable and inadequate manufacturing executives. They are, no doubt, not entirely separate, but their intercorrelations are unknown.

Several aspects of personality that the Procter and Gamble Company seeks in prospective foremen have been described (J. H. Taylor, 1957). These include the desire to be a foreman, goals which are explored by a superintendent in a depth interview, sustained energy, and acceptability. This is the first reference encountered in a written report that states that selection depends upon whether the interviewer likes the candidate, although this is probably always an important consideration.

Personal Data. Ghiselli (1955a) found personal data to correlate only .08 with proficiency criteria for somewhere between 100–499 foremen. Later results suggest that this result is low for a thorough and carefully prepared data sheet. Parsons (1958) found personal data items to be by far the most valid predictors in an extremely careful study at Lockheed. Fourteen significant items correlated .53 with ratings in a standardization group and .54 in a second group. These correlations were significant at the 1% level. The significant items were grouped into five areas as follows:

I. Ambition
  A. Participating in evening school or correspondence courses
  B. Coming to Lockheed at an early age
  C. Expecting to attain a high position
  D. Expecting to obtain a top salary

II. Flexibility
  A. Working less than sixteen years during longest period of tenure
  B. Living eight years or less at present home address

III. Mathematics
  A. Disliking another school subject rather than mathematics

IV. Sociability
  A. Having a number of very close friends
  B. Belonging to professional organizations

C. Liking social groups and active sports rather than reading, music and art, or movies and television
D. Telling jokes often

V. Vigor
A. Participating in active military service
B. Stating that present health is excellent.[4]

Personal data items had previously been shown to be valid at Lockheed with several groups of supervisors (Stockford, 1957). With one group of 139 supervisors an objective criterion was predicted 9 per cent over chance by community stability items.

General Electric (1957a) in one study found that:

> the more effective foremen were younger than the less effective foremen, had less total work experience and shorter service as foremen. They more often had been recruited from functional service jobs rather than directly from hourly-rated production jobs.[5]

One of the things Procter and Gamble seeks in prospective foremen is evidences of leadership in the community and in the Armed Forces (J. H. Taylor, 1957). These are believed to transfer to behavior in the plant.

The Individual Background Survey which was developed for the Standard Oil Company (New Jersey) is the most thorough approach published for personal data (Standard Oil Company, 1951, pp. 41–47). This has been found valid in predicting rankings of supervisors in two refineries. It was also found valid for Harvard MBA's in predicting earnings five years after college.

Inventories. Ghiselli and Barthol (1953) found that the weighted mean validity coefficient of personality inventories for 44 groups of foremen was only .18. Their review included 6,433 cases. Some of the more recent studies with positive results will be presented briefly here. Adamson (1957) obtained biserial correlations with ratings of .46 for self-sufficiency and of .37 for sociability for only 18 Canadian supervisors in a Canadian water and power company. These scales were from the Bernreuter

[4]Stuart O. Parsons, "A Study of the Prediction of Success of Manufacturing Supervisors in an Aircraft Corporation." Ph.D. dissertation, University of Southern California, 1958.

[5]"The Effective Manufacturing Foremen — An Observational Study of the Job Activities of Effective and Ineffective Foremen," Research Study by General Electric, Public and Employee Relations Research Service, 1957.

Personality Inventory. Guilford's personality tests have been found valid in two studies. Hable (1957) found that Objectivity on the Guilford-Zimmerman Temperament Survey had a validity coefficient with the ratings of 173 foremen at the Carrier Company that was significant at the 1% level. Mackie (1948) found several scores on a Guilford personality test to be different for higher-rated foremen in two separate groups. In one group of 289 production foremen there were higher scores in Objectivity, Cooperativeness, and Agreeableness and lower scores in Nervousness, Depression, and Cycloid Tendency. For 120 foremen in maintenance and tooling the higher-rated foremen had higher mean scores in Cooperativeness, Agreeableness, and Thinking Introversion. Here, as in other studies, the higher-rated managers showed superior adjustment.

Two components on the Humm-Wadsworth Temperament Scale (Owen, 1951) were reported as being valid for first-line supervisors. Scores on the Manic component were positively correlated with ratings and those on the Epileptoid component were negatively correlated.

Bruce (1953) reported a correlation of .24 between the Ess-Ay Inventory and ratings of 107 foremen in a tobacco manufacturing company. "This test offers an over-all score purportedly indicative of persuasive ability."

The Huttner Supervisory Aptitude Test, a personality inventory, correlated .42 with rankings of 146 Supervisors in Pillsbury Mills (Huttner & Stene, 1958).

Forced Choice. Parsons (1958) found that the Ascendancy score on the Gordon Personal Profile correlated .22 with ratings of Lockheed supervisors. This was significant at the 1% level.

Ghiselli and Barthol (1956) found that high-rated supervisors were different from low-rated ones in the way that they perceived themselves. Ghiselli's adjective check list was given to four groups of production supervisors and three groups of office supervisors in seven different organizations. There were 267 persons who filled out the forced-choice list of 64 pairs of adjectives. Ratings by superiors one or two levels above were compared with the answers. Supervisors were split into a high and a low group on

Table 8-3

ITEMS DIFFERENTIATING HIGH- AND LOW-RATED SUPERVISORS

Superior Supervisors		Inferior Supervisors	
See themselves as:	Do not see themselves as:	See themselves as:	Do not see themselves as:
energetic	noisy	ambitious	arrogant
loyal	affected	dependable	moody
kind	shallow	jolly	stingy
planful	unstable	resourceful	frivolous
clear-thinking	nervous	efficient	intolerant
enterprising	opinionated	intelligent	pessimistic
progressive	self-pitying	thrifty	hard-hearted
poised		ingenious	
steady		sociable	
appreciative		good-natured	
responsible		reliable	

Source: E. E. Ghiselli and R. P. Barthol. "Role Perceptions of Successful and Unsuccessful Supervisors," *Journal of Applied Psychology,* 40(1956), 241–244.

the basis of ratings. Eighteen of the pairs of adjectives were discriminating at the 5% level. Results are shown in Table 8-3.

Ghiselli and Barthol have attempted to interpret the results in Table 8-3 although they recognize the difficulty of explaining such forced-choice findings. Their interpretation is interesting even though it is doubtful that anyone else would have exactly duplicated it independently:

> The "good" supervisor sees himself as active, purposeful, and forward looking. He is favorably disposed toward his company and identifies himself with his job. He views his responsibilities broadly, that is, of having a job to do rather than a series of assigned tasks. He feels that he must exercise certain independence of thought and action: plans and decisions are an integral part of his work and cannot be left solely to his superiors.

His orientation toward production is through people. He sees himself as respecting the rights and dignity of others, but is somewhat reserved. He considers himself to be stable and to display an evenness of temperament. He feels that he is worthy of the respect and confidence of others and that people can trust him. One gets the over-all impression of maturity and calmness.

The most outstanding self-perception of the "poor" supervisor is his sales approach to human relations. He sees himself as a good fellow who is well liked but he does not show any need to understand and respect others. He seems to have a narrow approach to his job and sees himself as being highly skilled in carrying out instructions. He gives no indication of leadership qualities, but instead relies on his own ingenuity and intelligence to complete a job. He tends to be self-oriented rather than company-oriented; his efforts are for his own ends rather than those of the company. He does believe, however, that he possesses the qualities that management could well use to advantage.

These descriptions are in accord with the findings that poor supervisors are more production-oriented than are good supervisors. It is our interpretation that the poor supervisor tends to view production as an end in itself and as his personal responsibility. The good supervisor tends to view production as a means to an end (over-all company success) and that his main responsibility is working with the people who are the direct producers. . . .

It is reasonable to ask why the poor supervisor is the way he is. He does not wilfully try to be a poor supervisor. He persistently does the wrong thing, and this is possibly because he thinks these behaviors are expected of him. We assume that there is some foundation for his beliefs and that they arise from a misinterpretation of the expectations of higher management. The authors suspect that part of the trouble arises from a misunderstanding of the precepts in current thinking about proper supervision. Among these precepts we might find the following: The good supervisor (a) has the good will of his subordinates, (b) does his job with intelligence and ingenuity, (c) is reliable and conscientious, (d) wants to succeed, (e) "sells" his orders rather than dictates them.[6]

---

[6]E. E. Ghiselli and R. P. Barthol, "Role Perceptions of Successful and Unsuccessful Supervisors," *Journal of Applied Psychology* (1956). Reprinted by permission of American Psychological Association.

Ghiselli and Barthol conclude that these five precepts sound all right but that while the poor supervisor sees himself in those five ways, higher management still rates him as a poor supervisor. There are two essentials that were missing from the poor supervisor:

> (a) respect for other individuals, and (b) identification with the job. We hypothesize that higher management and the good supervisor are ego-involved in their jobs, while the poor supervisor views it as a way to make a living. . . .[7]

Projective Tests. Parsons (1958) found that Social Responsibility on the Industrial Rorschach had a correlation of −.25 with ratings of Lockheed supervisors which was significant at the 1% level. This does not fit into any theory, is unconfirmed, and may simply be a statistical accident. A "Mental Vision" test, which appears to be similar to the Thematic Apperception Test (TAT) had an "approximate validity coefficient" of .51 for General Mills supervisors (Dooher & Marting, 1957b, p. 164). The number of cases is not given but the total number of foremen was said to be 800 and it was stated that all but one foreman took the series of tests offered. The Worthington Personal History was reported as being valid for supervisors at the Glenn L. Martin Company (Swint & Newton, 1952). The Worthington Personal History is an unlikely but intriguing device which is an application blank with incomplete directions. It is interpreted as a projective test. Forty supervisors were hired whose histories were favorable; 40, whose histories were unfavorable. "Seven of the men in the latter group have requested demotion; none of those in the first group has."[8]

Group Discussion. Performance on a group discussion problem was significantly different between supervisors who were rated high and those who were rated low in two of three military depots (Glaser, Schwarz, & Flanagan, 1958). The differences were significant at the 1% level in two depots but not significant at the 10% level at the third. At each of the three depots the population

[7] *Ibid.*

[8] E. R. Swint and R. A. Newton, "The Personal History — A Second Report," *Journal of the American Society of Training Directors* (January-February, 1952). Reprinted by special permission of the *Journal of the American Society of Training Directors.*

studied consisted of 20 supervisors rated high and 20 rated low.

Interests. Ghiselli's (1955a) literature survey found that interests had been reported as correlating only .15 with proficiency criteria for foremen. One thousand or more cases had been reported. Interests as measured by the Production Manager Scale on the Strong Vocational Interest Blank correlated .38 with ratings of 30 foremen and assistant foremen at the Coleman Lamp and Stove Company (Shultz & Barnabas, 1945). The Kuder Preference Record has had validity reported with two groups of production supervisors. Stockford (1957) found that Persuasiveness scores predicted an objective criterion 35 per cent over chance for 139 aircraft supervisors, and Administrative Interests predicted the criterion 24 per cent over chance. Owen (1951) found that the Social Service Scale on the Kuder was valid for a group of first-line supervisors. Cuomo and Meyer (1955) obtained a correlation of .44 between a Personal Interest Inventory ("An unpublished inventory developed and validated in other studies against a "Human Relations Ability" criterion) and rankings of 45 General Electric foremen. Presumably this is the inventory which Meyer developed at Detroit Edison where it was also found to have some validity. The Meyer inventory sounds as if it is a combination interest inventory and personal data sheet.

J. H. Taylor (1957) has written that the Procter and Gamble Company looks for depth of the man's interest in his chosen field in considering him for a supervisory job in production. They like an intensity of interest which is determined in an interview. This appears to be contrary to the conclusion that breadth rather than depth is favorable for management potential, but there may be no real contradiction. The interview may simply be determining enthusiasm or persuasiveness rather than vocational interest.

Summary

The performance of production managers is mainly communicating with people — primarily subordinates through interviews or meetings.

The ability of production managers is above average for the general population although how far it is above average varies with the situation. The personality of the production manager is somewhat better adjusted than the average, but he is more defensive than managers generally. Production managers dislike competitiveness and humanitarian interests.

Ability and mechanical aptitude tests have shown that the higher-rated managers or supervisors made better scores. There have been longer range follow-up studies to show the pay-off from scientific selection than with other functions of management. Personal data have been shown to be valid for differentiating superior production supervisors. There is not enough consistency of results to say exactly what is the best background for a production supervisor but there is a suggestion of where to begin looking in the published results.

Ghiselli and Barthol have found differences between good and poor supervisors which have led to the interesting conclusion that the key to the personality of the successful supervisor is a genuine respect for people rather than the belief that the supervisor can do his job through salesmanship.

Chapter 9

OFFICE MANAGERS

The term "office manager" is used here to include the finance and accounting manager, the credit manager, and the office supervisor. There was some discussion of studies including office supervisors in Chapter 8 in those instances where they had been included in reports with larger groups of production supervisors.

Performance

Normative Data. Spencer (1956) has given some interesting insights into the performance of financial officers of companies headed by members of the Young Presidents' Organization. The differences in the way the finance officer sees his job versus the way the president sees the finance officer's job appear to be significant for understanding the personality of the finance officer. There are, of course, great individual differences. Finance officers are said to see their job generally as a policing one, not a creative one. They are interested in the accounting system, in operating it accurately, and improving its efficiency. The backward look is the main function in their view.

Presidents take for granted that their financial officers will efficiently and accurately perform their accounting duties. What the presidents want most in financial officers is sound advice on the future with respect to financial needs and the tax situation.

Another aspect of the situation which appears to be salient to the finance manager's personality is the uniqueness of his power position within the company. He is a watchdog on the efficiency of the organization and all its major officers. No one, however, is able to grade his performance in the same way that he grades the performance of others. There can be conflicts when the other officers do not know or approve the rules of the game by which they are graded by the finance officer. There might also be conflicts just because of the unpopular position of the policeman in any organization.

Two factor analyses were made of the performance of office supervisors in two insurance companies by two of Wherry's former students (Grant, 1955; Roach, 1956). In neither instance were the factors orthogonal, *i.e.*, entirely independent. Six factors were found in the Prudential Company which were more or less related to one or more of the fifteen factors found in the Nationwide Insurance Company. The difference in number of factors was no doubt due mainly to the difference in number of items that went into the two studies. There were only 20 items in the Prudential study versus 328 in the Nationwide analysis. In both instances there was a general factor that was interpreted as a halo effect which was more the result of the raters' bias than of the behavior of supervisors. Table 9-1 shows a comparison of the supervisory behavior factors found in Prudential and Nationwide. In addition to those shown, there were six factors in the Nationwide analysis which had no counterparts in Prudential. These were (1) Personal Compliance; (2) Rewarding Performance and Thoroughness of Employee Evaluation; (3) Company Loyalty; (4) Personal Drive (Motivation); (5) Impartiality; and (6) Poise and Bearing.

Roach (1956) concluded from the Nationwide study that personality was much more important to the job of office supervisor than was technical knowledge. This did seem to be borne out by his factors, and to some extent was also true of the factors found in the Prudential Company by Grant (1955). The factor analysis method, however, limits to some extent the results one can obtain. It would be impossible to find personality factors by the analysis if the investigator had not in his planning included personality variables which could constitute such factors. Factors not found could not, therefore, be isolated by the analysis if, in the original planning, variables had not been conceived which could permit their emergence.

While there were some similarities of results in the two analyses, there were obviously differences as well. One implication of these differences is to spotlight the lack of certainty about supervisory performance. Here, in two insurance companies,

Table 9-1

COMPARISON OF RESULTS OF TWO FACTOR ANALYSES OF SUPERVISORY BEHAVIOR IN TWO INSURANCE COMPANIES

Prudential		Nationwide	
I	Halo effect	XV	Bias or halo
II	Skill in dealing with others	VII	Group spirit
		XI	Consideration
		XII	Open-mindedness
		XIII	Cheerfulness
		XIV	Approachability
III	Judgment	VI	Acceptance of responsibility (Decision making)
IV	Effectiveness in supervising the work	III	Direction of group performance
V	Effectiveness in planning the work	III	Direction of group performance
VI	Effectiveness in improving operating efficiency	II	Job knowledge

Source: Prudential results adapted from D. L. Grant. "A Factor Analysis of Managers' Ratings." *Journal of Applied Psychology*, 39(1955), 283–286; Nationwide results adapted from D. E. Roach, "Factor Analysis of Rated Supervisory Behavior." *Personnel Psychology*, 9(1956), 487–498.

factor analyses were performed by men who had learned the methods at the same university, Ohio State, but who reached considerably different answers. In more divergent situations there would have been presumably even fewer generalizations that would have been common to the dimensions of supervisory behavior.

Validity. Randle (1956) found that ratings of three performance characteristics discriminated between finance and accounting executives who were judged to be promotable and those who were judged to be inadequate. Position performance and administration were discriminating to the extent that 49 per cent of the promotable versus 7 per cent of the inadequate executives were judged outstanding in the former, and 44 per cent versus 7 per cent in the latter. Thirty per cent of the promotable and none of the inadequate finance and accounting executives were rated as outstanding in Quality. Quality was defined as "Accuracy and thoroughness. High standards." Position performance and administration were also discriminating for the functional fields of sales, manufacturing, and engineering and research, but quality was not.

Ability

Normative Data. Huttner, Levy, Rosen, and Stopol (1959) concluded that a group of administrative and accounting executives were high in numerical ability but relatively low in verbal ability. They did not publish results but presumably these will be published later. Thorndike and Hagen had results that confirmed the high numerical ability, as far as numerical operations went, of treasurers and comptrollers. These two occupations had relatively lower ability in reading comprehension although there were no verbal tests exactly comparable to the Thurstone Primary Mental Ability Tests used by Huttner, *et al.* Results of Thorndike and Hagen are shown in Table 9-2. The Thorndike and Hagen study is unusual in that the tests had been given to the men in their teens and early twenties when they were Air Force air crew members during World War II. Consequently the results were swayed relatively little by the influence of business experience since a large proportion of the men had come into the Air Force directly from school.

Terman and Oden (1959) included 44 executives in banking, finance and insurance among their follow-up of the gifted group at mid-life. This classification constituted 5.8 per cent of their entire population and was the greatest number in any occupational

Table 9-2

TEST PROFILES FOR FINANCE AND OFFICE MANAGERS

	Company Treasurers and Comptrollers	Office Manager	Credit Manager
Perceptual speed	B+	B−	B−
Reading comprehension	B+	C+	C+
Arithmetic reasoning	B+	B−	C+
Mathematical knowledge	A−	B−	C+
Numerical operations	A+	B+	B
Mechanical principles	C	C	C
Two-hand coordination	C+	C+	C+
Psychomotor coordination	B−	B−	C

Source: Adapted from R. L. Thorndike and E. P. Hagen. *Ten Thousand Careers: A Summary Report of the Survey of Post-War Education and Employment.* New York: Columbia University, undated.

grouping except general management executives and managers where there were 79. Terman and Oden classified managers of accounting, statistics, marketing research, etc., as a separate group which numbered 35 or 4.6 per cent of their sample. This is further convincing evidence for the high intelligence of people who succeed in finance and accounting. The tests were completely uncontaminated by business experience since they had originally been given when the men were boys at an average age of 11 years.

Validity. Randle (1956) found that technical knowledge and intellectual ability were discriminating between finance and accounting executives who were judged to be promotable and those judged to be inadequate. Seventy-two per cent of the promotable executives were rated as being outstanding in technical knowledge as compared to 33 per cent of the inadequate ones. Forty-six per cent of the promotable executives were rated as being outstanding in intellectual ability contrasted to 13 per cent of the inadequate executives. The technical knowledge result is interesting in two ways. Although technical knowledge was discriminating for finance and accounting executives and for engineering and research executives, it was not discriminating for sales or for manufacturing executives. Second, the level of technical knowledge was high for finance and accounting executives and was exceeded only by the technical knowledge of engineering and research executives. Among all the 30 characteristics rated, technical knowledge was highest in the per cent of engineering and research, and finance and accounting executives who were rated outstanding.

Creativeness was not discriminating for finance and accounting executives although it did discriminate the promotable executives in sales, in manufacturing, and in engineering and research. Creativeness is considered here as an ability although it may well be due in part to some nonintellectual aspect of personality. While all highly creative people seem to be well above average in ability, not all highly able people are creative. There seems to be some component or components necessary from the nonintellectual. While apparently one can succeed as a financial or accounting executive without a high level of creativeness, it would be going too far to conclude that creativeness would not be an asset.

Frederick (1957) presented data showing that accountants who became managers in a public accounting firm had scored higher at the time of employment on an Accounting Achievement Test than had accountants who were not promoted to management. Stevens and Wonderlic (1934) showed a relation between the number of items missed and skipped on the Otis Self-Administering Test of Mental Ability and criticisms found in superiors' reports of office managers in branches of a finance company. An Arithmetic Reasoning Test had a tri-serial correlation of .20 with job performance as reflected by promotions, demotions, or continued status for 117 assistant managers in a life insurance company (Grant, 1954, p. 285). Meyer (1951) developed a Social Judgment or Human Relations Test that correlated .36 with ratings of the human relations performance of 77 office supervisors.

Personality

Normative Data. Huttner, Levy, Rosen, and Stopol (1959) concluded that administrative and accounting executives were "more constricted, less sociable, and more withdrawn" than other executives they studied. Rosen (1959), reporting the results of the TAT and a Sentence Completion Test, concluded that the same above-mentioned group of administrative and accounting executives was so different in personality from production managers, sales managers, and research managers that administrative and accounting executives were not comparable with these other managers. Huttner, *et al.*, (1959) went on to conclude that the administrative and accounting executives of a number of companies showed "the least signs of original thought or creativity, and are also the least optimistic group, with more frequent indications of overt depression."

Argyris (1954) interviewed managers and other employees in a bank and reported interesting answers from bank employees and conclusions that largely support and to some extent document popular stereotypes. He was not studying managers so much as employees, but his findings are relevant to management to the extent that managers were promoted from within. Bank employees described themselves as:

1. People who consider themselves more capable of receiving direction than of giving direction (70%).
2. People who feel more confortable if they are in situations where they initiate action only for themselves (46%) or where others initiate action for them (27%).
3. People who prefer to be followers (47%) or who have specific reservations about undertaking leadership (26%).

Argyris wrote that:

> The pattern that emerges from these comments is this: the "right type" seems to be quiet, passive, obedient, cautious, and careful.

> From these statements, it is possible to make further inferences. An employee of the "right type" apparently has (a) a strong desire for security, stability, predictability in his life; (b) a strong desire to be left alone and to work in relative isolation; and (c) a dislike of aggressiveness and/or hostility in himself or in others.[1]

Argyris concluded that there was a self-selection to the extent that people of the above type gravitated to the bank, were hired, remained, and were promoted, so that the type became purified. He pointed out that there were some differences among people in the bank that he studied.

On an "Initiative Scale" Ghiselli (1956a) found that supervising and higher level office clerks had an average score that was little above that of routine clerks and a little below the average of middle management personnel. The differences between the supervising clerks and the other groups mentioned did not appear to be statistically significant.

Validity. Randle (1956) found that four personality characteristics were discriminating between promotable and inadequate finance and accounting executives. Rated outstanding on drive were 47 per cent of promotable executives, and 20 per cent of the inadequate ones; on leadership, 34 per cent and 7 per cent respectively; initiative, 37 per cent and 13 per cent; motivation, 33 per cent and 7 per cent. It is noteworthy that acceptance as well as creativeness was not discriminating although both were discriminating for sales executives, for manufacturing executives, and for engineering and research executives.

Smith (1954) showed four significant differences between 12 high- and 12 low-rated credit managers at Sears. Fifty-one managers were studied from whom the two extreme groups were chosen. The highly-rated managers had higher scores on Social Leadership and Objectivity from the Guilford-Martin Personality Inventory, and on Economic and Political Values from the Allport-Vernon-Lindzey Scale of Values. Smith concluded that

---

[1]Chris Argyris, "Human Relations in a Bank," *Harvard Business Review* (January–February, 1954). Reprinted by permission of *Harvard Business Review*.

the valid characteristics for credit managers were essentially the same as those for successful Sears managers generally, and consequently that these personality traits were true for managers generally.

Interests. — *Normative Data.* Strong (1943) developed separate occupational scales for Certified Public Accountant, for Accountant, and for Banker on the Strong Vocational Interest Blank. The interests of Banker and Accountant were more similar than those of Certified Public Accountant and Accountant. The accountants in the standardization group included auditors, comptrollers, and treasurers as well as accountants. From a factor analysis (Strong, 1943, pp. 319–320) the interests of office managers, bankers, and accountants were found to be highly negative on a factor which seemed to represent creative interests wherein Architect had the highest loading. C.P.A. and Accountant were the only two occupations with positive loadings in a factor that may mean interest in numbers. In a factor that may be interpreted as interest in competitive business activities, Accountant was on the low side but not so low as Production Manager. Sales Manager was high on that factor.

Validity. Frederick (1957) presented data showing a positive relation between scores on the Strong Vocational Interest Blank and increases in earnings for Certified Public Accountants. Men who scored "A" or "B+" had greater increases in earnings than those who had lower scores on the Certified Public Accountant scale.

Attitudes. Nagle (1954) correlated ratings of productivity by higher management with attitudes of employees toward their immediate office supervisors. There were 14 supervisors and 223 employees in the study. The correlation for the 14 cases was .86, which was significant at the 1% level. Also significantly correlated with the productivity ratings was the sensitivity of the supervisors toward their employees' attitudes toward supervision and toward the company. In other words, the accuracy of supervisors in predicting how their employees would answer such questions on the questionnaire was correlated in each of these two instances at the 1% level with ratings of productivity in their departments.

Summary

Accounting and finance managers are very able, especially with numbers, in which they have high interests as well as ability. They are less able verbally. They are relatively lacking in creative ability and creative interests, although their superiors would like more creativity.

Chapter 10

RESEARCH AND ENGINEERING MANAGERS

Although recently there has been high interest in research management, primarily with a view to motivating scientists and engineers in large organizations, there is very little solid literature on the qualifications of research and engineering managers. Only two studies that give any data have been found.

Huttner, Levy, Rosen, and Stopol (1959) tested a sizable number of research and engineering managers as well as sales managers, production managers, and accounting managers. They used an interview and an extensive test battery consisting of Thurstone's Primary Mental Abilities, the Minnesota Multiphasic Personality Inventory, and the Bernreuter Personality Inventory. There were two projective tests in the battery, the Thematic Apperception Test (TAT) and a Sentence Completion Test, the results of which were not available. Rosen (1959) did publish conclusions from the projective and other tests for the group of production managers studied. These were summarized in Chapter 8. No specific quantitative results have been published for research or other managers, but several conclusions and interpretations have been. The number of research and engineering managers has not been reported, but the entire group of executives numbered approximately 250.

Huttner, *et al.*, concluded that research and engineering managers as compared to other executives were high in abstract reasoning, in spatial relations, and in personality tendencies consistent with creativity, and that they were low in speed of routine calculations, in word knowledge and fluency, in dominance, in mental adjustment, and in knowledge of business. They were inclined to subtle depressions.

Randle (1956) studied 1,427 executives including 300 research and engineering executives primarily from ratings of superiors

Table 10-1

CHARACTERISTICS DISCRIMINATING BETWEEN PROMOTABLE AND INADEQUATE EXECUTIVES BY FUNCTIONAL AREAS

Characteristic	Per cent present as an outstanding quality							
	Sales		Manufacturing		Engineering & Research		Finance & Accounting	
	Pr. Ex.*	In. Ex.	Pr. Ex.	In. Ex.	Pr. Ex.	In. Ex.	Pr. Ex.	In. Ex.
Position performance	50	18	48	3	47	3	49	7
Drive	47	27	52	10	36	4	48	20
Intellectual ability	44	23	41	3	47	4	46	13
Leadership	43	14	47	4	38	2	34	7
Administration	34	3	49	3	34	4	44	7
Initiative	36	23	49	6	30	1	37	13
Motivation	a	—	31	1	34	8	33	7
Creativeness	34	18	31	3	39	4	b	—
Acceptance	52	27	52	20	48	12	—	—
Planning	—	—	45	7	29	8	—	—
Flexibility	—	—	37	7	—	—	—	—
Analysis and judgment	—	—	50	7	—	—	—	—
Technical knowledge	—	—	—	—	73	46	72	33
Accomplishment	—	—	—	—	28	4	—	—
Socialness	—	—	—	—	43	19	—	—
Quality	—	—	—	—	—	—	30	0

*Pr. Ex. = Promotable Executives
In. Ex. = Inadequate Executives

[a]Motivation for Sales Managers not discriminating but Promotable 41%, Inadequate 32%. Both groups as highly motivated as other areas.

[b]Creativeness for Finance and Accounting not discriminating and neither group creative. Promotable: 13%, Inadequate: 7%.

Source: Adapted from C. W. Randle. "How to Identify Promotable Executives," *Harvard Business Review*, 34(3), 1956, 122–134.

and associates. The characteristics which he found discriminating for the four functional fields of research and engineering, manufacturing, finance and accounting, and sales are shown in Table 10-1. Randle's variables are probably all contaminated through the raters' knowledge of over-all ratings. Thirteen characteristics were discriminating between those research and engineering executives judged promotable and those judged inadequate. This was the largest number of discriminating characteristics for the four functional fields studied, although the number for manufacturing executives was only one less, *i.e.*, 12. Nine characteristics were discriminating for finance and accounting executives and eight for sales executives. This relative complexity of the requirements for research managers was supported by Hemphill's (1958) factor analysis, where it was found that there were more factors present in the research manager's job than in any others that were studied.

Two performance characteristics that Randle found discriminating for sales, for manufacturing, and for finance and accounting executives were also discriminating for engineering and research executives. Position performance was rated as outstanding for 47 per cent of the promotable engineering and research executives but for only 3 per cent of the inadequate ones. "Position performance" was defined as "how well the executive carries out the duties of his present job." Administration was rated outstanding for 34 per cent of the promotable executives but for only 4 per cent of the inadequate ones. Administration was defined as "Organizing own work and that of others. Delegation, follow-up, control of position activities."

Accomplishment was discriminating for engineering and research executives but not for any of the other functional fields. Accomplishment was defined as "Effective use of time. Amount of work produced." One might wonder how accomplishment differed from position performance. Twenty-eight per cent of the promotable engineering and research executives were rated as outstanding in accomplishment as contrasted to 4 per cent of the inadequate ones.

Planning was discriminating for engineering and research executives and for manufacturing executives but not for those in sales or finance and accounting. Engineering and research executives were more similar to those executives in manufacturing than to those in sales or finance and accounting. Twenty-nine per cent of the promotable engineering and research executives were rated as outstanding in planning versus 8 per cent of the inadequate ones.

Two ability characteristics were discriminating for research and engineering executives — intellectual ability, which was discriminating in all of the four functional fields, and technical knowledge, which was discriminating also for those in finance and accounting but not for those in the other two functional fields. Forty-seven per cent of the promotable engineering and research executives were outstanding in intellectual ability, but only 4 per cent of the inadequate ones were outstanding. Seventy-three per cent of the promotable research and engineering executives and 46 per cent of the inadequate executives were judged to be outstanding in technical knowledge. These are the highest percentages for any characteristic in any of the functional fields. Technical knowledge, therefore, is more generally possessed by research and engineering executives than any other characteristic is possessed by any group of executives.

Seven personality characteristics were discriminating for research and engineering executives. Three of these — drive, leadership, and initiative — were discriminating in each of the three other functional fields. Thirty-six per cent of the promotable research and engineering executives had outstanding drive, versus 4 per cent of the inadequate ones; 38 per cent of the promotable executives had outstanding leadership versus 2 per cent of the inadequate ones; and 30 per cent of the promotable research and engineering executives had outstanding initiative versus 1 per cent of the inadequate ones.

Motivation was discriminating for research and engineering as well as for manufacturing and finance and accounting executives. It was not discriminating for sales executives. Sales executives were generally more highly motivated than the others, so much so that even the inadequate executives were so highly motivated that this characteristic did not prove discriminating for the promotable ones.

Creativeness was discriminating for research and engineering executives, as might be expected; it was also discriminating among sales executives and those in manufacturing, but it was not discriminating for finance and accounting. Thirty-nine per cent of the promotable research and engineering executives were judged outstanding in creativeness versus 4 per cent of the inadequate ones.

Acceptance was discriminating for research and engineering executives, as well as for sales and manufacturing executives, but not for finance and accounting executives. Forty-eight per cent of the promotable research and engineering executives were judged outstanding in acceptance but only 12 per cent of the inadequate ones were outstanding.

Socialness was discriminating for research and engineering executives but not for the three other functional fields. Forty-three per cent of the promotable ones were judged outstanding in socialness versus 19 per cent of the inadequate ones. The definition of socialness was "Makes friends easily. Works 'comfortably' with others. Has sincere interest in people." There may be a substantial overlap with acceptance, which was defined as "Gains confidence of others; earns respect." There may also be a considerable overlap with leadership, which was defined as "Receives loyalty and cooperation from others. Manages and motivates others to full effectiveness."

Randle's characteristics and data have suggestions for the construction of a forced-choice rating scale since they show nondiscriminating versus discriminating characteristics. It might be of interest to compare his discriminating characteristics with the priority found by E. R. Henry.

Summary

Research managers appear to require greater versatility for their work than those in any other functional fields. Apparently they not only have to be competent scientists but must also have administrative skills for dealing with subordinates and political skills for dealing with peers and superiors. On the average, however, they are not as dominant, enthusiastic, and as optimistic as sales managers.

Chapter 11

PERSONALITY THEORY AND MEASUREMENT

The attempt to understand the makeup of successful business managers may lead to a personality theory which could throw light on some of the results reviewed in previous chapters. There are wide differences of opinion about personality, differences of opinion as to what personality is and how it develops. There is not only lack of agreement as to what are the important dimensions of personality, but there is also no agreement that it is legitimate even to inquire into the dimensions of personality since the concept of dimension implies an analytic approach which is opposed by a number of students while endorsed by others.

Beyond the problem of trying to improve the selection of general managers, a personality theory of managers may be cf broader social interest. Since the executive personality has been described as being similar to the American personality generally, except that the executive personality is more extreme in the direction in which Americans differ from others, current social questions of conformity and of the emphasis on the sales personality may be clarified by such an examination.

There is a great diversity of personalities among successful business managers. This has been documented among the major functional fields of sales, production, accounting, and research, where there were some differences, although more similarities were emphasized in the reports than differences. Research managers in particular and accounting managers were described as differing in personality from the other groups of business managers that have been studied. The personality of general managers seems to resemble that of sales managers more than it resembles the personality of managers of the other functional fields, although general managers may come from any of the fields. The same data that are used to demonstrate similarities can often be used to support the thesis that managers differ from one another. The great diversity within all groups may be the most practical fact.

The greatest diversity of personality among successful business managers is shown through the lack of evidence rather than its presence. Aside from wide agreement on the high ability of managers and their similarities in family background, there is little quantitative evidence that has been supported by cross-validation about the personality pattern of the successful business manager. This then points to diversity, or to the weakness of our personality measuring devices, or to both. The greatest agreement on the description of the nonintellectual aspects of the personality of successful business managers has come from the few clinical studies with emphasis on projective devices. While it is recognized that it is unreasonable to expect the same kind of quantification here as with psychometric scales, still it seems desirable to wait until the clinically oriented students have published a more complete account of their findings before becoming convinced by their conclusions.

There are other major reasons for diversity of personality aside from the differences of the functional fields and the uniqueness of personality that have been mentioned but that have not been thoroughly documented. There was one piece of evidence about company differences from Hemphill's factor analysis (1958). There was an indication of differences in management levels in Randle's (1956) study and from inferences made about other evidence. There was a historical account of different values put on the personality of the Protestant virtues of individual thrift and hard work versus the trend to winning cooperation from people. There have been opinions and some evidence about differences with size of company as with the Young Presidents who, in relatively smaller companies, insist that they are more independent and aggressive than managers in the corporate bureaucracies. Possible differences associated with company size may also be related to differences due to the trend of company growth or stability.

The ability of general managers is high although usually not so high as that of staff men in accounting, engineering, or law. General managers are typically brighter than 90 per cent of the population. There are great differences between companies. Sears, to take the most outstanding example known, has fantastically high ability among its managers.

The average general manager is better adjusted than the average of all other employees. He is highly dominant and independent, and his high ego is balanced by greater objectiveness than the average person. Most general managers want to be liked more than the average man, are more on the defensive than most people, and are ambitious to succeed, although they are afraid of failure. The interests of general managers are probably broader and shallower than those of people who remain in a functional field. The breadth that seems to be most often present includes an interest in sales, in production, and in people.

Sales managers as a group are not as bright as most managers of equal rank, but they are more articulate and dominant. They are generally optimistic and somewhat manic. Their talkativeness, coupled with their relative inaccuracy, aggressiveness, and optimism, leads to some conflict within the management team. The interests of sales managers are primarily in business competition and, secondarily, service and administrative work. They think that they are helping people, and they have a moderate interest in the paper work of reports.

Production managers have worked up from the bottom of the company more often than the other major managers; therefore, they are the least likely to be college trained. Their ability pattern is strong in the practical ability of mechanical knowledge, space relations ability, and numerical reasoning. They are relatively weak in verbal comprehension and fluency. Manufacturing managers are sometimes more interested in things than in people. A high percentage are critical and suspicious of people.

The average accounting and finance manager is very able, especially with numbers. He has relatively little imagination and creativity. He values security more than most managers. He is pessimistic and at times depressed. He values independence in the work situation and does not like to interact with others. This causes trouble when accounting managers grade the efficiency of others by cost and production figures without getting acceptance on the rules by which the grading is done.

The characteristics of research and engineering managers have not been so fully reported as have those of general managers and managers of sales, production, and accounting. There are a couple of pieces of evidence, however, that the requirements for success demand the highest amount of versatility in research and engineering management. One study shows more factors present in their job (Hemphill, 1958), and another study showed more discriminating characteristics for research and engineering managers compared to those in the other major functional fields. The average research manager is high in abstract thinking and in space relations but relatively low in verbal reasoning and in speed of numerical computations. He is less dominant and well-adjusted than the sales manager and to some extent the production manager. How he compares with finance and accounting managers in the nonintellectual aspects of personality is not known. Accounting as well as research managers are not so well-adjusted as are general managers, sales managers, and production managers. Research and accounting managers have more indications of depression than the others.

The literature does not contain any specific comparisons of line versus staff managers except insofar as all of the major functional fields usually may be considered as staff to the general managers whose results have been reviewed separately. Learned, Ulrich, and Booz (1951, pp. 188–9) have suggested that in some situations a staff position modifies personality because of its subordinate status. This may frustrate the staff man and consequently lead him to defensive reactions of aggression against the line or to attempts to overcompensate by bragging.

Determinants of Personality of Managers

Hall and Lindzey (1957, p. 548) have listed dimensions to be considered in describing a personality theory. Some of these dimensions provide a useful outline for discussing the determinants of the personality of business managers. This is a hazardous undertaking since it means trying to say why business managers have the personality that they do when there is by no means complete agreement on what their personality is. Nevertheless it still seems to be desirable to discuss possible determinants, although there is little evidence but mainly opinions about almost all of these dimensions as applied to managers' personality.

Early Development Experience. Early developmental experience with parents or a substitute father figure have been offered as explanations of managers' basic motivation in several instances. Parental influence has been the most frequently mentioned source of motivation. There seems to be some lack of agreement as to what are the ideal relations with parents for successful managers but the consensus appears to be that managers are trying to outdo their fathers and that they got along well with their mothers. Warner and Abegglen concluded that the mobile managers had been rejected by their fathers, felt close relations with their mothers, and had a substitute father figure, usually a teacher. They found that competition with the father also applied to what they called the "birth elite" although they did not stress this competition as much as some writers have.

Quite a few of the Young Presidents were reported to have been trying to outdo their fathers or at least to prove that, relative to their fathers, they, too, could accomplish something. Pertinent is the fact that a large number of top managers have had fathers who were successful businessmen. The influence here seems to be in large part on personality, although, of course, nepotism and subtler but still fairly crude forms of family influence have played a large part in some situations. Over 40 per cent of the Young Presidents were in companies controlled by their families. While no doubt most of these had to have some minimum qualifications to get and hold their jobs, it is unlikely that any significant percentage of them would have gotten their jobs had family influence been absent. Nepotism had a much smaller place in the top management positions in the largest companies, for although family pressure no doubt is prominent in getting men jobs even in the largest companies, it is less important for promotion to the top spots than in the smaller companies.

Personality adequate for successful management cannot develop, it has been said, where the parental relations varied too much from the ideal mentioned above. Where the son was so hostile to his father that this carried over to resistance to all authority or where the son was so attached to his mother that he did not become independent emotionally, he could not function effectively as a manager.

Field Emphasis. There is some evidence in a few studies for a field emphasis, or an emphasis on the situation, in shaping personality, although this appears to be less important to the personality than the early development experience. There is convincing evidence that the situation is extremely important for management practices, especially the example of the boss. This has been the conclusion from the two most rigorous studies which have shown short-time training not to have the desired influence on behavior where classroom theory differed from the bosses' examples. The goals of managers have been interpreted in one study to have changed depending upon their situation. In another study the attitudes of foremen were reported as changing first to coincide with those of management, but when a group was demoted, its attitudes changed again to be in agreement with the attitudes of rank and file employees. Interests of business managers have been shown to have changed more than those of men in other occupations.

The effectiveness of many management acts is being recognized more and more as a function of the situation. Consequently, it is being emphasized that the manager's behavior changes with the situation, primarily to adapt to what his boss expects and secondarily to what his subordinates and peers expect.

Group Membership Determinants. College education and religious preference influence personality because of the group membership. The influence of education will also be discussed as a social learning phenomenon. College graduation is the single most important variable correlating with top management position. The traditional explanation has been that college graduation assured a company that a man had at least a minimum of ability and motivation. This applied only to the advantage that a college man had for employment, rather than for promotion.

The policies of some companies, whether written or not, favor promotion of college graduates. This study has not attempted to explore these policies, but it is highly doubtful whether the information is available; it is also probable that there has been a fairly rapid change in policies toward favoring college-trained men that did not apply to the top managers of 1950.

Mills (1956) has interpreted the value of the college education for managers in terms of group membership determinants. He thought that the "power elite" selected others to management who were from their colleges, their college clubs, and their clubs after college. Mills made an impressive case for the continuation of power by the elite who attended Ivy League colleges, especially Harvard. He went further to document the conclusion that the controlling business positions are held not only by Harvard graduates but mainly by those who went to expensive prep schools and belonged to the right clubs at Harvard. This is interesting material, but other studies of top managers by Newcomer, Warner and Abegglen, and by Havemann and West, while supporting the importance of college, do not show by any means the same advantage for Harvard or for the rest of the Ivy League. This is not to say that Mills is wrong either in his data or in his interpretation. He was studying a different group of managers, a more select group including more owners of the largest corporations than other students have reported. While Mills' interpretation for owners may be correct, the scope of the present study is managers rather than owners.

Group membership may make a difference, as Dalton has opined, by managers choosing new managers similar to themselves, not consciously, but because they wish to have managers who will be congenial and loyal. While these objectives are laudable, they also pose some threat to the open society.

The various groups considered — college, clubs, prep schools, religious denominations — taken together make up social class. There is no doubt that the socio-economic class does have some influence on personality, although exactly what and how much has not been proved. Belonging to the upper class may make children more confident and more dominant, and may lead them to set higher levels of aspiration for business management success.

It may lead them to take more chances in going into new risk companies because their parents can stake them to new tries if the first one fails or because they know that they can always get a job if their new venture does not succeed.

The upper class may be better adjusted through having less anxiety. There is overwhelming evidence from paper and pencil tests, mainly of the inventory type and to a lesser extent of the forced-choice type, that managers are better adjusted than the general population and that the higher-level managers are better adjusted than the lower-level ones. Since the higher-level managers come overwhelmingly from the upper classes, the important variable may be the security of group membership in the upper class.

Learning Process. Dalton (1959) has made the interesting point that since so many managers are not in positions for which their college education trained them, the advantage of college for management must be something other than classroom education. While he presented results from only one company, it is likely that his results are fairly representative and that a majority of college graduates who are in management positions have not been trained in college specifically for their field of work. Dalton ascribes the value of the college education to its training in politics and in learning to make compromises and presumably dealing with a variety of people on a variety of matters. This would be classified in Hall and Lindzey's terminology as the learning process, although it is social learning rather than intellectual learning. This has intriguing possibilities for the graduate school of business. If college provides this social learning, can the graduate school add more, and if so, exactly what, and how? Gordon and Howell's results plus those of Ward and others suggest that what business says it wants and what it rewards is human relations. This relates back to the classroom, but in a way that gets into the social learning process suggested by Dalton, since it is feelings and consideration that are desired rather than the more intellectual academic subjects.

Purpose. Purpose as defined by Hall and Lindzey (1957) means "the importance of conceiving of the human organism as a striving, seeking, purposive creature . . ." Like most Americans, managers want to succeed, but managers have an even greater desire for success than average Americans. They have the purpose of getting ahead. This may have to be masked politely to some extent and under some circumstances but nevertheless this purpose seems to be practically universally present in studies that have touched on the point. While the term has dropped out of favor, a personality trait of "will," which seems to be the opposite of neuroticism, has been isolated. While all managers seem to possess a will to get ahead, it has been written up especially in describing the aggressive egos of the Young Presidents. Managers may have purpose for various reasons, and specific goals have been reported as changing within the life span of individual managers with success. The purpose is to succeed and this means to many managers to become managers or to get promoted. It may also mean money, status, power, equalling or beating Dad, or other things. "The power, prestige, and status associated with high income are dominant themes for individuals with business contact . . . patterns of interests." (Darley and Hagenah, 1955)

Reward. The rewards for the general manager are several. While one thinks often of money, it has been shown that the income of some groups of physicians and lawyers exceeds that of managers. There is no doubt satisfaction in being a manager, but again the job satisfaction of the physicians in Terman's group far exceeded that of managers. In spite of these evidences of relatively less reward in comparison to physicians and lawyers, still the rewards for the general manager in our society are very great. In addition to income and job satisfaction, people put a very high status value on the job of the manager.

Contiguity. Contiguity was defined by Hall and Lindzey as "Association, the spatial and temporal linking of two events . . ." Some behavior of managers can be explained by contiguity, or being in a certain place at a given time. This is what apparently is often meant by luck which some put so prominently as a reason for the success of some managers. The Harvard MBA's who were friends of a classmate who shortly after graduation became president of a company were exemplifying contiguity when they also shortly became officers of the company. Getting to know fellow country club members might also operate in this way.

Heredity. The ability requirements for being at the 90th percentile in intelligence means that managers probably have to inherit superior mental ability. None of the studies found have dealt specifically with the relative contribution of heredity and environment to ability, but since the writer is of the opinion that heredity is the major determinant, it appears that superior heredity is necessary but not alone sufficient.

Self Concept. The self concept is implied in some of the evidence about managers' personality, especially that of the Young Presidents. Their "aggressive egos" show a well-developed self concept. Other descriptions of managers include an account of well-developed superegos. The self concept of successful managers has been described as including objectivity and often some consideration of others as well as for the self. The self concept is probably set mainly by relations with parents and to some extent by other features in the environment. The pertinence of self concept to understanding managers has been demonstrated by Ghiselli in his series of studies showing the self concepts of various levels of managers and of other employee groups related to status and performance ratings. Self concept more than most of the other dimensions raises the question of possible changes with different management positions.

Organismic Emphasis. Hall and Lindzey have defined organismic emphasis as meaning to ". . . emphasize the importance of considering the individual as a total, functioning unit . . ." The most obvious place where an organismic emphasis has been encountered in this study has been over the question of method of appraising personality. While clinicians have insisted on an organismic emphasis, or the necessity of viewing the personality as a whole rather than segmenting it by various test scores, the evidence marshalled by Meehl is that this clinical approach has not been proved superior to a statistical one; and, in fact, the evidence favored a statistical approach as superior. The comparisons of the two approaches were in educational and not in business situations. There are loyal defenders of the clinical method in appraising the personality of business managers but no clear-cut results have been presented to allow a comparison with statistical approaches.

The interview generally represents an attempt to appraise personality through an organismic emphasis or seeing personality as a whole. Although the interview is almost universally used in selecting managers when they are being obtained from outside the company, there is almost no literature on its validity for this purpose. In spite of questions about its reliability, as well as its validity, it will no doubt continue to be used. If the interview is to be used, it should only be used for getting information which can not be obtained in other ways. Almost no one today uses the interview rather than a test to measure intelligence. The interview, however, is still used to gather some items of information about a person's background which could be done more reliably as well as inexpensively with an application blank.

Wagner (1949) in a thorough and critical review of the literature on the interview pointed out that using all of the data might produce less accurate results than just using some of the data that were valid for a specific prediction. This statement has been borne out by Meehl's review, by Berdie (1958), and by an unpublished study by the writer.

Ward found that the interview seemed to make prediction of grades at the Harvard Graduate School of Business Administration poorer than doing without the interview. After his study the interview was no longer used by Harvard. Conceivably the interview could be valid for a different criterion of business management success and not for scholarship.

Uniqueness. Uniqueness of personality is contrary to the search for generalizations about personality which is the object of the great majority of studies reviewed. It is, consequently, not unexpected that almost none of them contribute to the understanding of the extent to which personality is in fact unique. One exception is Shartle's observation that the same management job can be performed equally well with an entirely different pattern of performance. While Shartle was explicitly emphasizing performance in contrast to personality, still his example has pertinence for its suggestion about differences, if not uniqueness, of personality. It may be significant only to high managers. Perhaps lower managers are more often expected to conform than to show unique performance.

Psychological Environment. Psychological environment is a concept that is not explicitly mentioned in the management literature, but nevertheless it may have meaning for some of the data. It comes into Likert's relative and adjustive theory of management. Likert says that the effectiveness of various management practices depends to a considerable extent on the expectations of and the way these practices are perceived by the manager's boss, his subordinates, and his peers. These perceptions substantially are the psychological environment. While this reference is to the psychological environment of those who surround the manager at work, rather than to the psychological environment of the manager himself, this too is of increasing interest in current research. There are more and more studies of the perceptions of managers, their perceptions of people in general, of subordinates, of bosses, of themselves. These perceptions, or the psychological environment, are believed to be important, and in effect to constitute the personality.

Multiplicity of Motives. The major motives for business managers appear to be rather few, although agreement is lacking on exactly how they should be classified. The fundamental motive seems to be that of the ego, or wanting to be important. Other students have emphasized the presence of a self-actualizing or achievement motive. Power appears to be an important motive for some managers. Although leading to success in some situations, it is not so clearly desirable as is achievement. The primary motives of ego and achievement are combined in various situations with secondary motives of service to customers, and consideration for employees.

Continuity of Development. Tuddenham (1957) showed that personality ratings had some stability over a period of nineteen years. His study included 32 males who averaged 14 years of age at the time of the initial ratings. They were rated nineteen years later by different raters. The reliability over this period of time averaged .27. The most stable rating for males was on drive-aggression. The implications here for a personality of management are that some aspects of personality have a considerable stability so that they must not depend entirely on situational causes. Several of the least stable variables, however, are particularly important for management, *i.e.*, self-confidence, leadership, and popularity. Consequently, there is no proof that prospective managers can be spotted as early as age 14.

Personality Structure. Although some writers believe that it is not useful to think in terms of personality factors and although they may be correct, it still seems to be worthwhile to take a look at some ideas and information about the presence of personality factors. Even if the factor analytic approach is followed, Anastasi and Foley (1949, p. 528) have expressed the opinion that the pattern of factors emerging from a particular analysis would depend upon the cultural setting. A number of writers (Hinchliffe, 1959; Barber, 1957) have recorded the suggestion that personality depends largely on social class; but Barber, after reviewing the literature carefully, reported little demonstration of the influence of social class on personality. There is an impressive amount of indirect evidence that has been presented above that would strongly suggest the influence of social class on personality. Successful business and professional men have sons who are also college graduates and who often are successes in management. Managers are more dominant and better adjusted than rank and file employees. Primarily managers are from the middle and upper classes and not from the lower class.

While the traditional distinction between abilities and nonintellectual factors of personality has been used herein, Anastasi and Foley (1949, p. 510) and others have pointed out that factors may cut across both ability and nonintellectual factors of personality. Their example is a relation between "ability in drawing and certain personality characteristics . . ." From the test results of managers there have been suggestions of an association between speed in verbal and routine numerical problems with mistakes and optimism for sales managers, and relatively higher abstract reasoning, slower routine reactions, and less optimism for research managers. One might wonder whether the mathematical accuracy of accounting managers is associated with compulsiveness. Creativity probably includes nonintellectual factors as well as requiring superior general ability, and depending upon the field, high educational ability or practical ability or both. In spite of the possibility that factors should be considered as crossing both intellectual and nonintellectual lines, the traditional classification of discussing mental ability separately from nonintellectual factors will be followed.

Mental Ability. The organization of mental ability can be conceived in different ways from the same correlations of tests and criteria. British writers have differed from American, and although the writer has followed Thurstone and the American trend, it now seems that the British conception is more useful as well as being simpler. The British theory (Vernon, 1950) states that mental ability can be conceived as consisting of a hierarchical structure. At the top is a general ability. Below this there are two abilities, educational and practical. Educational ability can be split into verbal and numerical abilities. The second level cannot be measured without measuring verbal and numerical abilities. Practical ability can be split into mechanical and spatial abilities. Vernon's conclusion, which is substantially confirmed in the literature on managers, is that predictions are just as accurate using only these levels as attempting to isolate factors that are more specific.

Nonintellectual Factors. There is only a small amount of agreement, if any, as to what are the nonintellectual factors of personality. Personality research has concentrated on people in mental hospitals, which no doubt explains why the only personality trait about which there is complete agreement is that of neurotic instability. This neurotic factor is separate from psychotic factors. Of particular interest for managers is the positive extreme of the neurotic factor about which there is not so much unanimity of agreement but which has been referred to as will or perseverance (Tyler, 1956, pp. 173 ff.). Descriptions of will that appear to have relevance for managers are "tendency not to abandon tasks in face of obstacles . . . 'readiness to forego an immediate gain for the sake of a remote but greater gain.' "

The two most ambitious attempts to isolate nonintellectual factors have been by Guilford and Cattell. Both have come out with about the same number of factors, but their labels for the names of the factors have varied in some instances. By correlating questions on inventories, Guilford and Guilford (1936,

1939 a and b) and Martin (1945) have named thirteen factors, some of which have been referred to in studies above, especially in the study at Sears. These are:

1. Social Introversion-Extraversion (sociability as against shyness).
2. Thinking Introversion-Extraversion (introspective as opposed to objective orientation of the thinking process).
3. Depression (cheerful optimistic disposition as opposed to chronic depressed mood).
4. Cycloid Disposition (stability of mood as opposed to marked fluctuations).
5. Rhathymia (happy-go-lucky or carefree disposition as opposed to inhibition or over-control).
6. General Activity (tendency to engage in over-activity as opposed to inertness).
7. Ascendance-Submission (social leadership vs. social passivity).
8. Masculinity-Femininity (resemblance to characteristic masculine vs. characteristic feminine responses).
9. Inferiority Feelings (confidence vs. lack of confidence in oneself).
10. Nervousness (calmness vs. jumpiness, irritability).
11. Objectivity (tendency to view oneself and surroundings objectively vs. tendency to take things personally).
12. Cooperativeness (willingness to accept things and people as they are vs. overcriticism and intolerance).
13. Agreeableness (lack of quarrelsomeness as opposed to belligerent, domineering attitude).

Lovell (1945) factor analyzed the scores on Guilford's thirteen scales based on his factor analysis and found that the relations could be explained mainly by four factors. These were:

1. Drive-Restraint (high loadings on general drive, carefreeness, sociability and social ascendance).
2. Realism (high loadings on objectivity, masculinity, freedom from nervousness, and freedom from inferiority feelings).
3. Emotionality (high loadings on stability of emotional reactions, freedom from depression, and extravertive orientation of the thinking process).

4. Social Adaptability (high loadings on lack of quarrelsomeness and tolerance).[1]

Cattell (1957) has made the most ambitious attempt to determine personality factors. He set out to isolate those factors which existed by seeking leads from three sources, ratings, questionnaires, and objective tests. His design was to find factors on which there was agreement by these three methods, and then to subject the same population to the three methods as a cross check. His first major step was to look for the verbal description of personality which had been summarized by Allport and Odbert. To this list he had a psychologist and a student of literature add other adjectives from the psychological and psychiatric literature. The total was 171 different characteristics of personality. He had 100 adults rated on these 171 characteristics. A cluster analysis reduced the number of variables to 35. Next, 208 men were rated on these 35 clusters. A factor analysis reduced the matrix to twelve factors listed below:

1. Cyclothymia vs. schizothymia.
2. Intelligence vs. mental defect.
3. Emotionally mature, stable character vs. demoralized general emotionality.
4. Hypersensitive infantile emotionality vs. phlegmatic frustration tolerance.
5. Dominance vs. submissiveness.
6. Surgency (optimistic enthusiasm) vs. melancholy shy desurgency.
7. Positive character integration vs. immature, dependent character.
8. Charitable, adventurous rhathymia (happy-go-lucky attitude) vs. obstructive, withdrawn schizophrenia.
9. Sensitive, imaginative, anxious emotionality vs. rigid, tough poise.
10. Neurasthenia vs. vigorous, obsessional, determined character.
11. Trained, socialized, cultured mind vs. boorishness.
12. Surgent cyclothymia vs. paranoid schizophrenia.[2]

---

[1]Constance Lovell, "A Study of the Factor Structure of Thirteen Personality Variables," *Educational and Psychological Measurement* 5 (1945), 335–350. Reprinted by permission of *Educational and Psychological Measurement*.

[2]R. B. Cattell, *Personality and Motivation Structure and Measurement* (World Book Co., 1957). Reprinted by permisson of World Book Co.

Several of Cattell's factors are similar to those of Guilford, but the differences have defied an attempt to show the extent of agreement. Cattell has not been able to demonstrate the same factors from objective tests, questionnaires, and ratings on the same population. Part of the difficulty has been that he could not get cooperation from a large group of subjects on all three procedures.

The British have a hierarchical view of personality generally similar in relative simplicity to their view of ability that again has distinguished their approach from the American. Eysenck (1947, p. 30) has proposed that types are the major classification, then traits, next habitual responses, and finally specific responses. Americans have started with traits and worked back to types.

Ability to judge people may be considered as a personality trait that has been said to be of importance to business managers. There have been a few laboratory studies of this but none of them included business managers as subjects. Studies referred to in previous chapters might be construed as showing that supervisors who were better judges of people had more productive work groups. Nagel's study, especially, showed that supervisors who were more accurate judges of their employees' attitudes had higher production. Fiedler's results might be attributed to better judgment about individual differences although this is not his interpretation.

Laboratory studies have been reviewed by Taft (1955) and reported by Vernon (1933) and Estes (1938). Taft concluded that the following characteristics had correlated with ability to judge people's personality: "high intelligence and academic ability (with analytic judgment especially); specialization in the physical sciences; esthetic and dramatic interests; insight into one's status with respect to one's peers on specific traits; good emotional adjustment and integration . . . and social skill . . ."

Interests. Vocational interests have been reduced to five factors (Strong, 1943, pp. 319–320), (1) scientific creativity; (2) mathematics-accounting; (3) business competition; (4) humanitarian; and (5) sociability. Interests seem to depend upon self-concepts rather than on experience with particular occupations (Tyler, 1956, p. 216).

Darley and Hagenah (1955, pp. 103–133) have presented several relationships between measurements of interests on the Strong Vocational Interest Blank and measurements of personality, which add to knowledge of business managers even though the results were all obtained with students. The Interest Blank results are given in terms of norms for mature business groups so that the student results can be extrapolated to the personality pattern of businessmen. "The economically conservative, socially aggressive, physically robust individuals will probably have 'business contact' interests . . ." This confirms results on the personality of sales managers whose interests are in the business contact or competitive group. Students with interest in the business contact group had higher scores on social adjustment and lower scores on the theoretical scale of the Allport-Vernon Scale of Values than average college students.

The definition of the Occupational Level scale from the Strong test is suggestive of the interpretation about ambition and class. Darley and Hagenah defined it, quoting from Darley:

> in the context of level of aspiration: "The degree to which the individual's total background has prepared him to seek the prestige and discharge the social responsibilities growing out of high income, professional status, recognition, or leadership in the community. . .". This definition, while rhetorically fascinating, may be a little overextended. However, the scale does distinguish student groups accepting or rejecting the interests characteristic of those in families of occupations at widely separate points on the income scale.[3]

This suggests that one should look at Occupational Level scores in relation to management success.

Attitudes. Attitudes can be expressed by two major factors, Conservative-Radical, and Tough Minded-Tender Minded according to Eysenck (1947). This conclusion followed from a study of economic, social, and political attitudes of wide variety. Big businessmen had a higher percentage who were rated ultra-conservative on a conservative-radicalism scale than small businessmen (Centers, 1949, p. 57).

---

[3]John G. Darley and Theda Hagenah, *Vocational Interest Measurement: Theory and Practice* (University of Minnesota Press, 1955). Reprinted by permission of the University of Minnesota.

The considerable change of attitudes to conform with those in the organization has been presented colorfully by Whyte in *The Organization Man.* Although mainly opinion, Argyris (1957) has also presented some evidence that agreed with Whyte's pessimistic stand on the influence of big business on attitudes. More specific evidence was given in the studies reported by Dalton and Larke, above.

A somewhat contrary point can be inferred from the data presented by Stouffer (1955) on a Scale of Willingness to Tolerate Nonconformists. Industrial leaders who were presidents of Chambers of Commerce were essentially as tolerant as the average of community leaders, as tolerant as the presidents of labor unions, and substantially more tolerant than a cross section of people.

Methods of Measuring Personality

There is considerable question as to what if any methods are valid for measuring personality, especially in the hiring situation. Some of the issues have caught the attention of businessmen from Whyte's article in *Fortune* and from his later book, *The Organization Man.* Whyte has attacked personality testing as being an invasion of privacy, invalid because of its fakability which he has attempted to increase and because of lack of valid norms. The invasion of privacy argument is essentially a value judgment where anyone is entitled to his opinion. The question of valid norms has been treated in earlier chapters wherein it was pointed out that norms to be valid do have to be local to the company and to the job. Fakability will be discussed below. Tyler (1956, pp. 188–9) has concluded that the old-fashioned methods of ratings and letters of recommendation still appear to be more useful than personality tests.

Projective Tests. Kelly (1958, p. 332) has made a quotable distinction between projective and objective tests. "When the subject is asked to guess what the examiner is thinking, we call it an objective test; when the examiner tries to guess what the subject is thinking we call it a projective device." The literature that has been reviewed in previous chapters has contained several references to the Thematic Apperception Test (TAT) and Sentence Completion Test, which are projective tests.

More (1957) made an interesting study on the extent of agreement among several measures of personality, including projective tests, when independent rankings were made by different people. Sentence Completion was used in combination with the TAT. Rosenzweig's Picture Frustration was the other projective test used. There was also a patterned interview and a biographical statement. A psychologist had available the results of the Wonderlic, of a non-verbal test, and of a numbers test for all the subjects along with the other measures mentioned above. Subjects were 63 pharmacists. Only 31 of them took the Picture Frustration test. They were rated on personality traits judged important for the job and for their promotion potential to a management job. Results showed significant agreement among all the devices, except between the Rosenzweig and the combination of Sentence Completion (SC) and TAT. Correlations with a final ranking depending upon the over-all judgment showed a correlation significant at the 1% level for all four, but lowest for the Rosenzweig. Best was the biographical summary, but its correlation with final ranking, .79, was probably not significantly higher than the combination of SC-TAT, .78, or the patterned interview, .74. There was no validity criterion.

Faking. There have been numerous studies in the classroom showing that personality and interest inventories can be faked by students. More crucial is the question: are they faked in the employment situation? Davids and Pildner (1958) found less faking on projective tests, including the TAT and a Sentence Completion Test, than on self-rating scales. There was no evidence that the projective tests had been faked at all. The study was unusual in simulating an employment situation. Subjects were college students. There was a control group. This appears to be a crucial study which indicates that more valid results about personality could be obtained from projective devices in an employment situation. Heron (1956) proved that applicants did better on emotional adjustment in an employment situation than did a control group. Heron also reviewed a study by Green who found that applicants seemed to be faking on the Kuder Preference Record and on all scales of Guilford's STDCR except R. R meant Ascendance-Submission or social leadership vs. social passivity.

Forced-choice tests apparently are not quite as susceptible to faking as the self report personality inventories, but they also have been shown to be fakable to a slight extent. This was the conclusion of two studies with Gordon's Personal Profile. Rusmore (1956) found a difference of about 5 per cent in a simulated employment situation as contrasted to a simulated vocational guidance situation. Gordon and Stapleton (1956) found only "moderate" increases from a guidance to an employment situation.

Different from faking, but somewhat related, is the question of motivation on an intelligence test between administration for research and for promotion. Jennings (1953) found higher scores when the test was taken for promotion that were significant at the 5% level of confidence.

Summary and Conclusions

The personality theory that best fits the data on business managers is a relatively simple one. Ability need be analyzed no finer than verbal and numerical ability, and a practical ability including mechanical and spatial abilities for production managers especially. On the nonintellectual side, the most prominent part of personality is drive or will to control energy in pursuit of a goal rather than being disorganized in a neurotic way. This is the achievement drive. The expenditure of energy is usually in communications where at least some minimum level of verbal skills is also required. Drive needs to be accompanied usually by confidence and enthusiasm, which seems to be particularly present among sales managers.

Parental influence comes out as a major determinant of the personality of managers. The most effective father appears to be a business success who somehow influences his son to compete with him. This assumes that the son will have the ability to graduate from college and does so. If he wants to be the president of a large company, he is favored if he is a white Protestant. For the personality development to head smaller companies, there is also a correlation with the incidence of fathers who were successful business or professional men. The Jewish religion is modal in the smaller companies.

There are many business managers, especially at levels lower than presidencies, who are successful but whose fathers were neither successful business nor professional men. Even there the business manager's relationship to his mother and to either his father or a father substitute seems to be important in his personality development by giving him the dominance and self-confidence that are required in top management, in sales, or in production management. The story is somewhat different and not as clear for accounting management and for research management.

While the self-concept of the manager, developed from early influences, seems to be highly important, there are also some changes in behavior that occur with the business situation. There seems to be a flexibility which is often required to adjust to the situation.

Chapter 12

SUMMARY AND CONCLUSIONS

There is a good deal known about the performance of managers, but the prediction of management success is still in the primitive stages. There is no agreement on what is management success and no agreement on what is personality; so there can be no agreement on what personality it takes to be a success as a manager. Still, there are some definitions of management success and some attempts to measure personality that deserve attention.

Business goes on satisfying the stockholders, customers, and employees to a great extent in spite of the existence of these fundamental problems which have not been answered. Graduate schools of business continue to admit only a fraction of their applicants and continue to graduate men who get management jobs; so the practical problem remains as to who should be admitted and almost automatically therefore moved toward management. This chapter will attempt to summarize some of the highlights and conclusions from the literature. Some desirable research will be discussed in the next and last chapter.

The question of who is a success at management depends logically on the definition of management and what managers do. The difficulty of generalizing is well-recognized. The duties of managers differ by levels, functional fields, growth situation, to some extent by industries, size of company, by company, and time. There have been a few studies of what general managers do, more of what production foremen do, and one of the behavior of field sales managers (Davis, 1957).

Managers' Performance

Because of the situational nature of leadership one would not expect any substantial number of immutable personality characteristics of successful managers or many rigid rules of successful management practice. There has been a growing interest in supervisory practices and a diminution of interest relatively in personality characteristics of managers. One authority has gone so far as to define leadership in terms of performance rather than personality. While performance needs to be emphasized, it is still necessary to stress that performance depends on personality as well as on the situation. Performance depends in part on the way the manager sees people, including himself, and on what his needs are.

There has been and still is a controversy over the relative effectiveness of democratic versus autocratic management. The controversy can be largely, if not entirely, resolved by the situational theory of leadership formulated by Likert which includes a consideration of the personality of the leaders and the led. What the key people in the situation want and how they see the situation determines the effectiveness of management practices to a great extent. The importance of effective communication which includes acceptance has led to increasing stress on participation among all levels of employees down to and including the rank and file level, although the situation limits the extent of participation for a particular work group. There is greater acceptance where ego involvement occurs through genuine participation in decision making. The fact that top managers have such aggressive egos may be responsible for their having relatively less consideration for rank and file employees than do lower level managers, as found by Fleishman.

The relative merits of democratic versus autocratic management depend to a considerable extent upon the length of time under consideration. It appears that for immediate results an autocratic approach can get highest productivity, but this is at the expense of the human side of the organization. For long-range results over a year or more, it seems that a participative approach is necessary for optimal productivity as well as morale.

One implication of the studies on management practices in relation to productivity and morale is the need for flexibility of performance, which means greater demands on the personality. A great part of this flexibility comes automatically. Rigid personalities have been found to be unsuccessful managers. Managers adapt naturally to the example of their superior's behavior and probably to the expectations of their subordinates as well, within the limits of what is often a conflict between the expectations of superior and subordinates. The effective manager certainly needs to know when to talk as well as when to listen. The need for flexibility should be qualified by the desirability of sincerity rather than by the insincere sales approach that Ghiselli found to be ineffective. Ghiselli concluded that the heart of successful supervision seemed to be a genuine respect for people, and the key difficulty of unsuccessful supervisors was a sales approach to human relations.

All managers have to communicate successfully in the sense of influencing people and not just in being understood by them. This means that they have to relate to people to the extent that they are accepted as the boss by their subordinates and also supported by their superior in their management position. Successful communication is a complex process that involves several variables. The manager has to have a message to communicate. This calls for a certain amount of ability and technical knowledge about the business in question. Successful communication seems also to require that the manager know something about the knowledge of his subordinates, and what they expect and how they perceive their situation. The manager may succeed through luck or through trial and error without analyzing communication in this way, but these steps appear to be generally desirable.

At levels below the top, the management job includes communicating and relating upward to one's superior and horizontally to peers as well as downward. The same processes of expectations and perceptions of bosses and peers are present as in the case of subordinates.

The fundamental that "management gets work done through people" still needs emphasis since not all managers spend enough time at this for most effective performance. Sales managers in particular and some presidents spend considerable time in selling which, for the long-term good of the company, should be spent in managing.

General Managers. The first job of top managers, according to a survey of the Young Presidents' Organization, is staffing the key jobs of officers — the officers of sales, production, and finance. This means choosing the right person and, if the choice turns out to be a mistake, getting rid of the person chosen and getting someone who is right. No doubt larger companies have more room for transfers at this juncture. Procrastination when one is sure that the officer is not suited for the job is the biggest error that Young Presidents say that they make.

Second in time and importance is the motivation of the president's immediate subordinates. This a complex job that involves persuasion and much more than financial incentives. Spencer has made the analogy to the family; the president lives with his vice-presidents and immediate subordinates. Problems are similar to those in the family in that they may take equally long to solve, if they are ever solved completely.

One emphasis of the key duty for highly successful top managers is innovation. This means being able to put across the idea for a new product or service, although it does not mean that the top manager originated the new idea. Planning has been stressed as being essential for top management and at lower levels. It has often been shown to be what has discriminated between more effective managers and those who were less effective. Less effective managers were more frequently swayed by the always numerous immediate demands of the job. Another essential of top management that has been stressed is coordination of the staff so that successful teamwork results.

Sales. The job of the sales manager has many of the same elements as that of the president. The sales manager's job consists of picking efficient subordinates, training them, and motivating them to sell and to become qualified for more responsible jobs. Somehow the sales manager's job seems to be more completely concerned with people than that of the other major managers studied, although all managers' jobs have essential tasks of dealing with people. The sales manager, perhaps because of higher turnover among salesmen than among many other employees, seems to be more concerned with personnel matters.

Production. The production manager's job is to make things efficiently at a low price; things that sell at a good profit. The production manager's job is perhaps more task oriented than that of any other major manager. Certainly the production manager needs to be people-minded as well as production-minded, but the expectation in the factory is that the great stress will be on production.

Finance. The financial manager is expected to take an accurate backward look and to keep the books straight. This much is taken for granted by his president, but it is sometimes regarded as the main job by the financial manager. Presidents, on the other hand, want financial managers to look toward the future for the financing needs of the company and the tax situation.

Research. It is not quite as clear what the research manager's job should be as for the other managers although it appears that it means staying in close touch with scientists to help and ec-courage them but not to dictate what they do. A couple of pieces of evidence suggest that the job of the research manager requires an extreme degree of versatility.

Success Criteria

The criterion of successful management has not been satisfactorily solved and there is no prospect of any single solution. There have been a number of objective criteria discovered or developed and some of them have been predictable, but objective criteria do not seem to be generally useful for research or for administration. Company growth may be a reliable criterion, but it is not generally accepted as valid for the competence of the top manager since there seem to be too many variables outside his control that are significant for growth.

Sales. Sales may be reliable for the sales manager's efforts, but the uncontrolled variables of economic swings and differences in territories have kept it from being generally accepted as a valid measure of sales managers' competence. Sales quotas seem to be used more for the motivation of sales effort than for a yardstick of success.

Production. Reliable objective criteria have been developed for production managers at Lockheed and in a few other companies, but even within these companies they have been generally rejected in research procedure in favor of ratings. Perhaps objective production criteria have been discounted because of the lack of broad comparability from one department to another.

Finance. Although objective criteria have been developed for small work groups in offices, there have been no instances found of the application of an objective criterion for financial or accounting managers. Spencer has pointed out that the financial officer grades all the other managers but in turn is not graded. This is said sometimes to be a source of conflict.

Research. Objective criteria for research groups have been shown to be possible, but the extent of the influence of the manager on research output of subordinates is somewhat in doubt. While there has been some demonstration of the importance of the research manager on scientists' morale, the most significant correlates of scientific success seem to be the intrinsic motivation in science that the research worker brings to his job and, secondarily, his freedom to pursue a problem of his choice. The latter is largely company policy although it may be modified by the manager's behavior. Company loyalty, which is to some extent a function of the manager's behavior, has not been found to be positively correlated with research productivity. Those scientists who put a greater value on the organization than on science appear to be less productive than those who have the opposite values. To recapitulate, although there can be an objective criterion of research productivity, this criterion seems to be correlated little if any with the actions of the research manager and therefore is not useful as a measure of the manager.

Summary. To summarize, the most widely used criterion of management success seems to be ratings for functional managers while for general managers it is the fact that the person is occupying the position. E. R. Henry has reported that a forced choice rating has been used by Standard Oil (New Jersey) companies that has been effective as a criterion across company lines. It looks as if it could be tried for general managers as well as for functional managers although separate norms might need to be developed.

Whether it or any other rating is sufficiently valid in terms of objective results remains to be demonstrated. Pay is the most useful criterion cutting across management groups for such diverse populations as alumni, but it is less useful for more homogeneous groups.

Managers' Personality

There is less agreement on the fundamental nature of personality than there is on the nature of business management success. Even the place of mental ability in the total personality is not completely clear. There are some suggestions that the pattern of mental ability is correlated with particular patterns of nonintellectual personality traits, but this has not been clearly proven. In fact, a number of students of personality object to attempts to analyze in terms of traits, preferring to look at personality as an indivisible whole. Mental ability can be conceived as consisting of a general ability factor with subordinate factors of educational ability and practical ability. Educational ability is divisible into numerical and verbal abilities; practical ability is divisible into mechanical and spatial abilities. Even though this concept is not accepted by a number of the leading research people in the United States, who prefer a more complicated analysis of mental factors, the more complicated pattern does not seem to offer any advantage for understanding managers. The mental ability of managers and students even when measured with tests that have more apparent analytic refinement seem to be no more predictive of manager success. The Educational Testing Service's Admission Test for Graduate Study in Business seems to be an adequately valid predictor of scholastic grades. Although it has not been used long enough to follow up in business, it will probably be adequate to give about as much as a measure of mental ability can contribute to predicting success in management.

Personality can be defined as including, in addition to ability, a number of nonintellectual factors, plus interests and attitudes. There is some doubt that it is useful to attempt to measure personality for selection purposes in terms of specific traits. The analyses of pencil and paper tests as well as of ratings and objective tests have, however, sugested about 12 personality factors that may be combined into approximately four types which are not yet clearly identified. There seems to be a factor of will or perseverance of importance to managers' success which, at its other extreme, is neurotic instability. There is also an extraversion or social factor. There is less agreement on the identification of other personality factors, although an achievement factor perhaps correlated with will appears to be crucial. A power need that includes influencing others seems to be present in some managers.

Measurement Methods. The inventory or self-report measures of personality have a fatal transparency that makes them too easily fakable in employment situations as well as in the laboratory or classroom. While it has been argued that this fakability can be overlooked if their validity is established as it has been in a few specific instances for supervisors but not for high level managers, this seems highly questionable. Since some would doubtless be faking more than others, the best liars would be rewarded.

Forced-choice measures of personality such as the Gordon Personal Profile are not as easily fakable as are inventories, although they are fakable from five to nine percentile points. There has been no evidence presented on the fakability of the adjective check list of Ghiselli on which there are some interesting results for management selection.

Projective devices such as the Thematic Apperception Test and the Sentence Completion test have proved resistant to faking in one crucial study. The validity of these projective tests has been claimed by a few people but is not clearly established.

The best ways to measure personality at present are with personal data sheets, which resemble application blanks except that they are more complete, and with ratings. There are several studies that show personal data to be a significant predictor for supervisory success. The Individual Background Survey constructed for the Standard Oil Company (New Jersey) is one approach that is unusually thorough and that is based on a considerable amount of research.

Interests. Interests seem to be divisible into a few broad factors, (1) scientific creativity; (2) mathematics-accounting;

(3) competitive business activities; (4) humanitarianism; and (5) sociability. Such factors emerged from the occupational scales of the Strong Vocational Interest Blank. Two other interest scales appear to have some place in considering the personality of managers — Occupational Level, which gives some index of one's aspiration level, and Masculinity-Femininity. This interest blank is useful in vocational guidance but because of its fakability is of less clear use for selection.

Attitudes. The fundamental factors of attitudes appear to be two, (1) radicalism-conservatism; and (2) tough-minded versus tender-minded. There is some information about businessmen's attitudes on radicalism-conservatism, but none on tough-minded versus tender-minded. Maybe there should be, in terms of some of the issues of democratic leadership and management practices. Perhaps the autocratic manager is more tough-minded. Students interested in sales were more conservative than the average college student, and big businessmen were more conservative than small businessmen.

Theory. Relations to one's parents appear to offer the best explanation for the development of a personality similar to that of successful general managers. Who the parents are, especially what is the father's occupation, has already been discussed. Relations with parents regardless of their socio-economic status are also crucial. Many Young Presidents have been reported to be competing with their fathers whom they respected but wanted to match or outdo. The mobile elite, who by definition did not have highly successful fathers, occupationally were still trying to prove themselves worthy of the acceptance they had not had from their fathers, and often had developed an identification with some other father figure who inspired them to great effort.

General Managers. The variables most highly correlated with a white man arriving in general management in the United States were: (1) college graduation; (2) father's occupation, either business or professional; (3) for the largest companies high status Protestant religion, for the smaller companies, Jewish; (4) intelligence at or above the 90th percentile for the general population; and (5) personality pattern of high will, wanting to succeed in management, high energy, dominance, aggressiveness far above average, and superior mental adjustment.

The above cluster of variables has been interpreted as being the upper and upper-middle socio-economic class, and they are essentially that, but the problem is somewhat more complex. Certainly there are many good managers from the lower class, and not all upper class men in business get to top management. Top managers, though, do come mainly from the upper and middle class and these class memberships no doubt work in subtle ways for the ingroup to perpetuate itself. One of the necessary steps in the appointment of a president is usually the nomination or approval of his predecessor. This approval is generally readier for one's friends or for people with a similar background. The extent is not clear to which it is desirable to put a value on acceptance of colleagues for appointment to general management. On the one hand, the acceptance of a boss is essential for effectiveness. On the other, it seems to be perpetuating a class system antithetical to the American dream of equal opportunity for all.

Supporting the emphasis on communication in the definition of management are the results of two studies on survival in management positions. Pederson at Lockheed found that managers were demoted more often, and Bentz found at Sears that managers were often fired, who were relatively low in persuasive interests.

There is some evidence that breadth of interests in production, in people, in sales contact, and in office work is desirable for general managers.

Functional Fields. The personality of managers in the functional fields of sales, production, accounting, and research are more or less similar to those of general managers. Similarities are greatest in sales and production; they are less for accounting and research.

Sales. Sales managers are interested in power, status, and and in persuading people. They are verbal-minded, are less theoretical in their interests than people generally, and are not as bright and are more inaccurate than managers generally. They are optimistic, enthusiastic, masculine, and dominant.

Production. Production managers are interested in things and in numbers. They are highly competent in mechanical aptitude and in numerical operations and less so in verbal skills. They welcome responsibility and are afraid of failure. They are practical and put a high value on status.

Finance and Accounting. Finance and accounting managers are interested in making order out of chaos. They are highly able in quantitative reasoning, but less so in verbal. They are critical and less optimistic than sales or even production managers. Ordinarily their imagination and creativity are low.

Research and Engineering. Research and engineering managers are high in abstract reasoning, but relatively lower in speed of routine computations and in verbal skills. They are creative and less optimistic than sales or production managers.

Graduate Schools of Business

Putting the information on undergraduate alumni follow-ups together with the studies of graduate schools of business alumni, the following conclusions emerge. Present intellectual standards are probably high enough for maximum success in general management, although the decision-making process on applications could probably be routinized more conveniently with no loss in validity.

There is some carry-over between leadership in college and in business. There is evidence that holding major offices in college is favorable. There is evidence in some studies that participation in athletics is favorable, but in other studies this is not supported. The ideal student to become a successful general manager is one who is high in scholarship, has held offices, is endorsed by his undergraduate professors, and is more masculine than average.

The biggest improvement that graduate schools of business can make in their percentage of alumni who become general managers is to have more good applicants from whom to choose, although some improvement can probably be made in refining the selection process. The next and last chapter will discuss a research program for exploring the personality requirements for successful general managers. It will propose a program based on the information presently available on business careers and the interests and other qualifications required for study of success in business.

Chapter 13

FUTURE RESEARCH

Before suggesting future research, a proposal will be made for a method of selecting students to a graduate school of business which would simplify present procedure, and for a counseling program. Future research suggested consists of two large programs, one for selection of students, the other in several companies. Both programs are aimed at increasing the understanding of personality requirements for business managers.

Selection of Students

It is proposed that the selection of students for a graduate school of business be continued for the present by essentially the same methods now in use except that the procedure be routinized. Not only would this make the selection easier administratively, but the literature suggests that a statistical rather than a clinical approach is more valid. Five variables are now often considered in the selection of MBA students. These are:

1. Undergraduate grades, possibly corrected for experience with students from colleges throughout the United States.
2. Score on the Admission Test for Graduate Study in Business.
3. Recommendations by references, usually undergraduate professors.
4. Major offices held in college.
5. Undergraduate varsity athletics.

There is a wide-spread belief that students who work their way through college are good bets because of the achievement need that this demonstrates. These working students, however, earn less after graduation than those who don't work in school (Havemann and West, 1952). The reason may be the family advantage. In any event, self-support was considered but on the evidence is not recommended as positive.

It is recommended that the selection procedure be organized into two measures, one for scholastic aptitude and the second for potential leadership. Minimum scores would be set for scholastic aptitude which would be the first hurdle. Unless the applicant passed the scholastic aptitude hurdle he would not be considered further. For those who meet the scholastic aptitude requirement, actual admission would be earned by those who possess the highest leadership potential.

Scholastic Aptitude. Scholastic aptitude would be determined from scores on the Admission Test for Graduate Study in Business plus undergraduate grades corrected for national norms. In addition to considering the total test score, there would also be a separate minimum requirement on the Quantitative Score and on the Language Score. All scholastic aptitude requirements would be based on minima to obtain the grade requirement for graduation.

There are various valid ways for using the predictors, but perhaps the method suggested as follows might be tried. First set two minimum scores, one on the Quantitative and the other on the Language part of the Admission Test. The minimum Quantitative score would be set from the correlation with the course, *e.g.*, Statistics, or courses with which it correlated highest. Similarly a minimum on the Language Score would be set after finding which course or courses it predicted best. It would be necessary to obtain the minimum score on both Quantitative and Language as a high score on one would not offset a low score on the other if it were below the minimum necessary for a passing grade.

From those candidates remaining, a regression equation would be used in which Total Score on the Admission Test would be combined with undergraduate average grades. A score would be set to predict a passing average in all courses. Applicants would not be admitted who scored below this level.

Leadership Potential. From those who qualified in scholastic aptitude students would be admitted on the basis of leadership potential. Of three variables currently in use, Williams (1959) has shown validity for recommendations and for major offices held in college and his masculinity finding suggests validity for varsity athletics. Equal weight would be given to recommendations and to major offices held in college. Participation in varsity athletics should receive less weight. A simple point system would be established for each of the three to provide a convenient scoring method.

While father's occupation is highly correlated with high management positions, it does not seem consistent with public policy to recommend that it be used as part of the entrance standard. It may be appropriate to carry out research on personality that will reveal an applicant's relations with his parents, and this in turn may be useful.

Counseling

It is recommended that a counseling program be adopted which would be integrated with continuing research on student selection. Immediately on arriving each student should take the Vocational Interest Test which would be useful for educational as well as for vocational guidance. Soon after the Vocational Interest Test is scored each student should have a thorough interview with his Faculty Advisor. The primary purpose of this would be for counseling the student, but the interview would also yield an important by-product for research purposes by giving an opportunity for personality appraisal. The Faculty Advisor would study the information in the student's folder which would include the results of the Vocational Interest Test, the application, undergraduate transcript, Admission Test Score and the results on the three personality tests recommended below to be taken for research purposes before the student arrives. There would be an analysis of these three tests provided to the Advisor who would not be expected to learn the details of their interpretation. These are the Sentence Completion Test, Thematic Apperception Test, and Adjective Check List. Where there had been a research interview before admission, there would be a check list of the interviewer's judgment of leadership potential which would also be in the student's file to be studied before the interview after enrollment.

The primary purpose of the interview after arrival would be for educational and vocational guidance based on the student's personality and abilities as indicated in the interview and from the records mentioned above. Knowledge of the personality desirable in general managers and in sales, production, accounting, and research, might be heightened in Faculty Advisors by a study of this report. The Advisor in explaining the results of the Interest and Personality Tests would take the opportunity for obtaining support or modifications of the initial interpretations by the reactions of the student. After the interview the Advisor would record his judgments of the student's personality on a rating scale that would be prepared for that purpose.

Research on Student Selection

The next research study on student selection should be to refine the variables in the Leadership Potential measure. This should take two directions: (1) looking in detail at past results; and (2) developing more refined measures, if possible, in the future.

Alumni records from alumni surveys should be analyzed in detail for:

Recommendations
Offices
Undergraduate varsity athletics

Williams' criteria, earnings and administrative level, should be correlated against each of the three variables above, using the *eta* coefficient to look for non-linear relationships, and breaking each predictor variable into as many separate variables as would be meaningful. Professors' recommendations should be considered separately from those by employers and military commanders as well as in combination with them. Offices should be scrutinized as to level, to see whether president of the student body, for example, should have more weight than the manager of the baseball team. Varsity athletics should be looked at to see whether football, for example, was more predictive of management success than tennis.

At the same time, or growing out of the research above, the application blank should be studied to determine the optimal biographical information; in addition the recommendation form should be studied. The biographical statement might be a revision of the Individual Background Survey which was developed for the Standard Oil Company (New Jersey) and which has proved valid with groups of supervisors. The purpose of investigating the recommendation form would be to attempt to increase its reliability and validity.

Additional research on student selection should be in three locations: (1) before the student arrives; (2) while in school; and (3) in business.

Before the Student Arrives. Efforts should be made to develop some valid test of personality to supplement the leadership potential measure described above. The best bets at the moment appear to be the projective ones of Sentence Completion and Thematic Apperception Test, and the forced-choice Adjective Check List developed by Ghiselli. Where students applying to a graduate school of business are available, there should be an interview for research purposes on which a judgment as to leadership potential could be based.

While in School. Research after students arrive in school should be coordinated with the counseling program described above. There should be further leadership research while the student is in school from peer ratings, leaderless discussion groups, and instructor ratings.

Peer Ratings. Ratings on potential general management competence should be obtained in school on each student by other students. The number of raters would be the minimal number to give a highly reliable composite. The purpose of these ratings would be to provide a measure that would be both an intermediate criterion of leadership success and a predictor of success in business that can be followed up later on the job.

Leaderless Discussion Groups. Leaderless discussion groups appear to be a possible valid predictor of management success that can be put naturally into the educational program. Since so much of the training at a graduate school of business consists of discussion, such discussion could be a part of the course work. Development of ratings on leadership in such discussion groups might incidentally help in the improvement of grading practices.

The main purpose, however, for the leaderless discussion groups, as well as for the peer ratings, would be to give a realistic predictor that might improve the prediction of general management success, and in turn might be predictable from variables that could be obtained before the student's arrival at the school.

Instructor Ratings. Another variable that might prove to be a valid predictor of management success is instructor ratings at a graduate school of business. It might be well to have Faculty Advisors responsible for collecting such ratings from the other faculty members who have sufficient contact with students to make ratings. A standard rating form should be developed.

In Business. There should be a continual follow-up of alumni for research purposes and for alumni-school relationships. It might be well to have an interview with each alumnus between six months and a year after he is out of school, and again between four and six years after. The purpose would be to get his reaction to his job progress and to the curriculum and teaching methods.

Two other alumni follow-up methods should be used with or even without the interview which might prove too expensive to be used now. One is a description of the duties of the alumni using the method developed by the Executive Study. Second, it would be well to try to develop objective criteria of success or to have a rating of the job performance of each alumnus using the rating scale developed by the Standard Oil Company (New Jersey).

Research Within Companies

There would be better comparability of performance records to have a separate research program on management potential within a few companies. The choice of companies would depend upon their willingness to cooperate and upon their representativeness as employers. The effort here should be to profit from the experience of the Executive Study, Educational Testing Service, the Early Information of Management Potential, coordinated by Richardson, Bellows, and Henry, Inc., plus the current research within the American Telephone and Telegraph Company.

All appraisal would be done on the campus. Appraisal methods would be flexible in that new methods could be added or substituted whenever they promise to offer improvement as predictors of management success.

Whenever a man was hired from college or from graduate school, or whenever a man was promoted to a supervisor, he would be put through a thorough appraisal session lasting 2–3 days. The exact methods used would be subject to agreement in a workshop with representatives from the participating companies. Essentially the same measures would be considered that were shown above for prospective students to graduate schools of business.

Each appraisal group would be limited in size to perhaps 12 men. Results of the appraisal would be used only for research purposes. Results would be studied 10 years after the appraisal and at each 5-year period after that as long as there was interest in following up the results.

Each company would be asked to contribute to the research expense in proportion to the number of men involved as compared with the total cost. There would have to be a paid research staff, although a small amount of the research might be done by Ph.D. students as Ph.D. dissertation topics. This would be relatively slight, however, since there would be criteria available at the time of the appraisal and the only dissertation contribution would be the methodological phases of the program.

Preferably the appraisal phase should continue each year for ten years with as many modifications in the appraisal methods as indicated. That is, men entering management would be appraised for 10 years, but the procedures might differ from one year to another. After appraisal, however, the first follow-up would be 10 years later.

Summary

The results hoped for from these studies of graduate students of business and beginning managers would be a better understanding of the performance and personality of business managers. The focus would be on the qualifications to be successful general managers. There would be by-products of the qualifications essential for success in the functional fields of sales, production, office, and research and engineering management.

BIBLIOGRAPHY

Acton Society Trust. *Management Succession: The Recruitment, Selection, Training, and Promotion of Managers.* London: Acton Society Trust, 1956.

Adams, J. *et al. What Industry and Business Look for in the College Graduate (Bachelor Level).* Western College Placement Association, 1959.

Adamson, D. "Shawingan Water and Power Company," *Selection of Management Personnel,* M. J. Dooher and E. Marting, eds. Vol. 1. New York: American Management Association, 1957. Chapter 5, 85 ff.

Anastasi, A., and J. P. Foley, Jr. *Differential Psychology,* Second Edition. New York: The Macmillan Company, 1949.

Anikeeff, A. M. "Attitudes on Social Issues of Business Administrators and Students in a School of Business Administration," *Journal of Applied Psychology,* 38(1954), 407–408.

————. "Attitudinal Comparison of Business Employees and Students in the School of Business Administration," *Journal of Applied Psychology,* 39(1955), 65–66.

Arbous, A. G. "The Validation of Test Procedures for the Selection and Classification of Administrative Personnel: Summary of Report," *Bulletin of the National Institute for Personnel Research* (Johannesburg), 3(1), 1951, 27–33.

Arbous, A. G., and Joy Maree. "Contribution of Two Group Discussion Techniques to a Validated Test Battery," *Occupational Psychology,* 25(1951), 73–89.

Argyris, C. "Human Relations in a Bank," *Harvard Business Review,* 32(5), 1954, 63–72.

————. *Personality and Organization.* New York: Harper & Bros., 1957.

Balinsky, B., and H. W. Shaw. "The Contribution of the WAIS to a Management Appraisal Program," *Personnel Psychology,* 9(1956), 207–209.

Barber, B. *Social Stratification.* New York: Harcourt, Brace, & Co., 1957.

Barnabas, B. Personal communication. 1958.

Bass, B. M. "Comparison of the Leaderless Group Discussion and the Individual Interview in the Selection of Sales and Management Trainees," *Ohio State University, Abstracts of Doctoral Dissertations 1949-50*, No. 61, 1951.

———. "Leadership Opinions as Forecasts of Supervisory Success," *Journal of Applied Psychology*, 40(1956), 345–346.

Baumgartel, H. "Leadership, Motivation, and Attitudes in 20 Research Laboratories," *Dissertation Abstracts*, 16(1956), 1518.

Bavelas, A. Personal communication. April 29, 1959.

Bellows, R. M. "Procedures for Evaluating Vocational Criteria," *Journal of Applied Psychology*, 25(1941), 499–513.

Bendix, R. *Work and Authority in Industry: Ideologies of Management in the Course of Industrialization.* New York: John Wiley & Sons, Inc., 1956.

Benge, E. J. "Promotional Practices for Technical Men," *Advanced Management*, 21(3), 1956, 10–12.

Benjamin, R., Jr. "A Survey of 130 Merit-Rating Plans," *Personnel*, (American Management Association), 29(1952), 289–294.

Bentz, V. J. "A Study of Psychological Components Related to Success and Failure of Sears Executives." Unpublished study by Sears, Roebuck & Co.

Berdie, R. Personal communication. 1958.

Bingham, W. V., and W. T. Davis. "Intelligence Test Scores and Business Success," *Journal of Applied Psychology*, 8(1924), 1.

Brooks, E. "What Successful Executives Do," *Personnel*, (American Management Association), 32(3), 1955, 210–225.

Brooks, T. "Promotion Practices," *State of New York Industrial Bulletin*, (August, 1958), 3–7.

Bruce, M. M. "The Prediction of Effectiveness As a Factory Foreman," *Psychological Monographs*, No. 362, 1953, 67.

———. "Validity Information Exchange," *Personnel Psychology*, 7(1954), 128–129.

Carlson, S. *Executive Behaviour: A Study of the Work Load and the Working Methods of Managing Directors.* Stockholm: Strombergs, 1951.

Carter, G. C. "Measurement of Supervisory Ability," *Journal of Applied Psychology*, 36(1952), 393–395.

Cattell, R. B. *Personality and Motivation Structure and Measurement.* Yonkers, New York: World Book Company, 1957.

Centers, R. *Psychology of Social Classes: A Study of Class Consciousness.* Princeton: Princeton University Press, 1949.

Cleven, W. A., and F. E. Fiedler. "Interpersonal Perceptions of Open-Hearth Foremen and Steel Production," *Journal of Applied Psychology,* 40(1956), 312–314.

Coates, C. H., and R. J. Pellegrin. "Executives and Supervisors: Informal Factors in Differential Bureaucratic Promotion," *Administrative Science Quarterly,* 2(2), 1957, 201–215.

Colby, A. N., and J. Tiffin. "The Reading Ability of Industrial Supervisors," *Personnel,* (American Management Association), 27(2), 1950, 156–158.

Comrey, A. L., W. S. High, and R. C. Wilson. "Factors Influencing Organizational Effectiveness. VI. A Survey of Aircraft Workers." *Personnel Psychology,* 8(1955), 79–100. (a)

————. "Factors Influencing Organizational Effectiveness. VII. A Survey of Aircraft Supervisors," *Personnel Psychology,* 8(1955), 245–257. (b)

Comrey, A. L., J. M. Pfiffner, and W. S. High. *Factors Influencing Organizational Effectiveness: A Final Report.* Final Technical Report: Contract N6-ONR-23815. The Office of Naval Research. University of Southern California, 1954.

Creager, J. A., and F. D. Harding, Jr. "A Hierarchical Factor Analysis of Foreman Behavior," *Journal of Applied Psychology,* 42(1958), 197–203.

Cuomo, S. "Validity Information Exchange," *Personnel Psychology,* 8(1955), 268.

Cuomo, S., and H. H. Meyer. "Validity Information Exchange," *Personnel Psychology,* 8(1955), 267.

Dalton, M. "Informal Factors in Career Achievement," *American Journal of Sociology,* 56(1951), 407–415.

————. *Men Who Manage.* New York: John Wiley & Sons, 1959.

Darley, J. G., and T. Hagenah. *Vocational Interest Measurement.* Minneapolis: The University of Minnesota Press, 1955.

Davids, A., and H. Pildner, Jr. "Comparison of Direct and Projective Methods of Personality Assessment Under Different Conditions of Motivation," *Psychological Monographs,* No. 11, (Whole No. 464), 1958, 72.

Davis, R. T. *Performance and Development of Field Sales Managers.* Boston: Harvard University Graduate School of Business Administration, 1957.

Dill, W. R. Personal communication. 1960.

Dooher, M. J., and E. Marting, eds. *Selection of Management Personnel,* Vol. 1. New York: American Management Association, 1957. (a)

————. *Selection of Management Personnel,* Vol. 2. New York: American Management Association, 1957. (b)

Dunnette, M. D., and W. K. Kirchner. "Validation of Psychological Tests in Industry," *Personnel Administration,* (May–June, 1958), 20–27.

Estes, S. G. "Judging Personality from Expressive Behavior," *Journal of Abnormal and Social Psychology,* 33(1938), 217–236.

Eysenck, H. J. *Dimensions of Personality.* London: Routledge and Kegan Paul, 1947.

Fiedler, F. E. *Leader Attitudes and Group Effectiveness.* Urbana: University of Illinois Press, 1958.

File, Q. W. "The Measurement of Supervisory Quality in Industry," *Journal of Applied Psychology,* 29(1945), 323–337.

File, Q. W., and H. H. Remmers. "Studies in Supervisory Evaluation," *Journal of Applied Psychology,* 30(1946), 421–425.

Fleishman, E. A. "The Measurement of Leadership Attitudes in Industry," *Journal of Applied Psychology,* 37(1953), 153–158.

Fleishman, E. A., E. F. Harris, and H. E. Burtt. *Leadership and Supervision in Industry.* Columbus: Bureau of Educational Research, The Ohio State University, 1955.

Foundation for Research on Human Behavior. *Assessing Managerial Potential.* Ann Arbor, Michigan: Foundation for Research on Human Behavior, 1958.

Frederick, M. L. "Testing the Tests," *Journal of Accountancy,* (April, 1957).

Gardner, B. B. "What Makes Successful and Unsuccessful Executives?" *Advanced Management,* 13(1948), 116–125.

Gaudet, F. J., and A. R. Carli. "Why Executives Fail," *Personnel Psychology,* 10(1957), 7–21.

General Electric, Public and Employee Relations Research Service. "The Effective Manufacturing Foremen: An Observational Study of the Job Activities of Effective and Ineffective Foremen." Research study, 1957. (a)

————. "Leadership Style and Employee Morale." Research study sponsored by and conducted in the large steam turbine and generator department during 1957. (b)

Ghiselli, E. E. "Correlates of Initiative," *Personnel Psychology*, 9(1956), 311–320. (a)

————. "Dimensional Problems of Criteria," *Journal of Applied Psychology*, 40(1956), 1–4. (b)

————. "Occupational Level Measured Through Self Perception," *Personnel Psychology*, 9(1956), 169–176. (c)

————. "The Measurement of Occupational Aptitude," *University of California Publications in Psychology*, 8(2), 1955, 101–216. (a)

————. "A Scale for the Measurement of Initiative," *Personnel Psychology*, 8(1955), 157–164. (b)

Ghiselli, E. E., and R. P. Barthol. "Role Perceptions of Successful and Unsuccessful Supervisors," *Journal of Applied Psychology*, 40(1956), 241–244.

————. "The Validity of Personality Inventories in the Selection of Employees," *Journal of Applied Psychology*, 37(1953), 18–20.

Ghiselli, E. E., and T. M. Lodahl. "The Evaluation of Foremen's Performance in Relation to the Internal Characteristics of Their Work Groups," *Personnel Psychology*, 11(1958), 179–188.

Gibb, C. A. "The Principles and Traits of Leadership," *The Study of Leadership*. C. G. Browne and T. S. Cohn, eds. Danville, Illinois: Interstate Printers & Publishers, 1958, 67–75.

Gifford, W. "Does Business Want Scholars?" *Harper's Magazine*, 156(1928), 669–674.

Glaser, R., P. A. Schwarz, and J. C. Flanagan. "The Contribution of Interview and Situational Performance Procedures to the Selection of Supervisory Personnel," *Journal of Applied Psychology*, 42(1958), 69–73.

Godfrey, E. P., F. E. Fiedler, and D. M. Hall. *Boards, Management and Company Success*. Danville, Illinois: Interstate Printers & Publishers, 1958.

Goode, C. E. "Significant Research on Leadership," *Personnel*, (American Management Association), 27(1951), 342–350.

Gordon, L. V., and E. S. Stapleton. "Fakability of a Forced-Choice Personality Test Under Realistic High School Employment Conditions," *Journal of Applied Psychology*, 40(1956), 258–262.

Gordon, R. A., and J. Howell. *Higher Education for Business*. New York: Columbia University Press, 1959.

Gowin, E. B. *The Executive and His Control of Men*. New York: The Macmillan Company, 1915.

Grant, D. L. "A Factor Analysis of Managers' Ratings," *Journal of Applied Psychology*, 39(1955), 283–286.

———, ed. "Validity Information Exchange," *Personnel Psychology*, 7(1954), 285, 301.

Greenewalt, C. H. "What Makes a Good Executive?" *Think*, (December, 1958), 6–9.

Guilford, J. P. "The Guilford-Zimmerman Aptitude Survey," *Personnel and Guidance Journal*, 35(1956), 219–224.

Guilford, J. P., and R. B. Guilford. "Personality Factors D, R, T, and A," *Journal of Abnormal and Social Psychology*, 34(1939), 21–36. (a)

———. "Personality Factors N and GD," *Journal of Abnormal and Social Psychology*, 34(1939), 239–248. (b)

———. "Personality Factors S, E, and M, and Their Measurement," *Journal of Psychology*, 2(1936), 109–127.

Guilford, J. S. "Temperament Traits of Executives and Supervisors Measured by the Guilford Personality Inventories," *Journal of Applied Psychology*, 36(1952), 228–233.

Hable, K. "Carrier Corporation," *Selection of Management Personnel*, M. J. Dooher and E. Marting, eds. Vol. 2. New York: American Management Association, 1957. Chapter 6, 109 ff.

Hall, C. S., and G. Lindzey. *Theories of Personality*. New York: John Wiley & Sons, 1957.

Harrell, T. W. "Testing Cotton Mill Supervisors," *Journal of Applied Psychology*, 24(1940), 31–35.

Harrell, T. W., and Margaret S. Harrell. "Army General Classification Test Scores," *Educational and Psychological Measurement*, 5(1945), 229–239.

Havemann, E., and P. S. West. *They Went to College*. New York: Harcourt, Brace and Co., 1952.

Hemphill, J. K. *Basic Dimensions of Executive Positions*, Research Memorandum 58-2. Princeton: Educational Testing Service, March, 1958.

Henry, E. R. Unpublished paper presented at Harvard Graduate School of Business Administration Symposium, March 13–14, 1959.

Henry, W. E. "Identifying the Potentially Successful Executive," *American Management Association Personnel Series, No. 127*, 1949, 14–19.

Heron, A. "The Effects of Real-Life Motivation on Questionnaire Response," *Journal of Applied Psychology*, 40(1956), 65–68.

Hinchliffe, B. "Bureaucracy, Objectivity, and Occupational Mobility of the Business Elite." Unpublished manuscript, Stanford Graduate School of Business, 1959.

Holbrook, S. *The Age of the Moguls.* Garden City, New York: Doubleday & Company, Inc., 1953.

Howe, R. J. "Price Tags for Executives," *Harvard Business Review*, 34(3), 1956, 94–100.

Husband, R. W. "What Do College Grades Predict?" *Fortune*, 55(June, 1957), 157 ff.

Huttner, L., S. Levy, E. Rosen, and M. Stopol. "Further Light on the Executive Personality," *Personnel*, (American Management Association), 36(1959), 42–50.

Huttner, L., and D. M. Stene. "Foremen Selection in Light of a Theory of Supervision," *Personnel Psychology*, 11 (1958), 403–410.

Jaffe, A. J., and R. O. Carleton. *Occupational Mobility in the United States, 1930–1960.* New York: King's Crown Press, Columbia University, 1954.

Jasinski, F. J. "Foreman Relationships Outside the Work Group," *Personnel*, (American Management Association), 33(2), 1956, 130–135.

Jennings, E. E. "The Motivation Factor in Testing Supervisors," *Journal of Applied Psychology*, 37(1953), 168–169.

Jones, Margaret H. "The Adequacy of Employee Selection Reports," *Journal of Applied Psychology*, 34(1950), 219–224.

Jones, O. R., and K. U. Smith. "Measurement of Supervisory Ability," *Journal of Applied Psychology*, 35(1951), 146–150.

Kahn, R., and D. Katz. "Leadership Practices in Relation to Productivity and Morale," *Group Dynamics*, D. Cartwright and A. Zander, eds. Evanston: Row, Peterson & Co., 1953.

Kahn, R. L., F. C. Mann, and S. E. Seashore, eds. "Human Relations Research in Large Organizations, Part 2." *Journal of Social Issues*, 12(2), 1956.

Katz, D., *et al.* *Productivity, Supervision, and Morale Among Railroad Workers.* Ann Arbor: Survey Research Center, Institute for Social Research, University of Michigan, 1951.

Katz, D., and R. L. Kahn. "Some Recent Findings in Human Relations Research," *Readings in Social Psychology*, G. E. Swanson, T. M. Newcomb, and E. L. Hartley, eds. New York: Holt & Co., 1952, 650–655.

Kay, B. R. "Key Factors in Effective Foreman Behavior," *Personnel* (American Management Association), 36(1), 1959, 25–31.

Keller, Suzanne. "The Social Origins and Career Lines of Three Generations of American Business Leaders." Unpublished Ph.D. dissertation, Columbia University, 1953.

Kelly, G. A. "The Theory and Technique of Assessment," *Annual Review of Psychology*, 9(1958), 323–352.

Klaw, S. "The Entrepreneurial Ego," *Fortune*, 54(August, 1956), 100 ff.

Knauft, E. B. "A Selection Battery for Bake Shop Managers," *Journal of Applied Psychology*, 33(1949), 304–315.

————. "Vocational Interests and Managerial Success," *Journal of Applied Psychology*, 35(1951), 160–163.

Krauss, I., and L. W. Porter. *Report on Survey of the Professional Literature on the Qualities Needed by Businessmen.* Unpublished.

Kurtz, A. K. "A Research Test of the Rorschach Test," *Personnel Psychology*, 1(1948), 41–51.

Larke, A. G. "How Foremen Get That Way," *Dun's Review and Modern Industry*, 65(January, 1955), 44 ff.

Lawshe, C. H. "How Can We Pick Better Supervisors?" *Personnel Psychology*, 2(1949), 69–73.

Learned, E. P., D. N. Ulrich, and D. R. Booz. *Executive Action.* Boston: Harvard University Graduate School of Business Administration, 1951.

Leavitt, H. J., and T. L. Whisler. "Management in the 1980's," *Harvard Business Review*, 36(6), 1958, 41–48.

Likert, R. "Effective Supervision: An Adaptive and Relative Process," Personnel Psychology, 11(1958), 317–332. (a)

————. "Measuring Organizational Performance," *Harvard Business Review*, 36(2), 1958, 41–50. (b)

————. "Motivational Dimensions of Administration," *America's Manpower Crisis, Institute on Manpower Utilization and Government Personnel, Stanford University, 1951.* Chicago: Public Administration Service, 1952, 89–117.

Likert, R., and D. Katz. "Supervisory Practices and Organizational Structures As They Affect Employee Productivity and Morale," *American Management Association Personnel Series, No. 120,* 1948.

Lovell, Constance. "A Study of the Factor Structure of Thirteen Personality Variables." *Educational and Psychological Measurement,* 5(1945), 335–350.

McConnell, P., and P. O'Neill. "A Study of the Selection Interview." Unpublished. 1958.

McMurry, R. N. Personal communication. 1959.

————. "The Executive Neurosis," *Harvard Business Review,* 30(6), 1952, 33–47.

Mackie, R. R. "Norms and Validities of Sixteen Test Variables for Predicting Success of Foremen." Unpublished Master's thesis, University of Southern California, 1948.

Mahoney, T. A., W. Dohman, and T. Jerdee. "Applying Yardsticks to Management," *Personnel,* (American Management Association), 33(6), 1957, 556–562.

Mann, F., and J. Dent. *Appraisals of Supervisors and Attitudes of Their Employees in an Electric Power Company.* Ann Arbor: Survey Research Center, University of Michigan. Ser. 1, Ref. 4, 1954.

Marchetti, P. V. "Manager-Employee 'Understanding' in the Retail Grocery and Meat Market," *Journal of Applied Psychology,* 38(1954), 216–221.

Marchetti, P. V., and R. L. Malone. "Understanding: A Key to Leadership?" *Personnel,* (American Management Association), 32(4), 1956, 327–334.

Martin, H. G. "The Construction of The Guilford-Martin Inventory of Factors G-A-M-I-N," *Journal of Applied Psychology,* 29(1945), 298–300.

Mee, J. F. "The Impact of Economic Evaluation on Educational Requirements," *The College Graduate in the American Economy, 1970.* Indiana Business Information Bulletin, No. 23, 1955, 39–50.

Meehl, P. E. *Clinical Versus Statistical Prediction: A Theoretical Analysis and a Review of the Evidence.* Minneapolis: University of Minnesota Press, 1954.

Merrihue, W. V., and R. A. Katzell. "ERI — Yardstick of Employee Relations," *Harvard Business Review*, 33(6), 1955, 91–99.

Meyer, D., and G. L. Pressel. "Personality Test Scores in the Management Hierarchy," *Journal of Applied Psychology*, 38(1954), 73–80.

Meyer, H. H. "An Evaluation of a Supervisory Selection Program," *Personnel Psychology*, 9(1956), 499–513.

————. "Factors Related to Success in the Human Relations Aspect of Work-Group Leadership," *Psychological Monographs*, No. 3 (Whole No. 320), 1951, 65.

Miller, H. G. *Summary Report on Student Research Project as Part of the Research in Executive Selection and Development*. Carnegie Institute of Technology, Graduate School of Industrial Administration. Undated.

Mills, C. W. *The Power Elite*. New York: Oxford University Press, 1956.

More, D. M. "The Congruence of Projective Instruments in Personnel Assessment," *Journal of Applied Psychology*, 41(1957), 137–140.

————. "The Foreman: A Personality Portrait," *Journal of Personnel Administration and Industrial Relations*, 1(1954), 60–75.

Morse, Nancy, and E. Reimer. "The Experimental Change of a Major Organizational Variable," *Journal of Abnormal and Social Psychology*, 52(1956), 120–129.

Nagle, B. F. "Productivity, Employee Attitudes and Supervisory Sensitivity," *Personnel Psychology*, 7(1954), 219–234.

National Industrial Conference Board. "Selecting Company Executives," *Studies in Personnel Policy, No. 161*, 1957.

Newcomer, Mabel. *The Big Business Executive: The Factors That Made Him, 1900-1950*. New York: Columbia University Press, 1955.

O'Neill, H. E., and A. J. Kubany. "Observation Methodology and Supervisory Behavior," *Personnel Psychology*, 12(1959), 85–96.

Owen, J. L. "A Validity Study of a Test Battery for the Selection of First Line Supervisors." Unpublished Master's thesis, Pennsylvania State College, 1951.

Parsons, S. O. "A Study of the Prediction of Success of Manufacturing Supervisors in an Aircraft Corporation." Unpublished Ph.D. dissertation, University of Southern California, 1958.

Patton, A. "Annual Report on Executive Compensation," *Harvard Business Review*, 36(5), 1958, 129–140.

Pederson, C. A. "A Case Study of Lockheed Aircraft Corporation's Program for the Selection of Management Personnel." Unpublished Ph.D. dissertation, Stanford University, 1946.

———. "Twenty-Five Years of Business School Graduates," *Stanford Business School Alumni Bulletin*, (July, 1953), 3–10.

Pellegrin, R. J., and C. H. Coates. "Executives and Supervisors: Contrasting Definitions of Career Success," *Administrative Science Quarterly*, 1(1957), 506–517.

Pelz, D. C. "Influence: A Key to Effective Leadership in the First-Line Supervisor," *Personnel*, (American Management Association), 29(3), 1952, 209–217.

———. "Motivation of the Engineering and Research Specialist," *American Management Association General Management Series, No. 186*, 1957, 25–46.

Pfiffner, J. M. "The Effective Supervisor: An Organization Research Study," *Personnel*, (American Management Association), 31(6), 1955, 530–540.

Pietrowski, R. F. "Predicting Success in Graduate School of Business, Stanford University." Unpublished report, Stanford Graduate School of Business, 1958.

Poe, W. A., and I. A. Berg. "Psychological Test Performance of Steel Industry Production Supervisors," *Journal of Applied Psychology*, 36(1952), 234–237.

Porter, L. W., and E. E. Ghiselli. "The Self Perceptions of Top and Middle Management Personnel," *Personnel Psychology*, 10(1957), 397–406.

Psychological Services, Sears Roebuck & Co., "Report on Executives." Unpublished report. March, 1956.

Radom, M. "Picking Better Foremen," *Factory Management*, 108(10), 1950, 119–122.

Randle, C. W. "How to Identify Promotable Executives," *Harvard Business Review*, 34(3), 1956, 122–134.

Richardson, H. M., and N. G. Hanawalt. "Leadership As Related to the Bernreuter Personality Measures: III. Leadership Among Adult Men in Vocational and Social Activities," *Journal of Applied Psychology*, 28(1944), 308–317.

Roach, D. E. "Factor Analysis of Rated Supervisory Behavior," *Personnel Psychology*, 9(1956), 487–498.

Roberts, D. R. *Executive Compensation.* Glencoe, Illinois: Free Press, 1959.

Roe, A. *The Psychology of Occupations.* New York: John Wiley & Sons, 1956.

Rosen, E. H. "The Executive Personality," *Personnel,* (American Management Association), 36(1), 1959, 8–20.

Rupe, J. C. "When Workers Rate the Boss," *Personnel Psychology,* 4(1951), 271–290.

Rusmore, J. T. "Fakability of the Gordon Personal Profile," *Journal of Applied Psychology,* 40(1956), 175–177.

Sarbin, T. R. "A Contribution to the Study of Actuarial and Individual Methods of Prediction," *American Journal of Sociology,* 48(1942), 593–602.

Schultz, R. S. "Standardized Tests and Statistical Procedures in Selection of Life Insurance Sales Personnel," *Journal of Applied Psychology,* 20(1936), 553–566.

Scott, E. L. *Leadership and Perceptions of Organization,* Research Monograph No. 82. Columbus: The Bureau of Business Research, College of Commerce and Administration, The Ohio State University, 1956.

Seashore, S. E. "The Training of Leaders for Effective Human Relations," *Some Applications of Behavioural Research,* R. Likert and S. P. Hayes, Jr., eds. Paris: UNESCO Publications Division, 1957, 81–123.

Shaffer, R. H. and G. F. Kuder. "Kuder Interest Patterns of Medical, Law, and Business School Alumni," *Journal of Applied Psychology,* 37(1953), 367–369.

Shartle, C. L. *Executive Performance and Leadership.* Englewood Cliffs, New Jersey: Prentice-Hall, Inc., 1956.

Shultz, I. T., and B. Barnabas. "Testing for Leadership in Industry," *Transactions of the Kansas Academy of Science,* 1945, 160–164.

Shuman, J. T. "The Values of Aptitude Tests for Supervisory Workers in the Aircraft Engine and Propeller Industries," *Journal of Applied Psychology,* 29(1945), 185–190.

Sinaiko, H. W. "The Rosenzweig Picture-Frustration Study in the Selection of Department Store Section Managers," *Journal of Applied Psychology,* 1(1949), 36–42.

Smiddy, H. F. "General Electric's Philosophy and Approach for Manager Development," *American Management Association General Management Series, No. 174,* 1955.

Smith, F. J. "A Study of the Psychological Components Related to Success Among Sears Retail Credit Managers." Unpublished study by Sears, Roebuck & Co., 1954.

Soar, R. A. "Personal History Data As a Predictor of Success in Service Station Management," *Journal of Applied Psychology,* 40(1956), 383–385.

Society for Advancement of Management and Foundation for Research on Human Behavior. *Planning and Training for Effective Leadership.* Ann Arbor: Foundation for Research on Human Behavior, 1956.

Speer, G. S. "Normative Data Information Exchange," *Personnel Psychology,* 10(1957), 236–237.

Spencer, L. M. "Annual Report of YPO Survey," *Enterprise,* (May, 1957).

————. "Characteristics of High- and Low-Profit YPO Companies," *Enterprise,* (October, 1958).

————. *Results of the YPO Wives' Survey.* New York: Young Presidents' Organization, Inc., 1955. (a)

————. *The President and His Executive Team: Preliminary Findings of the 1956 Survey.* New York: Young Presidents' Organization, Inc., 1956.

————. *What YPO Presidents Think About: Preliminary Findings of the 1954 Survey.* New York: Young Presidents' Organization, Inc., 1954.

————. "Portrait of Company Presidents," *Young Presidents' Organization Third Annual Survey Report,* 1955. (b)

Spicer, L. G. "A Survey of Merit Rating in Industry," *Personnel,* (American Management Association), 27(1951), 515–518.

Springer, D. "Ratings of Candidates for Promotion by Co-Workers and Supervisors," *Journal of Applied Psychology,* 37(1953), 347–351.

Standard Oil Co. (New Jersey), Employee Relations Department. *Made to Measure.* New York: Standard Oil Company (New Jersey), 1951.

————. *Employee Relations Research in Standard Oil Company (New Jersey) and Affiliates,* Vols. 1 and 2. New York: Standard Oil Company (New Jersey), 1955.

Steele, J. E. "Tests Used in Recruiting and Selecting College Graduates," *Personnel,* (American Management Association), 26(1949), 200–204.

Stevens, S. N., and E. F. Wonderlic. "The Relationship of the Number of Questions Missed on the Otis Mental Tests and the Ability to Handle Office Detail," *Journal of Applied Psychology,* 18(1934), 364–368.

Stockford, L. "A Controlled Testing Program Pays Off," *Selection of Management Personnel,* M. J. Dooher and E. Marting, eds., Vol. 1. New York: American Management Association, 1957, 138–155.

————. "Selection of Supervisory Personnel," *Personnel* (American Management Association), 24(1947), 186–199.

Stogdill, Ralph M. "Personal Factors Associated With Leadership: A Survey of the Literature," *Journal of Psychology,* 25(1948), 35–71.

Stouffer, S. A. *Communism, Conformity, and Civil Liberties.* Garden City, New York: Doubleday & Company, Inc., 1955.

Strong, E. K., Jr. "Interests of Public Administrators," *Public Personnel Review,* 6(1945), 166–173.

————. *Vocational Interests of Men and Women.* Stanford: Stanford University Press, 1943.

Stryker, P. "On the Meaning of Executive Qualities," *Fortune,* 57(June, 1958), 116 ff.

————. "The Executive Bonus," *Fortune,* 54(December, 1956), 127 ff.

Swint, E. R., and R. A. Newton. "The Personal History — A Second Report," *Journal of Industrial Training,* (January-February, 1952), 1–7.

Taft, R. "The Ability to Judge People," *Psychological Bulletin,* 52(1955), 1–23.

Tagiuri, R. *Research in Executive Selection: Some Needed Directions of Effort.* American Psychological Association Meeting, 1958.

Tannenbaum, R., and F. Massarik. "Leadership: A Frame of Reference," *Management Science,* 4(1957), 1–19.

Taylor, E. K., D. E. Schneider, and H. Clay. "Short Forced-Choice Ratings Work," *Personnel Psychology*, 7(1954), 245–252.

Taylor, J. H. "How Can We Identify and Select Prospective Foremen?" *Addresses on Industrial Relations*, 1957 Series, Bulletin No. 25. University of Michigan, Bureau of Industrial Relations, 1–17.

Terman, L. M., and M. H. Oden. *The Gifted Group at Mid-Life: Thirty-Five Years' Follow-Up of the Superior Child.* Stanford, California: Stanford University Press, 1959.

"The Nine Hundred," *Fortune*, 46(5), 1952, 135.

Thompson, P. O. "A Correlational Study of the Efficiency of Certain Aptitude Tests in Predicting the Success of Supervisors in an Aircraft Factory" Unpublished Master's thesis, University of Southern California, 1950.

Thorndike, R. L. "Who Will Be Successful 10 Years From Now? *American Management Association Personnel Series, No. 163*, 1955, 3–14.

Thorndike, R. L., and E. P. Hagen. *Ten Thousand Careers.* New York: John Wiley & Sons, Inc., 1959.

Tuddenham, R. D. *The Stability of Personality Ratings Over Two Decades.* Office of Naval Research Report, 1957.

Tyler, Leona E. *The Psychology of Human Differences,* Second Edition. New York: Appleton-Century-Crofts, Inc., 1956.

Uhrbrock, R. S. "Construction of a Selection Test for College Graduates," *Journal of General Psychology*, 41(1949), 153–193.

Vatter, P. A. "Factors Related to First Year Grade Averages at Harvard Business School — Class Entering September, 1957." Report, 1958. (a)

————. "Verbal and Quantitative Skills and Their Relation to Achievement at the Harvard Business School — Class Entered 1957." Report, 1958. (b)

Vernon, P. E. "Some Characteristics of the Good Judge of Personality," *Journal of Social Psychology*, 4(1933), 42–58.

————. *The Structure of Human Abilities.* New York: John Wiley & Sons, 1950.

Wagner, R. "The Employment Interview: A Critical Summary," *Personnel Psychology*, 2(1949), 17–43.

Wald, R. M., and R. A. Doty. "The Top Executive — A First-Hand Profile," *Harvard Business Review*, 32(4), 1954, 45–54.

Wallace, W. L., and J. V. Gallagher. *Activities and Behaviors of Production Supervisors, Technical Research Report No. 946*, Personnel Research Branch, Research and Development Division, The Adjutant General's Office, Department of the Army, April 30, 1952.

Ward, L. B. "The Interview As an Assessment Technique," *College Admissions, No. 2*. College Entrance Examination Board, 62–71.

————. "Tentative Summary." Unpublished, 1958.

Ward, L. B., *et al. Status Report of the Selection Study*. Harvard Business School, September 23, 1954.

Warner, L. W., and J. Abegglen. *Big Business Leaders in America*. New York: Harper and Brothers, 1955.

Weitz, J. "Selecting Supervisors With Peer Ratings," *Personnel Psychology*, 11(1958), 25–36.

Whisler, T. L. "Management Jobs and the Selection and Training of Men to Fill Them." Unpublished Ford Foundation study, 1958.

Whyte, W. H., Jr. "How Hard Do Executives Work?" *Fortune*, 49(January, 1954), 108 ff. (a)

————. "The Fallacies of 'Personality' Testing," *Fortune*, (September, 1954), 117 ff. (b)

————. *The Organization Man*. Garden City, New York: Doubleday & Company, 1957.

Williams, F. J. "Predicting Success in Business." Ph. D. dissertation, Graduate School of Business, Stanford University, 1959.

Wolfle, D. *America's Resources of Specialized Talent*. New York: Harper and Brothers, 1954.

Worthy, J. C. "Planned Executive Development: The Experience of Sears, Roebuck & Co.," *American Management Association Personnel Series No. 137*, 1951, 3–27.

Wyllie, I. G. *The Self-Made Man in America: The Myth of Rags to Riches*. New Brunswick, New Jersey: Rutgers University Press, 1954.

Yoder, D. "A Preliminary Evaluation of the Master's Program in Industrial Relations." Unpublished, 1959.

————. *Industrial Relations Center, University of Minnesota Chart Book*, 1958.

INDEX OF REFERENCES

Abegglen, J., 10, 70, 90–91, 98, 112, 146, 148
Acton Society Trust, 74
Adams, J., 53
Adamson, D., 120
Anastasi, A., 154
Anikeeff, A. M., 56
Arbous, A. G., 98
Argyris, C., 45, 133–134, 160

Balinsky, B., 93
Barber, B., 154
Barnabas, B., 91, 125
Barthol, R. P., 120–124, 126
Bass, B. M., 45, 55
Baumgartel, H., 50
Bavelas, A., 76
Bellows, R. M., 22
Bendix, R., 16, 19, 76–77
Benge, E. J., 71
Benjamin, R., Jr., 31–32
Bentz, V. J., 103–106, 173
Berdie, R., 152
Berg, I. A., 115
Bingham, W. V., 82, 101
Booz, D. R., 76, 145
Brooks, T., 67–68, 80
Bruce, M. M., 103–121
Burtt, H. E., 44–45

Carleton, R. O., 1
Carli, A. R., 94
Carlson, S., 15, 79
Carter, G. C., 116, 117
Cattell, R. B., 155, 157–158
Centers, R., 159
Clay, H., 31
Cleven, W. A., 30, 117
Coates, C. H., 19, 20, 73
Colby, A. N., 111
Comrey, A. L., 36, 46
Creager, J. A., 109–110
Cuomo, S., 116, 125

Dalton, M., 54, 72, 109, 148–149
Darley, J. G., 150, 159
Davids, A., 161
Davis, W. T., 82, 100–101, 164
Dent, J., 49
Dill, W. R., 28, 91
Dohman, A. W., 31–32
Dooher, M. J., 91–92, 115, 117, 124
Dunnette, M. D., 103, 116

Estes, S. G., 158
Eysenck, H. J., 158, 159

Fiedler, F. E., 30, 40, 43, 51, 117, 158
File, Q. W., 30, 111
Flanagan, J. C., 124
Fleishman, E. A., 44–45, 108, 165
Foley, J. P., Jr., 154
Ford, H., 19
Frederick, M. L., 132, 135

Gallagher, J. V., 109–111
Gardner, B. B., 10, 98
Gaudet, F. J., 94
Ghiselli, E. E., 6, 12, 22, 23, 36, 92, 95–97, 99, 113, 116, 119–126, 134, 151, 166, 171, 179
Gibb, C. A., 5
Gifford, W., 57, 65
Glaser, R., 124
Godfrey, E. P., 40
Goode, C. E., 13
Gordon, L. V., 162
Gordon, R. A., 2, 53, 75, 149
Gowin, E. B., 87
Grant, D. L., 116–117, 128–129, 132
Greenewalt, C. H., 76
Guilford, J. P., 102, 116, 121, 155, 156
Guilford, R. B., 155

Hable, K., 116, 121
Hagen, E. P., 82, 130–131
Hagenah, T., 150, 159
Hall, C. S., 145, 149–151
Hall, D. M., 40
Hanawalt, N. G., 88
Harding, F. D., Jr., 109–110
Harrell, M. S., 111
Harrell, T. W., 111, 115
Harris, E. F., 44–45
Havemann, E., 56, 65, 148, 175
Hemphill, J. K., 23–26, 139, 143, 145
Henry, E. R., 30, 34, 141, 169
Henry, W. E., 10, 98, 112
Heron, A., 161
High, W. S., 36, 46
Hinchliffe, B., 54, 154
Holbrook, S., 18, 19
Howe, R. J., 27
Howell, J., 53, 75, 149
Husband, R. W., 57, 65
Huttner, L., 81, 87–88, 93, 101, 112, 114, 121, 130, 133, 137

Jaffe, A. J., 1
Jasinski, F. J., 111
Jennings, E. E., 162
Jerdee, T., 31–32
Jones, M., 2
Jones, O. R., 93, 95

Kahn, R. L., 46–47, 50
Katz, D., 47, 50
Katzell, R. A., 28, 29
Kay, B. R., 41–42
Keller, S., 84
Kelly, G. A., 160
Kirchner, W. K., 103, 116
Klaw, S., 77–79, 87–88
Knauft, E. B., 93, 95, 99
Krauss, I., 12, 13
Kubany, A. J., 28, 42
Kuder, G. F., 56
Kurtz, A. K., 105, 107

Larke, A. G., 113, 160
Lawshe, C. H., 115
Learned, E. P., 76, 145
Leavitt, H. J., 16
Levy, S., 81, 87–88, 93, 101, 112, 130, 133, 137
Likert, R., 36–38, 40–41, 48–52, 153, 165
Lindzey, G., 145, 149–151
Lodahl, T. M., 6, 36
Lovell, C., 156

Mackie, R. R., 121
Mahoney, T. A., 31–32
Malone, R. L., 107
Mann, F., 49
Marchetti, P. V., 107
Maree, J., 98
Martin, H. G., 156
Marting, E., 91–92, 115, 117, 124
Massarik, F., 8, 10
McConnell, P., 54–55
McMurry, R. N., 12, 28, 67
Mee, J. F., 16
Meehl, P. E., 63, 151–152
Merrihue, W. V., 28, 29
Meyer, D., 89, 113, 115, 117, 125, 132
Miller, H. G., 63
Mills, C. W., 1, 148
More, D. M., 111, 161
Morse, N., 48

Nagle, B. F., 135, 158
National Industrial Conference Board, 71
Newcomer, M., 12, 28, 69–70
Newton, R. A., 124

Oden, M. H., 82, 130–131
O'Neill, H. E., 28, 42
O'Neill, P., 55
Owen, J. L., 115, 121, 125

Parsons, S. O., 114, 119–121, 124
Patton, A., 26, 27
Pederson, C. A., 71, 93, 99, 108, 173
Pellegrin, R. J., 19, 20, 73
Pelz, D. C., 39, 50
Pfiffner, J. M., 36, 52
Pietrowski, R. F., 62, 64–65
Pildner, H., 161
Poe, W. A., 115
Porter, L. W., 12, 13, 95–97
Pressel, G. L., 89
Psychological Services, 105

Radom, M., 113
Randle, C. W., 31, 40, 71, 100, 102, 114, 118–119, 130–131, 134, 137–141, 143

Reimer, E., 48
Remmers, H. H., 111
Richardson, H. M., 88
Roach, D. E., 128–129
Roberts, D. R., 26
Roe, A., 16
Rosen, E., 81, 87–88, 93, 101, 112, 130, 133, 137
Rupe, J. C., 33
Rusmore, J. T., 162

Sarbin, T. R., 63
Schneider, D. E., 31
Schultz, R. S., 105
Schwarz, P. A., 124
Scott, E. L., 36
Seashore, S., 37, 44
Shaffer, R. H., 56
Shartle, C. L., 5, 8, 15, 152
Shaw, H. W., 93
Shultz, I. T., 125
Shuman, J. T., 114, 116
Sinaiko, H. W., 107
Smith, K. U., 93, 95, 134
Soar, R. A., 105
Spencer, L. M., 10, 39, 54, 78, 83, 85, 86, 97, 100, 109, 111, 127, 169
Spicer, L. J., 31–32
Springer, D., 31
Stapleton, E. S., 162
Steele, J. E., 54
Stene, D. M., 114, 121
Stevens, S. N., 132
Stockford, L., 114, 120, 125
Stogdill, R. M., 6, 7
Stopol, M., 81, 87–88, 93, 101, 112, 130, 133, 137
Stouffer, S. A., 160
Strong, E. K., Jr., 55, 91–92, 102, 113, 135, 158
Stryker, P., 7, 27, 53, 76
Swint, E. R., 124

Taft, R., 158
Tagiuri, R., 26
Tannenbaum, R., 8, 10
Taylor, E. K., 31, 113, 120
Taylor, J. H., 12, 119, 125
Terman, L. M., 82, 130–131, 150
Thompson, P. O., 114
Thorndike, R. L., 82, 93, 130–131
Tiffin, J., 111
Tuddenham, R. D., 153
Tyler, L. E., 155, 158, 160

Uhrbrock, R. S., 54
Ulrich, D. N., 76, 145

Vanderbilt, C., 18
Vatter, P. A., 61
Vernon, P. E., 155, 158

Wagner, R., 152
Wald, R. M., 82, 88, 92
Wallace, W. L., 109–111
Ward, L. B., 9, 10, 11, 59–61, 90, 98, 112, 149, 152
Warner, L. W., 10, 70, 90–91, 98, 112, 146, 148
Weitz, J., 31
West, P. S., 56, 65, 148, 175
Whisler, T. L., 14, 16
Whyte, W. H., Jr., 1, 15, 24, 160
Williams, F. J., 60, 176, 178
Wilson, R. C., 46
Wolfe, D., 55
Wonderlic, E. F., 132
Worthy, J. C., 103
Wylie, I. G., 19

Yoder, D., 63, 79, 89

INDEX OF TOPICS

A

Ability, 55, 81–83, 111, 119, 125–126, 144, 145, 147, 154, 155, 162, 174
  academic, 158; *see also* Scholastic aptitude
  administrative, 13, 138, 141
  British theory of, 155
  creative, 114, 132, 136, 137, 144, 154, 174; *see also* Personality traits
  educational, 155, 170
  general, 155
  intellectual, 13, 53, 58, 61, 65, 71, 76, 92, 93, 99, 101–105, 113–116, 130–131, 137, 138, 140, 144–145, 151, 154, 155, 157, 158, 170, 172, 174; measurement of, 152
  judgment, 117, 138; of people, 158
  mechanical, 116–117, 126, 144, 162, 170, 173; *see also* Aptitude, mechanical
  numerical, 130–132, 144–145, 154, 155, 162, 170; *see also* Aptitude, arithmetic
  persuasive, 121; *see also* Ess-Ay Inventory
  practical, 155, 170
  reading, 111, 130
  spatial, 144, 162, 170
  test, 54
  to communicate, 53, 76, 173; *see also* Communications
  to get along with others, 53
  to deal with people, 141
  verbal, 136, 137, 144, 154, 155, 162, 170, 174
Absenteeism, 44–45
Academic ability, *see* Ability
Acceptance, *see* Personality traits
Accidents, 44–45
Accomplishment, 138–139
Accountants, 56–132
  Achievement Test, *see* Tests
  Certified Public, 135
  scale on Strong Vocational Interest Test, 135
  see also Managers, office
Accounting managers, *see* Managers, office
Achievement need, *see* Needs
Activities
  extra-curricular, 58
  of managers, *see* Managers
  of Young Presidents, *see* Presidents, Young
Adams-Lepley Personal Audit, *see* Tests
Adaptability, *see* Personality traits
Adaptability Test, *see* Tests
Adjustment, 88, 99, 112, 121, 126, 144–145, 149, 158, 159, 162, 173
  of general managers, 144
  of production managers, 112, 121, 126
  of supervisors, 88
  upper class, 149, 154
Admission Test for Graduate Study in Business
  Quantitative Score, 62, 176
  Verbal Score, 62, 176
  see also Tests
Administration, 41, 111
  ability, 13, 138, 141
  and promotion, 71, 130, 138
  defined, 100
  interests, 99, 125
  level, 178
Administrative Practices Course grades in, 59, 62, 66
Administrative skills, *see* Administration, ability
Advertising, 70
Advisor, Faculty, 177

A.C.E. Psychological Examination, 103
Age and promotion, 72
Aggressiveness, *see* Personality traits
Agreeableness, *see* Personality traits
Air Force Men,
  occupations of, 82
  tests of, 130
Aircraft industry, 46, 99, 108, 114, 116, 117, 119, 120–121, 124, 125; *see also* Lockheed
Alumni Survey, 59, 178
  follow-up, 180
Ambition, *see* Personality traits
American Telephone and Telegraph Co., 180
Analytic approach to personality, 142, 157, 170
Anxiety, *see* Personality traits
Appliance manufacturing company, 47
Application blanks, 152, 177–179
Approachability, *see* Personality traits
Appraisal
  of management potential, 181
  of personality, *see* Personality, appraisal
Aptitudes, 13
  arithmetic, 82–83, 92, 93, 119
  clerical, 117
  mechanical, 116
  scholastic, 66, 176
Architects, 135
Arithmetic reasoning test, *see* Tests
Army Alpha Test, *see* Tests
Army General Classification Test, *see* Tests
Ascendancy, *see* Personality traits
Aspiration, 159
  level of, 20
Assigned leadership test, 98
Assumed Similarity of Opposites Test, *see* Tests, Fiedler
Assurance in communications, 62
Attitudes, 11–49, 127, 135, 159, 170
  changes in, 160
  economic, 159
  influence of big business on, 160
  of business men, 159, 160
  of leader, 43, 44
  of managers, *see* Managers
  political, 159
  radical-conservative, 56, 159, 172
  social, 159
  to father, *see* Family
  to mathematics, 119, 135
  to mother, *see* Family
  to paper work, 36, 144
  tough-minded-tender-minded, 159, 172
Autocratic leadership, *see* Leadership
Autocratic management, 165, 172
Authority,
  adequate, 46, 76
  exercise of, 24

B

Background, *see* Family; Class; College
Bankers, scale on Strong Vocational Interest Test, 135
Behavior
B-B-S Inventory, *see* Tests
  of managers, 147
  of supervisors, 48
  see also, Performance; Activities
Bell Telephone System, 57
Bennett's Mechanical Comprehension Test, *see* Tests
Bernreuter Personality Inventory, *see* Tests
Big Ten Universities, 81
Birth elite, 90, 91, 146
Birthplace, 84, 87, 99
Biographical statement, 161; *see also* Personal data
Board Chairmen, 40
  qualifications for, 84
Boss, 144, 153, 166
Boorishness, *see* Personality traits
British
  theory of mental ability, 155
  theory of personality, 158
  see also England
Bureaucracies, corporate, 143
Business, 55
  administration major, 85
  analogies test, 61
  goals, 18
  graduate students, *see* Graduate business students

influence on attitudes, 160
schools, *see* Graduate schools of business
what it wants in college men, 53
reputation, 24
Businessmen
attitudes of 159, 160
interests of, 159
personality of, 159

C

California Test of Mental Maturity, *see* Tests
California, University of, 86
Calmness, *see* Personality traits
Carefreeness, *see* Personality traits
Carnegie Tech., 63, 91
Carrier Corporation, 116, 121
Caterpillar tractor plant, 46
Catholic religion, *see* Religion
Caution, *see* Personality traits
Chamber of Commerce presidents, 160
Charitableness, *see* Personality traits
Cheerfulness, *see* Personality traits
Chesapeake and Ohio Railroad, 47
Clerical
aptitude, 117
aptitude test, *see* B-B-S Inventory
groups, 49
work, 1
Class, socio-economic
and ambition, 159
lower, 173
middle, 173
upper, 148, 149, 154, 173
Clinical approach, *see* Personality appraisal
Club membership, 72, 73, 148, 151
Coleman Lamp and Stove Co., 125
College, 56, 174
athletics, 58, 174, 175, 177, 178
application blank, 177, 178
background, 85, 86, 147, 149
grades, 57, 60, 62, 64, 66, 175, 176, 177
graduation from, 147, 148, 163, 172, 178
majors, 85
offices held, 60, 66, 174, 175, 177
recruitment from, 53, 55
students, 89, 159, 174, 175
value of, 149
Columbia University, 56, 75, 86
Community leadership, *see* Leadership
Communication, 9, 10, 11, 15, 42
ability, 53, 76, 173
assurance, 62
down, 46
effective, 165, 166
of foremen, 110, 125
presidential, 78
skills, 162
Company differences, 143
Competition
with father, 146
see also Family
Compensation
Key, 61
see also Earnings; Salary
Competence, job, 46
Compulsiveness, *see* Personality traits
Conference Practice, 46
Confidence, *see* Personality traits
Conformity, 142
Conservative attitude, 159, 172; *see also* Attitudes
Consideration, *see* Personality traits
Consistency, *see* Personality traits
Contacts with scientists, 50
Continuity, 153–154
Contiguity, 150–151
Control, 71
course, 62
hierarchical, 48
Cooperation, *see* Personality traits
Cornell University, 86
Correlation, 46, 59, 60, 61, 62
earnings and undergraduate record, 66
eta, 46
multiple, 62
pressure with production and satisfaction, 38
tests, and criteria, 155
Cost reduction, 49
Counseling, 175, 177–178, 179
tests for, 177
interview, 177–178, 179
Creativity, *see* Personality traits
Credit managers, *see* Managers, office

Criterion, 3, 40, 58, 71
administrative level as, 178
contamination of, 22
dimensions of, 22
earnings as, 21, 26, 28, 57, 178; *see also* Earnings
issues, 22
job evaluation as, 23
judgment as, 22; *see also* Personality traits
morale as, 44
objective measures as, 44, 46, 128
problem, 18
promotion as, 21; *see also* Promotion
ratings as, 98, 99; *see also* Ratings
Cultural
background, 154
setting, 157

D

Daring, *see* Personality traits
Dartmouth, 57
Decision-making, *see* Personality traits
Democratic management, 165
Dependability, *see* Personality traits
Dependance, *see* Personality traits
Depression, *see* Personality traits
Desurgency, *see* Personality traits
Determination, *see* Personality traits
Determinants of personality, *see* Personality determinants
Detroit Edison, 49, 117, 125
Differences
between industries, 2
due to time, 2
of company policy, 2
with growth pattern, 2
Differential Aptitude Test, *see* Tests
Differentiation
of duties, 51
of role, 47
Directors
managing, 79; activities of, 80
Discussion, 50
groups, 179
Dismissal, 78, 167
Drive, *see* Personality traits
and promotion, 71
Duties, differentiation of, 51

E

Earnings, 21, 26, 28, 57–58, 61, 65–66, 98, 150, 170, 178
Economic attitudes, 159
Edison, Detroit, 49, 117, 125
Education
and personality, 147
and promotion, 72, 84, 85
see also Colleges, Graduate School, Universities
Educational ability, *see* Ability
Ego defensiveness, *see* Personality traits
Egoism, *see* Personality traits
Emotional
immaturity, 147, 157
maturity 13, 59, 66, 123, 157
stability, 53
Emotionality, *see* Personality traits
Employee
attitude to company, 37
-centered supervisors, 35, 51, 77
participation, 165
questionnaire, 46
relations, 166
Relations Index, 28, 29
salaried, 77
self-concepts, 151
Energy, *see* Personality traits
Engineer, 70, 85
England, promotions in, 74
Enthusiasm, *see* Personality traits
Entrepreneurs, 77
Environment, 151, 153
psychological, 153
Environmental determinants of personality, *see* Personality determinants
Epileptoid, *see* Personality traits
Ess-Ay Inventory, *see* Tests
Eta, 46
Ethnic Origins, 72
Executive
activities, 80
adjustment, 88, 99, 112
bonuses, 27
effectiveness, 81
engineering, *see* Managers, research and engineering

entry occupations of 69, 70, 92
failure of, 94, 95
finance, *see* Managers, office
goals, 20
interests, 91, 125ff
job; factors in, 24–25; satisfaction, 82
manufacturing, 114, 118, 119–125; *see* also Manager, production
personality traits of, 87, 88, 118 119–125
Position Description, 23
rating scale, 33
research, *see* Managers, research
salaries, 27; *see also* Earnings
sales, 118; *see also* Managers, sales
Study, 180
see also Foremen; Managers; Supervisors
Expectancy Table, 63
Experience, early developmental, 146
Experimental group, 48
Extroversion, *see* Personality traits

F

Factor analysis method, 128
Factors
in executive job, 24–25
in failure, 94–95
in personality, *see* Personality determinants, traits
in promotion, 21, 68, 69, 71, 72, 73, 146; *see also* Promotion
in success, *see* Success
Factory, 50
Fakability of tests, 160–162, 171; *see also* Personality measurement
Failure
fear of, *see* Personality traits
reasons for, 94–95
Family, 73, 99, 176
background, 90–91, 143, 146, 148–149, 154, 172, 177
early experience with, 146, 147
father; attitude toward, 98, 112; influence of, 90, 146, 147, 150, 151, 163; occupation of, 61, 72, 84, 86, 99, 146, 172 177
mother; attitude toward, 91, 98; influence of, 146, 147, 151, 163
pressure, 146
Farmers, 61
Father-figure, 10, 146, 172
Father's occupation, *see* Family
Father-son relationship, *see* Family
Femininity, *see* Personality traits
Fiedler's Assumed Similarity of Opposites Test, *see* Tests
Field emphasis, 147
Finance, 168
course, 62
manager, *see* Managers, office
recruitment from, 70
Firing, *see* Dismissal
Fleishman's Supervisory Practices
Questionnaire, *see* Tests
Flexibility, 166
see also Personality traits
Forced choice ratings, 169
Forced-choice tests, *see* Tests
Ford Motor Co., 18, 19
Foremen, 44, 77
ability of, 92–93
attitudes of, 146
demotion of, 147
education of, 72
effective, 120
interests of, 125
interviews, 119
non-production, 45
production, 41, 42, 44–46, 109–125; *see also* Managers, production
proficiency of, 119
selection of, 113
see also Executives; Managers; Supervisors
Friendships, 74, 150

G

General Electric, 14, 18, 28, 42–43, 113, 116, 120, 125
General managers, *see* Managers, general
General Mills Company, 115, 117, 124
General Motors, 28, 42–43
Ghiselli Adjective Check List, *see* Tests
Gifted children, follow-up, 82, 130–131
Gordon Personal Profile, *see* Tests

Goals
Managers'; *see* Managers
organization, 19
Grades
college, 57–61, 62–66, 175–177
first year graduate, 61–65
graduate, 60–61, 66
reliability, 61
Graduate
business students, 61, 164, 181; M.B.A., 54, 59, 66, 150; Ph.D., 181; research on, 178–180; selection of, 174, 175–181
schools of business, 53, 59, 149, 152, 164, 174, 175–181; predicting success in, 53, 152; selection of students for, 174, 175–181
Grievances, 44–45
Group
cohesiveness, 37
discussion, 124, 179
experimental, 48
membership and personality, 147–149, 163
participation, 81
relations, 51
work, 46, 118
Guilford-Martin Personality Inventory, *see* Tests
Guilford Zimmerman
Aptitude Survey, *see* Tests
Temperament Survey, *see* Tests

H

Habits, 76
Halo effect, *see* Ratings
Harvard University, 59, 61, 63, 66, 76, 85, 86, 99, 148, 150, 152
Graduate School of Business Administration, 152
Heredity, 151
Hierarchical
control, 48
view of personality, 158
Hiring
appraisal for, 181
related to personality measures, 160
Hobbies, 87
Hostility, *see* Personality traits
How Supervise?, *see* Tests
Human Relations, 16, 65, 66, 77, 99, 134, 144, 167, 172
ability, 125, 149
sales approach to, 165
test of, 117
Humm-Wadsworth Temperament Scale, *see* Tests

I

Illinois, University of, 43, 81
Imagination, *see* Personality traits
Immaturity, emotional, 147, 157
Income, *see* Earnings
Independence, *see* Personality traits
Indiana, University of, 54
Individual Background Survey, *see* Tests
Industrial Rorschach, *see* Tests
Inferiority feelings, *see* Personality traits
Influence, 39
Inhibition, *see* Personality traits
Initiating structure, 44, 45
Initiative, *see* Personality traits
Inertness, *see* Personality traits
Innovation, 167
Insight, 158
Institute of Social Research, 46
Integration, personality, 157, 158
Integrity, *see* Personality traits
Intelligence, *see* Ability, intellectual
Interests, 13, 55, 99, 158, 170, 171–172
administrative, 99, 125
business competition, 158, 172
business contract, 159
clerical, 56
computational, 56, 108
dramatic, 158
esthetic, 158
foremen, *see* Foremen
human relations, 99, 144, 158, 172
literary, 56
math-accounting, 158, 171
measurement of, 159
mechanical, 56
numerical, 135, 136
persuasive, 56, 173
sales, 99
scientific creativity, 158, 171
sociability, 158, 172
tests, 60, 91; *see also* Tests: Kuder Preference Record,

Meyer Personal Interest Inventory, Strong Vocational Interest Test, Weschler Adult Interest Scale
Vocational, 153
see also Managers, interests of
International Harvester, 28, 44
Interview, 55, 152, 177
by superior, 71, 119
patterned, 161
research, 177, 180
student, 177, 179
see also Managers, selection of
Intolerance, 156
Introspection, *see* Personality traits
Introversion, *see* Personality traits
I.Q., 114–115
Ivy League Colleges, 148

J

Jewish religion, *see* Religion
Job
competence, 46
evaluation, 23
helpfulness, 46
identification, 124
placement, 72
satisfaction, 82, 108, 150
Judgment, 117, 138
correlated with personality characteristics, 158
good, 46, 76
of people, 158
test of, *see* How Supervise? test; Judgment Test
Jurgensen's Classification Inventory, *see* Tests

K

Kerr's Tear Ballot for Industry, *see* Tests
Knowledge
of business, 137
technical, 128, 131–132, 138, 140, 141, 166
test, 54
Kuder Preference Record, *see* Tests

L

Laborers, 70
sons, 61
unions, 77, 160
Language, 13
Lawshe Adaptability Test, *see* Tests
Leaderless group
discussions, 55, 179–180
tests, 98–99
Leadership, 5–6, 65–66, 164, 174
and productivity, 165
and promotion, 71
autocratic, 48, 165; related to morale, 107
community, 159, 160
definition, 8, 165
democratic, 165
industrial, 160
literature, 6, 13
measurement of, 176–177, 178–179
nominations, 36
potential, 176–177, 179
theory, 5–6, 165
typology, 9
see also Personality traits
Learning process, 149
Life insurance
agencies, 41
agents, 31
Likert's situational theory of management, 165
Lockheed Aircraft Corporation, 46, 99, 108, 114, 119, 120, 121, 124, 169
Loyalty to company, 169
Luck, 150

M

Macy, R. H., & Co., 102
Management, 1
autocratic vs. democratic, 165
business, 13
changes in, 16
definition, 14, 164
potential, 180
practices, 153, 165, 166
relative and adjustive, 153
situational theory of, 165
status, 89
success, 21, 71, 75, 164, 165, 166, 181; criteria of, 168–170; *see also* Success
theory, 35, 37
see also Managers

Managers
ability of, 81–83; 92, 93, 101–105, 108, 113–116, 118, 137–141, 144, 145, 154, 166, 168, 170, 173, 174; *see also* Ability
accounting, *see* Managers, office
activities of, 79, 110, 164
adjustment of, 88, 144
attitudes of, 113, 147, 159, 160, 172; toward employees, 105
autocratic, 165, 172
behavior of, 50
college attended, 86, 148; *see also* College
credit, *see* Managers, office
democratic, 165, 172
duties of, 164
education of, 72, 83, 147–149; *see also* College
engineering, *see* Managers, research and engineering
finance, *see* Managers, office
general, 39, 75–83, 167, 172; ability of, 81–83, 144; activities of, 164, 167; adjustment of, 144; definition of, 75; education of, 83, 174; income of, 82; interests of, 144, 173; job satisfaction among, 150; motivation of subordinates of, 167; personality of, 142–144; qualifications of, 75, 76, 172, 174; rewards of, 150; selection of, 142; success criteria for, 169, 180
goals of, 20, 90, 109, 147; shift in, 150
good, 2
innovation by, 167
interests of, 91–92, 99, 102, 112, 113, 171–173; general managers, 144, 172; office managers, 174; production managers, 112–113, 125, 144, 173; sales managers, 102, 108, 144, 159 173
job, 2, 19, 23
knowledge, technical, 166
manufacturing, 40, 114, 118; *see also* Managers, production
motives of, *see* Motivation
office (accounting, finance, and credit managers), 48, 118, 127–136, 137, 142, 163, 173; ability, creative, 132, 136, 144, 174; ability, intellectual, 130–131, 174; ability, numerical, 130–132, 144, 154; ability, reading comprehension, 130; ability, verbal, 136, 174; accounting, 132, 135, 173, 184; attitude, 1; attitude toward job, 127, attitude toward supervisors, 135; banking, 130, 133–134, 135, 136; credit, 134–135; finance, 118, 168, 169, 174; interests of, 174; performance of, 127, 128–129, 130, 135; performance of, administration, 130; performance of, effectiveness of, 129; performance of, factor analysis of, 128–129; performance of, group direction, 129; performance of, human relations, 133; performance of, quality of, 130; personality of, 128, 133, 134, 135, 144, 154, 174; personality of, differentiated from other managers, 133, 144; personality of, related to promotion, 134; power of, 127; promotability, 130–131, 134, 138–141; ratings, 132, 134, 144–145; success criteria for, 169; technical knowledge of, 128, 131; what presidents want in, 127
perceptions, 153
performance, 1, 2, 5, 7, 15, 40–41, 50, 100, 108, 109, 125, 138–139, 152, 154, 164, 166, 181; defined, 100; related to productivity, 35–52
personal data, 105, 108, 119–120, 126, 152
personal qualifications, *see* Managers, qualifications of
personality of, 1, 2, 89–91, 95–97, 100–102, 105, 108, 110, 111, 112, 119–125, 134–135, 144, 162, 165, 170–174, 181; compared with college students, 89; determinants of, 146–160, *see also* Personality determinants; measurements of, 171; theory of, *see* Personality theory; types of successful managers, 171
planning by, 167

production, 40, 109–126, 130, 132, 134, 135, 137, 163, 168, 173, 174; ability of, 111, 119, 125–126, 144, 174; ability of, creative, 114; ability of, in judgment, 117; ability of, mechanical, 116–117, 126, 173; activities of, 110–111, 164; adjustment of, 112, 121, 126; attitudes of, 113, 147; creativity of, 114; demotion of, 147; goals of, 109; intelligence of, 113–116; interests of, 112–113, 125, 144, 173; interests of, scale on Strong Vocational Interests Test, 125; job, 168; performance of, 109, 125; personal data, 119–120, 126; personality of, 111–112, 119–125, 174; personality of, adjustment, 121; personality of, and proficiency, 119, 120; personality of, in interviews, 119; personality of, self-perception of, 121–124; promotability of, 137–141; scale on Strong Vocational Interest Test, 125; success as, 121–124, 126; success as, criteria of, 169; unsuccessful, 121–124

promotability, 40, 101, 114, 137–141, 146, 147–149

qualifications of, 1, 76, 105, 107, 163, 181; general managers, 75, 76, 172, 174; sales managers, 107, 163

research and engineering, 50, 118, 130, 132, 134, 137–141, 142, 167, 173; ability, administrative, 138, 141; ability, intellectual, 137, 138, 140, 145, 154, 174; ability, job, 168; ability, to deal with people, 141; ability, verbal, 137, 154, 174; accomplishment of, 138; freedom needed by, 169; knowledge, of business, 137; knowledge, technical, 138, 140, 141; loyalty to company, 169; motivation of, 169; performance of, 50, 154; performance of, administration, 139; performance of, position, 139; performance of, quality of, 138; personality, 111–112, 119–125, 174; personality, compared to sales managers, 141; personality, creativity, 137; personality, depression, 137; personality, of promotable, 138, 140; promotable, 137–140; ratings, 137–140; selection of, 113; success, criteria of, 169; versatility, 141, 145, 168

sales, 40, 100–108, 130, 132, 134, 135, 137, 142, 163, 167, 173, 174; ability of, 101–105, 108, 118, 144, 154, 173; activities of, 164, 166; interests of, 102, 108, 144, 159, 173; job, 167; morale, subordinates, 105–108; motivation of, 168; performance, 100, 108, 154; personal data, 105, 108; personality of, 100–102, 105, 108, 144, 162, 173; promotable, 137–141; qualifications of, 107, 163; success, 168; success, criteria of, 169

selection of, 1, 113, 152, 167

self-concept, 163

staff, 145

successful, 18, 19, 56, 67, 142, 146–160, 164, 165, 166, 168

top and middle, 95–97, 165

Manic tendencies, *see* Personality traits

Manufacturing executives, *see* Executives; Managers, production

Martin, Glenn L., Co., 124

Masculinity, *see* Personality traits

Masculine-Feminine Scale, *see* Strong Vocational Interest Test

Masons, 72

Math
- ability, 155, 162, 170
- aptitude, 82–83, 92, 93, 119
- attitude toward, 119, 135
- interests, 56, 108, 135, 136, 158, 171

Maturity, emotional, 13, 59, 66, 123, 157

MBA's, 54, 59, 66, 150

Measurement of personality, *see* Personality, measurement of

Mechanical
- ability, *see* Ability
- Aptitude Test, *see* Tests
- Comprehension Test, *see* Tests

Medical Laboratories, 50
Melancholic, *see* Personality traits
Mental
  ability, *see* Ability, intellectual
  defect, 157
  Vision Test, *see* Tests
Merit and promotion, 68–69, 71
Meyer,
  Personal Interests Inventory, *see* Tests
  Social Judgment of Human Relations Test, *see* Tests
Michigan, University of, 43, 46–48, 50, 63, 81, 86
Miller Analogies Test, *see* Tests
Minnesota Mining and Manufacturing, 103, 116
Minnesota, University of, 63
  Industrial Relations Center, 109–110
M.I.T., 86
M.M.P.I., *see* Tests
Mobile elite, 90, 172
Morale, 44, 48, 165
  of subordinates, 105–108
Mother-son relationship, *see* Family
Motivation, 9, 11, 13, 118, 147, 168
  accomplishment, 13
  achievement, 153
  anxiety, 10
  belongingness, 50
  competitive, 9, 10
  consideration, 153
  ego, 50, 153
  internal, 50
  judgment of, 117
  material success, 9
  of subordinates, 167
  power, 105, 150, 153, 171
  prestige, 150, 153
  service, 153
  theory of, 20
  threatening, 38
  see also Needs

N

Nationwide Insurance Company, 128–129
Needs, 47
  achievement, 153, 171
  persistence, 107
  power, 105, 150, 153, 171
  security, 134
Nepotism, 86, 146
Nervousness, *see* Personality traits
Neurasthenia, *see* Personality traits
Neuroticism, 112, 150, 155
Nonintellectual factors in personality, *see* Personality factors
Norms, validity of, 160
Non-production
  departments, 44
  foremen, 45
  service, 44
Numerical ability, *see* Ability

O

Objective criteria, 46
Objective tests, 157, 158, 160, 168
Objectivity, *see* Personality traits
Observation study of foremen, 42
Obsessiveness, *see* Personality traits
Occupation of father, *see* Family
Occupational
  Level Scale, *see* Strong Vocational Interests Test
  mobility, 61
Office, 50, 60
  managers, *see* Managers, office
  supervisors, *see* Managers, office; Supervisors
Open-mindedness, *see* Personality traits
Operations, recruitment from, 70
Organization
  attitudes of, 160
  goal, 19
  of study, 16
  of work, 139
  planning, 71
Organization Man, 24, 68, 77, 78, 160
Organismic approach to personality, 151–152
Orderliness, *see* Personality traits
Ohio State University, 81
Owners, 148

P

Patterned interview, *see* Interview
Parental influence, *see* Family
Participative control, 48
Passivity, *see* Personality traits

Peer
  communications with, 166
  expectations, 147, 153
  ratings, *see* Ratings
Pennsylvania, University of, 86
Perceptions of managers, *see* Managers,
Performance, 41, 152, 165, 180
  measures, 32
  of managers, *see* Managers
  supervisors, 49
  see also Behavior
Permissiveness, *see* Personality traits
Personal
  characteristics, 32, 105
  data, 119–120, 152, 161, 171, 178–179
  demands, 24
  history, 95, 124, 161, 179
  Interest Inventory, *see* Tests
  relations, 2; *see also* Human relations
Personality
  American, 142
  analytic approach to, 142, 170
  appraisal, 151–152; clinical, 151–152; factor analytic, 154; statistical, 151–152; *see also* Personality measurement
  British theory of, 158
  defined, 5, 170; difficulties, 164
  determinants of, 146–160, 162, 163, 170–173; environmental, 146–151, 153–154, 157, 162, 163, 172; hereditary, 151, 152; situational, 147, 149, 150
  diversity of, 142
  factors, 154, 171; nonintellectual, 143, 154-156, 162, 170, 171; nonintellectual, agreement concerning, 155; nonintellectual, correlated with mental ability, 170; nonintellectual, integration of, 157, 158; nonintellectual, isolation of, 155, 157; nonintellectual, twelve found in managers, 171; *see also* Personality traits
  hierarchical view of, 158
  influences on, *see* Personality determinants
  inventories, 95, 128, 162, *see also* Tests
  interview, 152
  measurement of, 143, 159, 160–162, 164, 171, 179; correlations of, 161; forced-choice, *see* Tests; interview, *see* Interview; inventory, *see* Tests; methods, fakability of, 160, 161, 162, 171; methods, validity of, 160, 171; personal data sheet, 171; projective, *see* Tests; *see also* Tests
  of managers, diversity of, 142–143; manufacturing, 118, 119–125, *see also* Managers, production; related to American, 142; similarities, 143; successful, 142, 165; supervisory, 119–125; theory of, 143–163; theory of, summarized, 162–163; top and middle, 95–96; *see also* Managers, personality of
  organismic approach to, 151–152
  predictive of ratings, 95
  qualities, 53
  related to culture, 154, 157
  related to promotion, 118–119
  related to social class, 154, *see also* Class, socio-economic
  responses, 158
  self-perception, 95–96, 121–124, 151
  structure, 154–160; factors in, 154, 155, 162, 170–171
  tests, 95; *see also* Tests
  theory of, 5, 142–163; British, 158; disagreement concerning, 142, 146; of managers, *see* Personality, of managers
  traits, 6–7, 83, 87–89, 90 158, 170; acceptance, 118, 134, 138, 141; achievement need, 153, 171; activity, general, 156; adaptability, social, 157; adjustment, *see* Adjustment; aggression, 76, 108, 134, 143, 150, 151, 153, 159, 165, 173; agreeableness, 121, 156; ambition, 16, 53, 119, 123, 144, 148, 159; ambition, neurotic basis of, 112; ambition, related to background, 159; analysis of, 157; anxiety, 149, 157; approachability, 129; ascendancy, 121, 156, 162; aspiration, 159; assurance in

Personality traits, *continued*
communications, 62; boorishness, 157; calmness, 156; carefreeness, 156, 157; caution, 97; charitableness, 157; cheerfulness, 129; competitiveness, 144, 172; compulsiveness, 154; confidence, 156, 162, *see also* Self-confidence; conservativeness, 159; consideration, 44–45, 129, 151; consistency, 46; cooperation, 50, 102, 121, 156; creativity, 102, 114, 132, 133, 134, 135, 137, 138, 141, 144, 154, 172; cycloid disposition, 156; cyclothymia, 157; daring, 97; decision making, 15, 39, 129; defensiveness, 107, 112, 126, 144; dependability, 53; dependance, 88, 133, 157; depression, 133, 137, 144, 145, 156; desurgency, 157; determination, 157; dominance, 88, 99, 101, 102, 107, 144, 145, 148, 154, 156, 157, 163, 173; drive, 53, 65, 99, 118, 134, 138, 140, 156, 162, *see also* Will; ego-defensiveness, 107, 112, 126, 144; egoism, 78, 88, 153; emotionality, 156, 157; energy, 76, 162, 173; enthusiasm, 162, 173; epileptoid, 121; extroversion, 88, 156, 171; fear of failure, 112, 144; femininity, 156, 172; flexibility, 118, 119, 138, 163; followers, 133; hostility, 147; imagination, 76, 157, *see also* Ability, creative; independence, 88, 122, 143, 144, *see also* Self-sufficiency; inferiority, 105, 156; inhibition, 156; initiative, 71, 97–98, 118, 134, 138, 140; inertness, 156; innovation, 76; insight, 158; instability, 171; integrity, 53, 65; intolerance, 156; introspection, 156; introversion, 121, 156; irritability, 156; judgment of people, 158; leadership, 118, 120, 134, 138, 140, 141, 154, 156, 162; manic, 121, 144; masculinity, 60, 66, 113, 156, 172, 173, 177; maturity, emotional, 13, 59, 66, 123, 157; melancholia, 157; motivation, 53, 118, 134, 138, 140, 147; need persistence, 107; nervousness, 156; neurasthenia, 157; objectivity, 121, 134, 143, 151, 156; obsessiveness, 157; openmindedness, 129; optimism, 102, 144, 154, 156, 157, 173; orderliness, 76; passivity, 130, 156, 162; permissiveness, 40; perseverance, *see* Will; persuasiveness, 108, 121, 125; pessimism, 144; poise, 62, 157; popularity, 154; power, need for, 105, 150, 153, 171; quarrelsomeness, 156; realism, 156; related to failure, 94; related to family background, 90–91, 151, 163, *see also* Family; relating with people, 11, 123; respect for others, 124, 126; restraint, 156; rhathymia, 156, 157; rigidity, 157; schizophrenia, 157; schizothymia, 157; security, need for, 134; self-confidence, 62, 148, 154, 163; self-orientation, 123; self-sufficiency, 122, *see also* Independence; sensitivity, 157; shyness, 156, 157; social responsibility, 124; social skill, 158; sociability, 114, 120, 133, 138, 141, 156, 172; stability, 53, 119, 123, 156, 157; submissiveness, 156, 157, 162; surgency, 153, *see also* Optimism; suspicion, 144; sympathy, 46; tolerance, 157; tolerance, of frustration, 157; tolerance, of nonconformity, 160; understanding, 107–108; vigor, 120; will, 150, 155, 171, 172, *see also* Purpose
types, 158; of successful managers, 171
uniqueness, 152–153
verbal description of, 157
Perseverance, *see* Personality traits, will
Personnel, 167
Personnel Problems Test, *see* Test
Persuasiveness, *see* Personality traits; Ability

Pessimism, 144
Physical characteristics, 87
Physical sciences, 158
Pillsbury Mills, 114
Placement service, 54
Planning, 25, 39, 41, 42, 46, 138, 139, 167
Poise, *see* Personality traits
Political affiliation, 72
Political attitudes, *see* Attitudes
Political Values Scale, *see* Tests, Allport-Vernon
Popularity, *see* Personality traits
Position performance, 71, 100, 130, 138, 139
Power,
  elite, 148
  exercise of, 24
  motive, *see* Motivation; Needs
Practical ability, *see* Ability
Practical Judgment Test, *see* Tests
Practice effect on A.T.G.S.B., 62
Prediction
  clinical, 63
  from grades, 61
  of success, 56
  statistical, 63
  see also Predictors
Predictors, 2, 3, 57, 181
  A.T.G.S.B., *see* Tests
  activities, 58
  athletics, 58, 174, 175, 177–178
  college, grades, 57, 60, 62, 64, 66, 175, 176, 177; offices, 60, 66, 174, 175, 177; peer ratings, 179; professors' ratings, 60, 66, 180
  discussion groups, leaderless, 179–180
  emotional maturity rating, 59
  grades, 57, 60, 62, 64, 66, 175, 176, 177
  intelligence, 58
  interviews, 152, 177, 179, 180
  masculinity, 66, 172, 173, 177
  offices, 60, 66, 174, 175, 177
  peer ratings, 179
  professors' ratings, 60, 66, 180
Prep schools, 148
Presidents
  activities of, 166
  hobbies of, 87
  interests of, 91
  motivation of subordinates, 167
  nomination of, 74, 173
  qualifications for, 84–86, 163
  Young, 39, 54, 76–79, 127, 143, 146, 150, 151, 172; activities of, 79, 167; family background of, 146, 172; functions of, 78; personality of, 83, 87–88, 150–151; topics discussed by, 78–79; *see also* Executives; Managers
Pressure, 38
  for production, 46
Prestige, 159
  motive, *see* Motivation
Pride in work group, 46
Problem solving discussion, 50
Procter and Gamble Co., 54, 113, 119, 120, 125
Production, 43, 47, 50, 71, 168
  -centered, 55
  course, 62
  foremen, 41, 46, 110–111
  pressure for, 46
  rate, 46
  recruitment from, 70
  supervisors, 44
  see also Managers, production; Supervisors
Productivity, 35, 37–38, 48, 50
  and leadership, 165
  measurement of, 118, 158
Professions, 1, 82
Proficiency, 45, 97, 119
Profit, 21, 39
Projective Tests, *see* Tests
Promotion, 67, 74, 130–131, 134, 138–141
  appraisal for, 181
  criterion, 21
  experiences preceding, 71
  informal factors in, 73, 146
  merit, 68, 69
  methods, 68, 69
  of college graduates, 68, 147, 148
  qualifications for, 72
  ratings of potential for, 161, 181
  related to intelligence, 113–114, 118
  related to personality, 118–119, 138
  testing for, 162
Protestant religion, *see* Religion
Protestant virtues, 143
Prudential Insurance Company, 48, 128–129
Psychological distance, 43, 90, 117

Psychological environment, *see* Environment
Purchasing, 71
Purdue Rating Scale for Administrators and Executives, 33
Purpose, 149
  defined, 149
  in managers, 150
  see also Will

Q

Qualifications
  business wants, 53
  for managers, *see* Managers
Qualities
  of personality, 53
  wanted by business, 53
Quantitative
  Relations, 61
  Score, 62, 176; *see also* A.T.G.S.B.
Quarrelsomeness, *see* Personality traits
Questionnaires, 46, 155, 158

R

Race, 90
Radical attitude, 159, 172
Railroad-right-of-way gangs, 47
Ratings, 46, 58, 98, 99, 157, 158, 160, 169, 170
  by peers, 31, 116, 117, 179–180
  by professors, 60, 66, 180
  by subordinates, 22, 49
  by superiors, 29–30, 44, 49, 71, 93–95, 105, 109, 114–115, 121–122, 137–140
  compared to self-concept, 151
  contamination of, 139
  forced-choice, 31, 169
  halo effect in, 128
  of office managers, *see* Managers, office
  of promotion potential, 161, 181
  of research and engineering managers, *see* Managers, research and engineering
  of supervisors, *see* Supervisors
  related to adjustment, 121
  reliability of, 31, 160
  scales, 32, 33
  stability, 153
Realism, *see* Personality traits
Reading comprehension ability, 111, 130
Reading Comprehension Test, *see* Tests
Reasoning, deductive, 61
Recommendations, 160
  by professors, 174, 175, 177, 178
  forms, 179
  of superiors, 71, 74
Recreation, 73
Recruitment, methods of, 54
  from finance, 70
  from operations, 70
  from production, 70
Relating with people, *see* Personality traits
Relative and adjustive theory of management, *see* Management theory
Religion, 57, 72, 84, 86–87, 99, 147, 162, 163, 172
  Catholic, 57, 72, 84
  high status, 74, 84, 99
  Jewish, 57, 84, 87, 99, 163, 172
  of large vs. small company presidents, 86, 87, 163
  Protestant, 57, 74, 84, 87, 99, 163, 172
  see also Personality determinants
Requirements
  for production foremen, 42
  for promotion, 72; *see also* Promotion
  from College, 53
Research, 50, 174, 175–181
  and engineering managers, *see* Managers
  in student selection, 178–180; *see also* Graduate schools of business; Graduate students
  program for, 174, 175–181
  within companies, 180–181
Respect for others, *see* Personality traits
Restraint, *see* Personality traits
Rewards, 150
Rhathymia, *see* Personality traits
Rigidity, *see* Personality traits
Role
  differentiation, 47
  perception, 121–124
  theory of personality, 113
Rorschach Test, *see* Tests
Rosenzweig Picture-Frustration Test, *see* Tests

S

Salaries
Harvard MBA's, 59
see also Earnings; Income
Sales, 70, 71
work, 1
managers, *see* Managers, sales
Satisfaction, 38, 47, 82, 108, 150
Scale
Allport-Vernon, of Values, 105, 134, 159
occupational level, 159, 172
masculinity-femininity, 172
Political Values, 105, 134
production managers, 125
Social Adjustment, 159
Social Service, 125
Theoretical, 159
Willingness to Tolerate Nonconformists, 160
Schizophrenia, *see* Personality traits
Schizothymia, *see* Personality traits
Schools attended, 147, 149; *see also* Colleges
Scholarship, 65
Scholastic aptitude, *see* Aptitude
Science Research Associates Mechanical Aptitude Test, *see* Tests
Sears, Roebuck & Co., 103–108, 134–135
Security, need for, 134
Selection
for business, 13
for school of business, 13, 174, 175
studies, 17
Self-
concept of managers, 151, 158
confidence, *see* Personality traits
orientation, *see* Personality traits
perception, 95–96, 121–124, 151
sufficiency, *see* Personality traits
Sensitivity, *see* Personality traits
Sentence Completion Test, *see* Tests
Service departments, 44
Shyness, *see* Personality traits
Situation, 2, 6–7, 35–37
related to personality, 147, 149, 150
tests, *see* Tests
theory, 37, 38, 44, 52, 81, 147, 153, 165
Skills
communication, 162
social, 13, 158
technical, 13
verbal, 101, 112
see also Ability
Sociability, *see* Personality traits
Social
attitudes, *see* Attitudes
class, *see* Class
learning, 149
Nearness, 46
responsibility, *see* Personality traits
Service Scale, 125
skill, 13, 158
stratification, 53
Social Judgment of Human Relations Test, *see* Tests
Socio-economic status, 11
as a motive, 150
see also Status
Stability, 153–154
Staff Managers, *see* Managers
Standard Oil Co., 113, 117, 120, 171, 179, 180
Stanford University, 54, 62, 63, 66, 71
Statistical approach, *see* Personality appraisal
Statistics course, 176
Strong Vocational Interest Test, *see* Tests
Structure of personality, *see* Personality structure
Status
professional, 159
religion, 74, 84, 99
seeking, 150
socio-economic, 11
Subordinates
behavior of, 36
expectations of, 147, 153
interests of, 81
morale of, 105–108
parties of, 81
qualifications of, 36
ratings by, 22, 46, 121–124
status and personality, 145
Success, 40
as a business manager, 18, 19, 67, 164–166, 168; *see also* Managers

Success, *continued*
criteria, 168–170, 178
definitions by managers, 19, 150
Occupational Level Scores related to, 159
personality determinants related to, 146–160
predicting from college, 56
qualifications for, 83
Superego, 151
Supervision, 48
lack of close, 51
Supervisors, 49
ability of, 92, 111, 113–118, 158
adjustment of, 88
behavior, 48, 50, 81, 165, 166
education, 72
employee-centered, 35, 46, 51
first-line, *see* Managers, production
goals of, 20
good, 117, 166
high and low rated, 121–125
hiring, 125
interests of, 81
judgment of people, 158
judgment test, *see* Tests
office, *see* Managers, office
performance, 49
personal history, 95, 179
personality of, 95, 102, 119–125
production centered, 35
promotable, 49
ratings by, *see* Ratings
ratings of, 46, 121–124
role perception, 121–124
Supervisory Inventory, 95
Supervisory Judgment, 111
Supportive company, 37
Surgency, *see* Personality traits
Suspicion, *see* Personality traits
Sympathy, *see* Personality traits

T

Tap-to-Tap Time, 118
Task-oriented, job, 168
Taxes, 168
Teachers, influence of, 90, 146
Technical knowledge, 128, 131–132
Temperament, test of, *see* Tests, Guilford-Zimmerman Temperament Survey, 114,121
Humm-Wadsworth Temperament Scale, 121
Tests
ability, 54, 59, 60, 61, 63, 64, 66, 82, 91, 93, 101, 111, 114, 115, 116, 117, 118, 121, 124, 130, 132, 137, 170, 175, 177
Accounting Achievement Test, 132
A.C.E. Psychological Examination, 103–105
Adams-Lepley Personal Audit, 88
Adaptability Test, 115
Admission Test for Graduate Study in Business, 61–64, 66, 170, 175, 177
Allport-Vernon Scale of Values, 105, 134, 159; Political Values Scale, 105, 134; Social Adjustment Scale, 159; Theoretical Scale, 159
Analogies, 61
Arithmetic Reasoning, 132
Army Alpha, 82, 101
Army General Classification, 111
A.T.G.S.B., *see* Admission Test for Graduate Study in Business
B-B-S Inventory, 117
Bennett's Mechanical Comprehension, 116
Bernreuter Personality Inventory, 87–88, 101, 137
Business Problems, 59
California Test of Mental Maturity, 114; Short Form, 115
Deductive Reasoning, 61
Differential Aptitude, 116
Ess-Ay Inventory, 121
Fiedler's Assumed Similarity of Opposites, 117, 118
Fleishman Supervisory Practices Questionnaire, 108
forced-choice, 95, 96, 121–124, 141, 149, 162, 171, 179
Ghiselli Adjective Check List, 95–97, 121, 171, 177, 179
Gordon Personal Profile, 121, 162, 171
Guilford-Martin Personality Inventory, 102, 105, 120–121
Guilford-Zimmerman, Aptitude Survey, 116; Temperament Survey, 114, 121

How Supervise?, 117
Humm-Wadsworth Temperament Scale, 121
Huttner Supervisory Aptitude, 121
Imaginary Events, 59
Individual Background Survey, 59, 61, 66, 120, 171, 179
intelligence, 162; *see also* Tests, ability
interest, 54, 56, 60, 91, 92, 99, 108, 112, 125, 134, 135, 159, 162, 172, 177
inventory, 87, 88, 95, 101, 102, 105, 120–121, 125, 137, 149, 155, 171
Judgment, 117
Jurgensen's Classification Inventory, 95
Kerr's Tear Ballot for Industry, 108
Kuder Preference Record, 54, 56, 92, 99, 108, 125, 162
Mental Vision, 124
Meyer, Personal Interests Inventory, 125; Social Judgment of Human Relations, 117, 133
Miller Analogies, 63
Minnesota Multiphasic Personality Inventory, 87, 88, 101, 137
M.M.P.I., *see* Minnesota Multiphasic Personality Inventory
motivation for, 162
objective, 157, 158, 160, 168
Otis Self-Administering Test of Mental Ability, 115, 132
Otis Quick Scoring Test of Mental Ability, 115
Personality Interest Inventory, 125
personality, 54, 59, 61, 66, 87, 88, 90, 93, 95, 96, 97, 98, 101, 102, 103, 105, 107, 108, 114, 115, 117, 118, 120, 121, 124, 133, 134, 137, 159, 160, 161, 162, 171, 172, 177, 179
Personnel Problems, 59, 66
Political Values Scale, 105, 134
Practical Judgment, 61
projective, 90, 98, 107, 124, 137, 143, 160, 161, 171, 177, 179
Quantitative Relations, 61
Reading Comprehension, 93
Rorschach, 107; Industrial, 124
Rosenzweig Picture Frustration, 107, 160
Scale of Willingness to Tolerate Non-conformists, 160
Science Research Associates Mechanical Aptitude, 116
Sentence Completion, 111, 133, 137, 161, 171, 177, 179
situation, 98–99
Social Adjustment Scale, 159
Social Judgment of Human Relations, 117, 133
Strong Vocational Interest, 60, 91, 99, 112, 125, 134, 135, 159, 172, 177; Masculinity-Femininity Scale, 172; Occupational Level Scale, 159, 172; Production Managers' Scale, 125
Thematic Apperception, 90, 98, 124, 133, 137, 161, 171, 177, 179
Theoretical Scale, 159
Thurstone's Test of Primary Mental Abilities, 93, 101, 114, 130, 137
Wecshler Adult Intelligence Scale, 93, 103
Wonderlic Personnel, 54, 93, 114, 115, 160
Worthington Personal History, 124
Theory, 47
classroom, 147
leadership, 5–6; *see also* Leadership
management, 35, 37
motivation, 20; *see also* Motivation
personality, *see* Personality
Situation, 37, 38, 44, 52, 81, 147, 153, 165
Threatening, 38
Time, 56
Thematic Apperception Test, *see* Tests
Thurstone's Test of Primary Mental Ability, *see* Tests
Tolerance of non-conformists, 160
Tough vs. tender-minded attitudes, 159, 172
Traits, personality, *see* Personality traits
Turnover, 44, 45

U

Underachievement, 61
Understanding, *see* Personality traits
Uniqueness, of personality, 152–153
University
  California, 86
  Columbia, 56, 75, 86
  Cornell, 86
  Dartmouth, 57
  Harvard, 59, 61, 63, 66, 76, 85, 86, 99, 148, 150, 152
  Illinois, 43, 81
  Indiana, 54
  Michigan, 43, 46–48, 50, 63, 81, 86
  Minnesota, 63; Industrial Relations Center, 109–110
  Ohio State, 81
  Pennsylvania, 86
  Southern California, 46
  Wisconsin, 86
  Yale, 85, 86
Upper class, *see* Class

V

Values, 18
  Allport-Vernon Scale of, 105, 134, 159
  theoretical, 159
Verbal
  ability, *see* Abilities
  score, 62, 176
  skills, 101, 112
Versatility, 141, 145, 168
Vigor, *see* Personality traits
Vocational interests, *see* Interests
  Tests of, 54, 56, 60, 91, 92, 99, 108, 112, 125, 134, 135, 159, 162, 172, 177

W

Wages, 47; *see also* Earning; Salary
Wecshler Adult Intelligence Scale, *see* Tests
Will, *see* Personality traits; *see also* Purpose
Wisconsin, University of, 86
Wives, influence of, 73
Wonderlic Personnel Test, *see* Tests
Work
  acceptance rate, 46
  behavior, 45
  groups, 118, 158, 165
  -Rework Ratio, 46
  way through college, 57, 175
  week, 15
Worthington Personal History, 124

Y

Yale University, 85, 86
Young Presidents, *see* Presidents, Young

983

DATE DUE

2-27			
MAR 11 1969			
DEC 4 1974			
AP 6 '88			
FE 4 '85			

GAYLORD PRINTED IN U.S.A.